Contents

Part 3   The Reformed Model

Figures

Tables

Preface

This book was originally conceived as a follow-on from our comparative study of neo-corporatism (Inagami et al., 1994, in Japanese). The study looked at strains in national systems of labour–management–government interest intermediation, and whether these were (a) collapsing in an era of disorganized capitalism, or perhaps (b) being transformed by the growth of 'micro-corporatism' – company-level partnerships between management and labour, supported by weaker forms of national concertation.

Japan, of course, was well known for its co-operative enterprise-based industrial and employment relations, but it appeared to be going against the global trend of retreating national level concertation with the emergence of a weak form of national-level corporatism. If (b) were the case, Japan would not be the anomaly it first appeared.

At the same time, however, we recognized that Japan's co-operative enterprise-based industrial and employment relations – or the community dimensions of its firms – were coming under increasing strain, from a variety of sources. This book was intended to explore these strains, how they were being addressed, and hopefully to predict the outcome. Our working title was 'Japan's community firms: reform or collapse?' We believed the answer was 'reform,' and that 'collapse' prophets were relying on anecdotes and 'see, Japanese practices were strange after all' *schadenfreude*. And our question applied to the communitarian aspects of Japanese companies, not the companies themselves.

The Asian Crisis in 1997, and Japan's own growing financial crisis, followed by factory closures and restructuring in its manufacturing heartland from 1998, changed the meaning of the question. When companies themselves collapse, their communities can hardly be left intact. Reforms undertaken to avoid collapse could have a major impact on the community. The importance of looking at employment in its business context became increasingly clear.

The structure of the book to some extent reflects this evolution. It starts with a focus on the community firm and employment practices, and broadens the perspective to consider corporate governance and the implementation of consolidated management and related reforms. This is done through a number of surveys conducted in the late 1990s. In Part 2 the community firm, employment practices, corporate governance and management are considered in a specific business context – that of the general electric giant Hitachi. We chose Hitachi for a number of reasons, one of which was to consider both long-term and recent changes to Dore's 'Japanese factory', an archetype for our classic model employment practices and community firm. The timing was fortunate in that we were able to study Hitachi in a period leading up to crisis, and reforms set in train as a result of the crisis.

Inagami was primarily responsible for Part 1 and Whittaker for Part 2, with cross-fertilization of ideas shaping the progress of both. Our overall conclusions are presented in Part 3. We could have packaged our findings sensationally – in a message of collapse, or discovery of a completely 'new model' – but our interest was as much in continuity as discontinuity, and we found evidence of both. The community dimension persists in large Japanese firms, which we are primarily concerned with in this book, but the postwar 'classic model' is giving way (in some companies) to a 'reformed model', whose features will continue to crystallize in the coming years.

TAKESHI INAGAMI AND D. HUGH WHITTAKER

Acknowledgements

Ronald Dore's writing on the community firm over many years has provided inspiration and points of reference for us in writing this book. His help in facilitating our case study at Hitachi, his comments, and at times disagreements with our interpretations, are gratefully acknowledged.

There are many people at Hitachi we would like to thank for generously giving their time, and patiently and frankly answering our many questions. It is perhaps invidious to single out individuals, but the list would feature former Vice President T. Kashiwagi, who made the initial arrangements and opened the doors wide, K. Muneoka, H. Kanauchi, O. Yamamiya, T. Yamaguchi, T. Shigekuni, I. Yamazaki in the first half of the study, C. Onishi and K. Nezu, and especially T. Hatchoji, I. Hara, H. Hasegawa.

We would also like to thank Mr K. Itami of Japan Steel Corporation, and K. Fukuchi of Toray, F. Suzuki of JTUC's RIALS, and H. Oh of JIL.

M. Nitta and researchers at the Social Science Research Institute, Tokyo University kindly hosted Whittaker during a research sabbatical, which was supported by a Japan Foundation Fellowship. Travel support from the Japan Foundation Endowment Committee (UK) is also gratefully acknowledged, as well as support from ITEC/COE at Doshisha University.

The Centre for Economic Performance, LSE, hosted Inagami during sabbatical leave. Thanks to R. Dore, again, to R. Layard, R. Freeman and N. Rogers, and also to D. Marsden and H. Gospel.

We have both benefited from conversations with W. Brown of Cambridge University, and D. Gallie and M. Sako of Oxford University, on various occasions.

Anonymous referees' comments were very helpful for making our final revisions.

Finally, we would like to thank our families for putting up with our preoccupations and increasing administrative workloads.

Part 1

The End of the Community Firm?

1   Company as Community

Entering a minefield

In writing about companies-as-communities, or 'community firms' in Japan, we are entering a minefield.[1] The term eludes neat definition, and easy quantification. And for some people, it evokes negative reactions. The Japanese equivalent – *kigyo kyodotai* – can conjure up images of oppressive wartime control and 'feudal' communitarian institutions.[2] For some, it epitomizes Japan's 'corporate-centred society' and its associated patriarchal order. Community companies are male-dominated, discriminate against women, encroach on and distort family life (Osawa, 1993; Kumazawa, 2000). Collectively, they have created Japan's 'corporate capitalism', which perverts fundamental capitalist and market principles, breeds corruption and impedes healthy social development (Okumura, 1975, 1984, 1992). For others, they served a purpose during Japan's catch-up phase of development, but those days are over. Without a process of creative destruction, which includes 'Japanese-style management' and community firms, Japan will flounder in the twenty-first century (Tsujimura, 1998). Some of these criticisms, in fact, now find expression in official government publications, and the Japanese government itself has become one of the biggest critics.

On the other hand, community companies have their defenders, including the heads of some of Japan's most successful corporations, although they may not use the expression directly. Canon's president, for instance, declared:

---

[1] Throughout the book we use 'firm' and 'company' interchangeably. Japanese names appear with the surname first, followed by the given name.

[2] Cf., for instance, Kyochokai jikyoku taisaku iinkai, 1938. Fujita (1982: 230) notes that the material desperation of 1945–55 was lightened by the collapse of Japan's fascist regime. The communitarian elements of this regime were criticized by 'modernist' scholars such as M. Maruyama, H. Otsuka, T. Kawashima, K. Okochi and T. Fukutake.

    We have avoided using the expression 'corporate communities' because of possible confusion with groups of companies, or *keiretsu*, or company networks.

The advantage of lifetime employment is that employees absorb the company's culture throughout their careers. As a result, team spirit grows among them – a willingness to protect the corporate brand and stick together to pull through crises. I believe that such an employment practice conforms to Japanese culture and is our core competency to survive global competition.[3]

Mitarai's identification of lifetime employment and associated practices as his company's core competency resonates with growing recognition of the importance of communities for learning and innovation (Lave and Wenger, 1991; Wenger, 1998).

Given such divergent and often charged views, it is difficult to write a dispassionate account about how the community aspects of Japan's large corporations are changing. Our own prejudices and preferences will become clear during the course of this book, and particularly in Part 3, but our interests are not nostalgic. Japan is changing, and the community characteristics of large corporations are changing – must change – too. They must do this in order to remain core competences. To say this, however, is neither to predict, nor to advocate, their demise at the invisible hands of market forces.

As we enter the minefield, we begin with a skeletal definition of company-as-community, and add flesh throughout this chapter. In the community company, employment relations go beyond an economic contract to include what is sometimes called a psychological (or social) contract, which even if implicit, is tangible enough to influence effort and reward. This implicit contract involves an exchange of loyalty and effort for security, and is integrated into management priorities and the ordering of stakeholder claims. This in turn engenders a sense of membership and facilitates the development of shared norms and 'we-consciousness', which may become a source of motivation, but which may also override individual interests, especially in the short term. Various means are used to minimize them–us divisions within the company and foster a sense of membership, for core members at least, within the boundaries of the company.[4]

We use the expression 'community companies' instead of, for instance, 'organization orientation' because we want to draw attention to the norms and informal integrating mechanisms which complement or underpin formal organization structures. In the midst of organization reforms and restructuring, some form of organization structure will remain, but the community aspects may be lost. As with organization orientation, however, we consider the community company in polar opposition to a model

[3] F. Mitarai, *Nikkei Weekly*, 18 March 2002, cited in Jacoby, 2004, p. 168.
[4] There is a long history of writing about the social and ethical dimensions of Japanese companies; cf. Abegglen, 1958; Ouchi, 1981; Pascale and Athos, 1981.

of the firm featuring market-oriented, contractual employment, governance and management, and we are interested in how far large Japanese companies are moving towards this opposite pole in these dimensions.[5] Community *firms* is also used, however, in distinction from occupation or class solidarity, which may produce in-company cleavages.

Whether seen as a source of injustice or fairness, inefficient inertia or innovation-enabling competence, the community aspects of large Japanese companies matter, even if they are in many ways intangible. More directly tangible are *employment practices, corporate governance and management priorities, or ideologies*. Changes to these are likely to have an impact on the community aspects of such companies, and by entering the minefield, we gain a vantage point from which to observe these changes, their interaction, and their consequences.[6]

Community companies and company man

While our empirical interest is mainly in large Japanese companies, our theoretical interests and questions have been stimulated by developments in other countries. In the 1970s and 1980s 'lifetime employment' and seniority-based wages and promotion were popularized as peculiarly Japanese phenomena. Indeed they were enshrined as two of the three pillars or 'sacred treasures' of Japanese-style management, the third being enterprise-based unions. Yet the practice of recruiting new or recent graduates and employing them until retirement can – or could – be found in the public sector and large companies in many countries, even those with relatively high labour mobility, such as the USA and UK. And wages rising with age and tenure are – were – also common in those countries, at least for white-collar employees (Dore, 1973; Koike, 1983, OECD, 1997).

Even community firms may not be distinctively Japanese. Heckscher's (1995) study of middle managers in eight manufacturing companies in the USA identified long-term employment, internal promotion, a bureaucratic work ethic, company as a source of identity and object of commitment, sense of shared interests, firm-specific skills, paternalism and an implicit contractual exchange of loyalty for job security. He called these 'communities of loyalty'.

Heckscher, in turn, was building on a tradition of corporate studies in the USA. Kanter (1977) graphically depicted the organization and

---

[5] On the 'community model' versus the 'company law' model of the firm, see for instance, Dore, 1987, 2000.
[6] We are primarily concerned with large companies in this book. Small firms exhibit different community features; cf. Inagami and Yahata, 1999; Whittaker, 1997.

social world of managers, their wives and clerical workers in 'Indsco' in the 1970s. For managers, this world featured long-term employment and internal advancement, unlimited loyalty towards the company and blurring of work and private life, shared values, company-specific language, and gendered roles.[7] 'Organization man' was indeed a man. Earlier still, Whyte (1956) portrayed the rise of organization man, subjected to new collective social ethics in 'feudal communities', and Riesman (1950) identified 'other-directed' employees who had supplanted 'inner-directed' workers and owners of early capitalism.

Sampson (1995) suggests that company man was born in pre-industrial trading companies, like the British East India Company, and became widely diffused in large corporations by the end of the nineteenth century. Such corporations constructed their own community values and rules, usurping the centrality of the extended family, church and farm estate in society. Their values, rules and practices encompassed long-term (lifetime) employment, internal promotion, hierarchies, bureaucratic organization, loyalty to the company, patriarchy and paternalism.

In a general sense, then, community companies and 'company man' are widespread phenomena. Japan's distinctiveness lies not in their existence, but in their scope and specific features, which we will discuss below.

Observers of large organizations and company man the USA, however, noted a series of fundamental changes which occurred in the 1980s and 1990s. Heckscher's communities of loyalty either disintegrated, or were transformed. And when Kanter revisited Indsco in the early 1990s she found a paradigmatic shift away from 'corporatism'. In the Afterword to the 1993 edition of *Men and Women of the Corporation* (pp. 290–1), she cited six changes to work and career which occurred in the 1980s:

1. From fat to lean: a shift in employment assumptions that 'big is better' to 'smaller is beautiful' – cutting back on employment, relying on outsourcing and external suppliers, making organizations more flexible and cost-efficient, but straining people's endurance while undermining their security.
2. From vertical to horizontal: a change from hierarchical emphasis, vertical chains of command and promotion to cross-functional or cross-department teams, horizontal emphasis and collaboration.

---

[7] Regarding loyalty, one first line manager said of a former company: 'You won't believe this, but upper management expected you to come in on Sundays too – not to work, but just to be seen on the premises – supposed to show how much you loved the damn place . . . I did it a few times, and then said to hell with it – it's not worth it . . . I started to get passed over on promotions, and I finally asked why. My boss said they weren't sure about my attitude, and for me to think about it. Attitude! How does that grab you?' (Kanter, 1977: 65).

3. From homogeneity to diversity: increased access for women and minorities, globalization of professional labour markets, team diversity, managing and even affirming diversity.
4. From status and command rights to expertise and relationships: hierarchy-derived formal authority giving way to professional expertise for building expertise and leadership; increased emphasis on external relationship building.
5. From company to project: weaker attachments to the company, stronger attachments to profession or project team – sense of worth from these rather than bond with a particular company.
6. From organizational capital to reputational capital: shift in career assets from organizational capital derived from climbing internal career ladders to portable career assets of skills and reputation that can be applied anywhere.

Bennett (1990) also depicted the death of organization man, based on interviews of managers affected by restructuring and downsizing in major USA companies in the 1980s. While not fully developed, her image of 'new organization man' – someone who uses his (or her) skills as a weapon to move company as necessary rather than rely on a single company – is basically similar to those of Kanter and Heckscher. All three found community companies, which flourished in postwar USA, crumbling in the 1980s.

Cappelli (1999a, b) argues that these changes came about by the increasing penetration of market forces in employment relations, governance and management.[8] Jacoby (1997, 1999), on the other hand, sees two patterns of employment and industrial relations in large US corporations, a blue-collar internal labour market (job control) pattern, and a white-collar internal labour market pattern. The latter features long-term employment, internal promotion, seniority rights, flexible job contents, enterprise-based industrial relations and company-provided welfare. These features are similar to Japanese companies, but the US companies they are most commonly found in are non-unionized. Jacoby denies that 'welfare capitalism' is dead in the USA, but he acknowledges that both types underwent major changes in the 1980s, when greater risk was thrust on to employees.

Are similar forces – the quickening pace of technological innovation, intensification of global competition, increasing shareholder pressure, and so on – bringing similar changes to Japan? Or will the distinctive features of Japan's community firms forestall such changes, or create a different trajectory for transformation? Will change, if it is happening, be

[8] Cf. also Cappelli et al., 1997.

incremental, or discontinuous? These are questions we examine in this book.

Community firms in Japan: a selective review

Community companies and 'Japanese-style' management

Before we do so, however, we need a better understanding of community companies and their main features in Japan. In this section we will selectively review relevant research, without becoming entangled in debates which have often generated more theoretical heat than empirically grounded light.

We begin with Tsuda, who cited research into white-collar managers in the UK (Pahl and Pahl, 1971) and the USA (Kanter, 1977) to argue that community companies were a universal phenomenon, associated with 'modern management' (Tsuda, 1981: 337–50). All modern companies, he suggested, were communities, and Japanese companies were simply one variant. The decline of local communities in modern cities coincided with the rise of work as the central life interest of white-collar workers, resulting in the 'communitization of modern management'. A precondition for this was long-term, stable employment and living security provided by the company on the one hand, and long-term skill development by employees on the other. This in turn required managers to satisfy both the expectations of employees, and the need for economic efficiency, with inspirational qualities and authority, raising the work ethic to higher levels (Tsuda, 1976, 1977, 1981).

If anything was distinctively Japanese about lifetime employment for Tsuda, it was that it remained an implicit guarantee. What was distinctive about seniority-based wages was their application to blue-collar workers in the postwar period. Similarly, co-operative industrial and workplace relations were distinctive only in their particular manifestations, such as the *ringi* system.[9]

Tsuda's 'modern management' is dated from today's perspective, but it is worth noting his view of community companies as a universal phenomenon, and that lifetime employment and seniority-based wages were not distinctively Japanese. Here he drew on Koike's (1977) USA–Japan comparative studies. Subsequently, however, Tsuda's views underwent a metamorphosis. He downplayed the association of community companies with modern management, and came to see Japanese management

---

[9] *Ringi* is the 'bottom-up' circulation of a document to collect the signatures of relevant parties before a formal decision is made.

and community companies as developing in stages, from prewar familistic communities through 'Japanese-style' management (1945–85) to (legal) community companies (1985–), with each stage rooted in Japan's distinctive culture and differing fundamentally from the 'West'.

In contrast to Tsuda, Mito's (1976, 1991a, b) view of Japanese management and community companies was particularistic from the beginning, and linked to the 'logic of the *ie* (family or household)'.[10] Management based on this logic was quite different from that in the 'West', and for this reason, Western 'universal' theories failed to capture the distinctive reality of Japan. For Mito the logic of the *ie* had become the logic of the Japanese company, whose employees were *ie* members (1991a: 310).[11] Mito's premise of historical continuity also contrasts with Tsuda, for whom there was significant discontinuity between prewar and postwar Japanese management.

Iwata, too, stressed continuity. He argued that Japanese management should be understood in the context of workplace and company-based communities (1977: 57), rooted in a distinctive – and continuous – Japanese psychology, necessitating an 'indigenous management theory' (1978). Japanese people sought stable affiliation with a group, for instance, and based on this psychology, organization relations stressing stability gave rise to lifetime employment (1977: 11).[12] In contrast to Mito's 'logic of the *ie*', however, Iwata saw Japanese management as growing out of Japanese villages or *mura*.[13] The key features were: long-term, continuous employment and trading relations; emphasis on harmony; respect for status/position; emotional stability of group membership; avoidance of sudden change; coexistence of stability preference and stagnation avoidance; and unlimited responsibility of organization members.

---

[10] The 'logic of the *ie*' was: *ie* as community; *ie* as management unit, managed to transcend generations; kin and non-kin members; family members indentured for the sake of the *ie*; family trade or business, managed with the head's family and assets; head and family relations as parent–child relations, characterized by patriarchal benevolence and absolutism; stratification and ability-ism; discipline of members; household norms and rules; main and branch lines, characterized by parent–child relations, also found in relations with powerful families, forming extended units; and insider–outsider distinctions (Mito, 1991a: 309–10).

[11] The *ie* was elevated even further in the work of Murakami, Kumon and Sato (1979) as the key to understanding Japanese 'civilization', in contrast with that of the West. Different usage of concepts such as *ie* both complicated and intensified debates on Japanese management.

[12] This is an exemplary *Nihonjinron*, or theory of Japanese distinctiveness. Other Nihonjinron theorists in management include Odaka (discussed below), Hamaguchi and Kumon (cf. Hamaguchi, 1977; Hamaguchi and Kumon, 1982).

[13] 'If members took the *ie* as their fundamental collective unit, they would almost certainly face ostracism' (Iwata, 1977: 30).

Despite his emphasis on continuity, Iwata saw a number of serious challenges to Japanese management in the 1970s; problems arising from low growth and lack of opportunities for expansion, changing consciousness of youth, environmental challenges such as pollution, and relations with other 'cultures' (1977: 247–9).

Odaka (1981, 1984, 1995) incorporated the views of Mito and Iwata, though somewhat ambiguously. He saw Japanese management – including lifetime employment, seniority, harmony emphasis, bottom-up management and paternalism – as based on groupism, under which members perceived their group as a 'community of fate' which they dedicated themselves to. Their involvement was holistic, their status rose with seniority, and their interests became fused with the group, whose policies were decided by consensus, with regard for the welfare of members.

Groupism for Odaka, too, had long historical roots, dating back at least to the agricultural village communities of the Tokugawa period. Nonetheless, he thought that the merits of Japanese-style management's distinctive features could at the same time become demerits. Response to the demerits brought modification, while at the same time underlying principles were slowly becoming diluted by individualism.

On balance these authors stressed continuity rather than change in Japanese management, in the form of livelihood communities (Tsuda), the *ie* logic (Mito), national psychology (Iwata) and cultural roots of groupism (Odaka). And with the exception of Tsuda, they assigned these features a central role and contrasted them with the 'West'. Exceptionalism is one thing, but when it is linked to unchanging cultural features it runs the danger of becoming cultural reductionism.[14]

Our position, as suggested in the previous section, is closer to Tsuda's early view; community companies are not restricted to Japan, and can – or could – be found in other countries, even though there are distinctive Japanese features, which we will sketch at the end of this chapter. And while there may be continuities, we see Japanese management and

---

[14] All countries are exceptional in some respects. For British exceptionalism, see for instance Rubinstein, 1977; and Cain and Hopkins, 1993. For American exceptionalism, see Lipset, 1996. The issue is how these exceptional features are construed – within a framework allowing for comparison of variables and their combinations, or within an overarching cultural framework posited as unique. (Cf. Maruyama, 1984: 125–30.) To the debates about Japanese management we could add the 'structure of domination' views of Nishiyama and Okumura. Nishiyama characterized Japanese management as a structure of domination by employee-managers, which freed the companies from the imperatives of capital. He saw this 'post-capitalist' system as a new stage in evolutionary development, beyond American management, which in turn had succeeded European management (Nishiyama, 1980, 1983). Okumura's (1975, 1984) 'corporate capitalism' theory was highly critical of Nishiyama (and Japanese capitalism), but neither saw Japanese management as deriving from a distinctive Japanese culture.

community companies as historical and evolving. To some extent Iwata recognized this and Odaka began to elaborate on it.

Managerial familism

Another strand of research drew attention to continuities and disconti-nuities with prewar managerial ideology, notably managerial familism, which also likened the company to an *ie*, backed by Confucian familism, and employer–employee relations to parent–child relations. The head exercises wide-ranging authority over his wards in a patronage–loyalty relationship, and once the ward becomes a full member, the relationship is not easily broken (lifetime employment). Even under adverse conditions, living wages are paid, with consideration for age and family composition (seniority- or *nenko*-based wages). Welfare measures are an expression of paternalism, and there is a predilection towards minimizing or disguising conflicts of interest (co-operative industrial relations).

According to Hazama (1964, 1979), managerial familism fitted late development, the need to train workers internally, and then to retain them. It also served as a restraint against the burgeoning labour movement in the early interwar years. The Confucian ethics on which it was based, however, impeded the development of modern, contractual employment opportunities, and parity in labour–management relations.[15]

Hazama traced this ideology backwards to the merchant houses of Tokugawa Japan,[16] and forwards to its postwar transformation into 'man-agerial welfarism'. The latter shared such features as lifetime employment and seniority-based wages, but it was based on industrial democracy rather than Confucian familistic ideology, creating employment stability, 'fair' wages and labour–management understanding.[17] While the ideol-ogy underpinning community *companies* had changed, however, commu-nity *workplaces* had been destroyed during Japan's postwar high growth, exposing individual employees directly to the influence of centralized managerial authority.[18] This unhealthy development, he argued, needed

---

[15] Morishima (1982), by contrast, saw Confucian ethics – based on loyalty and piety rather than virtue – as instrumental in Japan's economic success.

[16] Cf. Nakano's (1968) classic study of merchant house management.

[17] Ujihara (1989 [1980]: 232–8), too, contrasted patriarchal familistic ideology of the pre-war period with 'shared labour–management norms of productivity improvement and a fair distribution of the results' of the postwar period. Noting the importance of an integrating management ideology, he suggested – over twenty years ago – that the insti-tutional features of these norms and the derived stability-emphasizing ideology formed during Japan's high growth period would need to be replaced by a new ideology.

[18] Hazama did not elaborate on this 'destruction', but no doubt he had in mind the spread of centralized personnel management and 'efficiency wages' in the steel industry, for instance, and centralization of the authority to call strikes; cf. Tekkororen and Rodo Chosa Kyogikai, 1980.

to be rectified by the recreation of workplace-based communities, semi-autonomous from the company.

Matsushima (1962) studied managerial familism at the Hitachi Mine in 1954–5, just prior to Japan's postwar takeoff. He painted a striking picture of the miners' housing, self-contained welfare facilities – public baths, hospital, theatre, club, barber, even crematorium – and parasitic shops, cut off from the wider world by mountains and *heimat* self-sufficiency.

Managerial familism, he argued, was not confined to the Hitachi Mine, but was a feature of large postwar Japanese companies. It included multi-generation and kin employment, lifetime employment, seniority wages, housing and other welfare measures normally provided by the state, disciplinarian in-house education and personalized superior–subordinate human relations. He predicted that this 'familistic, patriarchal and living security regime' would gradually change, however, in the face of the advancing labour movement, changing labour markets, technological innovation and development of a public welfare system (Matsushima, 1962, 1971).

Matsushima did not differentiate prewar managerial familism from postwar managerial welfarism like Hazama, but he predicted that managerial familism would decline. As we shall see, though, the living security he emphasized persisted, as an underlying principle of the 'classic model' of Japanese employment practices.

The community firm in comparison

Finally in this selective review, we look at an influential comparative study, which strengthened the view of company-as-community in Japan. In the late 1960s, as the ideology of managerial familism was declining in Japan, and a Royal Commission (the Donnovan Commission) was launched to investigate the UK's troubled industrial relations, a team of British and Japanese researchers set about comparing industrial relations in the two countries.[19]

In the presentation of his findings, Hazama (1974) contrasted association-like employment relations in Britain with community-like employment relations in Japan. (Conversely, however, he found community-like relations between unions and their members in Britain, and association-like relations in Japan.) He saw an inherent relationship between British association-like employment relations, individualism and

[19] The project was set up in 1966 to look at industrial relations in three industries – steel, electric/electronics and construction. The British team consisted of Ronald Dore, Keith Thurley and Martin Collick, and the Japanese team of Hazama Hiroshi and Okamoto Hideaki.

class formation. Community-like employment relations in Japan had a number of contrasting features, as well as pathologies, he argued.

Employment relations in Japan were more diffuse, and employees had higher and more complex expectations of this relationship. Large companies in Japan were able to recruit elite graduates and retain them, with the downside of fostering introversion and narrow-mindedness. The elite were relatively homogeneous (in consciousness, but not necessarily ability). Being homogeneous, they were relatively easily managed, and when multi-skilled, could be deployed flexibly.

Strong co-worker consciousness, too, irrespective of position in the hierarchy, was complemented by the minimization of distinctions between manual and non-manual workers, aiding communication and the spirit of mutual support. On the downside, weak respect for individuals was combined with a centralization of management. If management was rational, it was very efficient, but justice from an individual perspective could be sacrificed. Co-operative industrial relations, too, supported by single unions in most large companies, had the downside of unions sometimes becoming adjuncts of the company's personnel department.

Hazama's conceptual framework was based on Parson's (1951) pattern variables, particularly specificity and diffuseness of the functions of the group. The latter was linked to a community orientation. He placed these on one axis, and voluntary–coerced participation on another to create two types of community, voluntary and coercive. He saw many Japanese corporate communities as lying in the coercive-community quadrant.

Another major product of this project, more sympathetic to Japan, was Dore's (1973) *British Factory – Japanese Factory*. In this book Dore expanded on his earlier (1958) thesis of Japan skipping a stage – Riesman's inner-directed stage – of development in its industrialization. He contrasted the resulting organization-oriented 'welfare corporatism' of 'Japanese Factory' (Hitachi) with the early industrializer, market-oriented employment system of 'British Factory' (English Electric).[20] And like Hazama, he differentiated between welfare provision as institutionalized employee right – the postwar version – and welfare provision as an expression of paternalism – the prewar version.[21]

---

[20] Around the same time that Dore employed the term 'welfare corporatism', political economists began using the term 'corporatism' in macro-level analysis. Eventually the latter began to examine – tentatively – corporate level governance and industrial relations under the concept of 'micro-corporatism'. Dore used 'welfare corporatism' to provide a distinction from welfare statism on the one hand, and traditional paternalism on the other.

[21] The postwar version in terms of *institutions*, at least, as Dore perceived a lag in terms of informal relations between superiors and inferiors (1973: 219).

In chapter 8 of *British Factory – Japanese Factory*, titled 'The Enterprise as Community', Dore depicted the extensive welfare provision of Hitachi, and the importance of the company in the private lives and social identity of employees. Participation in sports club or recreation activities was virtually universal. Weddings, funerals, etc. involved virtually everyone from the workplace, irrespective of rank. For these ends, management directives could be extended outside the workplace. The union was actively involved in welfare measures, and the company in cultivating employees' minds. Employees' families were treated as adjunct members of the enterprise family. The priorities of the company took precedence over those of the family. When going on a holiday, the 'Hitachi man' would wear his company badge. Relations between company and employee were thus diffuse, and employees generally accepted this as a good thing.

Dore did not elaborate directly on the requisites for creating community companies, but he periodically returned to the conditions associated with ideal typical 'organization orientation', as opposed to 'market orientation'. In the latter, both the primary social as well as legal definition of the firm assigns ownership to the shareholders, who are its 'members'. The managers, as the shareholders' agents, contract at arm's length with the employees to provide labour, as they might contract with suppliers of parts or services. By contrast, in an organization-oriented system the primary social definition of the firm, as opposed to the legal definition, is of a community, belonging principally to the employees, who are its 'members'. Managers act as senior members of the firm community. A relationship of trust exists between them and other members of the community, not between them and shareholders, who are simply one group they have to keep happy, like the banks, insurance companies, suppliers and distributors. Agreed mergers may happen, but not hostile takeovers. This implies that the company-as-community is heavily influenced by their corporate governance (Dore, 1989, 1990).

At various points, too, Dore asked whether Britain was becoming more community- or organization-oriented, or what it could do to become so. Beyond changes in employment relations *per se*, this would involve tipping the scales away from shareholders in favour of employees by limiting hostile takeovers, promoting employee share ownership and industrial democracy. Again, he emphasized corporate governance, as well as the fairness of distribution rules.[22]

---

[22] Dore, 1987: 51f., 145–65. He listed four types of fairness – equal pay for equal work, equal percentage pay increases for all, equal shares in the fruits of shared effort (ESSE) and equal pay for enterprises of equal standing – and argued that ESSE meshed best with the community model of the firm, and was of growing importance.

Community roots remained shallow in British firms, however, and by the mid-1980s there was a strong neo-liberal counter-current, with a strengthening of market-oriented governance and employment relations. In the views of the writers cited earlier, these led to the demise of community-as-company in the UK (and USA). This counter-current, moreover, reached Japan and Germany in the 1990s. Dore took up the 'Darwinian clash' in *Stock Market Capitalism, Welfare Capitalism* (Dore, 2000). By this stage he had become equivocal about the prospects of survival of the Japanese system, and with it, the community firm, although he predicted that Japan would offer stiffer resistance than Germany. He actually found less evidence of substantive change than his forebodings suggested.

Implications

Let us now tease out some of the implications of this selective review, supplementing it with relevant 'middle range' theory.

First, as Hazama and Dore suggested, the primary unit of community companies is not the workplace or occupation, but the company itself. The company is a source of self-identity for members. Affiliation encourages spontaneous contributions to the group, solidaristic behaviour and mutual support. Collective norms and sanctions operate. Community companies are 'functionally diffuse'.[23]

Second, there are boundaries to such sentiments and behaviour, and closure with respect to membership and networks of social relations. These are reinforced by stability. (Conversely, frequent movement or change of members impedes community formation.) As a result, however, a gulf can open between internal behaviour, standards and even language, and those outside the community boundaries.[24]

Third, community companies emerge under certain conditions:
- Entry to a group with high social prestige and high entry barriers heightens the sense of affiliation and behaviour supportive of the group.
- When entry to the group depends on a comprehensive evaluation rather than specific abilities, affiliation tends to be status-related rather than contractual.
- Broad and deeply shared interests between members and the group promote community formation. When relations are diffuse, the scope for shared interests expands. When affiliation is long-term, shared interests tend to deepen.

[23] This diffuseness may be a requirement for their formation, but not necessarily their continuation.

[24] In other words, inside virtues–outside vices: Merton, 1948 [1968].

- Membership matters, and the identity and ideology of managers are especially important. When managers have strong employee characteristics – through internalized careers, the nature of their work and their remuneration – formation of community companies is facilitated. Conversely, when managers behave as agents of shareholders it is difficult to form a community at the corporate level; formation of shared interests between shareholders and managers takes priority, weakening shared interests with employees.
- Shared interests between manual and non-manual workers contribute to community formation.
- When 'pie distribution' accords with members' perceptions of distributional fairness, shared interests and sense of affiliation are strengthened.
- Where core members have internal career orientations, identity and affiliation with the group is strengthened, becoming moral in nature. To paraphrase Goldthorpe et al., a 'bureaucratic orientation to work' facilitates community formation.[25]
- If members can contribute to decision-making of the group spontaneously, their sense of identity and affiliation with the group is strengthened, as well as mutually supportive relations and solidarity.[26]
- Where affiliation is long-term and the livelihood of members becomes dependent on the fate of the firm, 'conflict' with other groups can mobilize employee energy and strengthen internal cohesion.[27]
- If the norms and values of a sub-group mirror those of the larger group, affective solidarity in the sub-group can strengthen attachment to the larger group.[28]

These propositions in essence boil down to three empirical issues: employment practices; corporate governance and priorities; value orientations or ideologies of community members, particularly managers.

Fourth, there are various types of community company, depending on the combination and strength of various features. Managerial ideologies have a particularly strong influence.

Fifth, there are both merits and demerits to community companies. On the plus side there is the living security for employees, 'egalitarian' distributional fairness, shared incentives for technological innovation

---

[25] Orientations to work are a basic ordering of the various needs and expectations of workers for their working lives. Goldthorpe et al. identified a 'solidaristic orientation' amongst 'traditional' manual workers, and 'instrumental orientation' among 'affluent' manual workers, and a 'bureaucratic orientation' among white-collar workers, as well as a fourth, 'professional orientation', which they did not elaborate on. They gave a multi-faceted view of Britain's 'affluent workers' (Goldthorpe et al., 1968a, b; 1969). Inagami (1981) contrasted the first two with the 'bureaucratic orientation' of Japanese blue-collar workers.

[26] Cf. Durkheim, 1893.   [27] Cf. Simmel, 1955 [1908]; Coser, 1956.

[28] Dore, 1973: 275.

(particularly of the incremental type) and productivity improvement, and an environment generally conducive to situated learning and innovation, mutual support and co-operative industrial relations. On the negative side the private interests of members can be subsumed into those of the company. The result is 'greedy institutions' (Coser, 1974) and 'company man'.[29] Company man is indeed a man, and women tend to acquire only quasi-member status. And finally, inside virtues–outside vices, if unchecked, can produce corporate scandals, in which the protection of corporate interests override accountability to customers and other external parties, as well as the law.

As Kanter (1977), Heckscher (1995) and, earlier Whyte (1956) show, such problems are not confined to Japan's community firms. What may be distinctive about community firms in Japan is, first, the relative weakness of countervailing tendencies – because of its late development, Japan 'skipped' the stage of small-scale 'inner-directed' capitalism, allowing for greater continuity with past (or invented) collective traditions, although there is an individualistic tradition in small firms (Whittaker, 1997). Second, they expanded to encompass regular blue-collar workers in the postwar period, which was an important factor in shopfloor-based learning, productivity improvement and innovation (cf. Udagawa et al., 1995). In this sense, 'communities of practice' were actively nurtured and harnessed for corporate goals, in the productive core of organizations. Third, there has been a strong emphasis on management through homogeneity and uniformity, which extends beyond the seniority or *nenko* principle. And fourth, postwar corporate communities built on welfare corporatism were different from those built on managerial familism, but Confucian-influenced paternalism did not completely disappear from managerial ideologies.

In this chapter we selectively reviewed writing on community firms, and discussed the conditions which foster their creation. We identified the need to pay particular attention to employment practices, corporate governance, and member value orientations or ideologies, particularly those of managers. Accordingly, in chapter 2 we look at the manifestation of these in the 'classic model'. This establishes a benchmark against which we examine changes and continuity, first in employment practices between 1975 and 2000 (chapter 3). In chapter 4 we examine the growing importance of white-collar professionals or 'creative workers' in large companies, and implications for classic model employment practices. Chapter 5 moves on to examine corporate governance, and

---

[29] One premise of the publicly sponsored movement to reduce working hours in Japan in the late 1980s was that, even if supported by loyal employees, companies had encroached excessively on the private lives of their members.

the impact of corporate governance reform on employment and industrial relations. In chapter 6 we look at management reform, especially consolidated management. We also examine related changes in group-wide employment and industrial relations. This yields insight into managers' priorities, or ideologies. Chapter 7 summarizes and concludes Part 1.

2 The Classic Model: Benchmark for Change

The demise of the community firm and 'Japanese-style' employment have been predicted for almost as long as they have been recognized. Consider this observation, written forty years ago:

> Technological innovation is necessitating changes in personnel management and there is a change of generation in the workplace . . . Managerially, it will not be possible to continue with *nenko* wages which were made possible by the lag between productivity improvements and increases in labour costs; generally speaking Japanese-style employer–employee and union–management relations are headed for a period of fundamental reform.[1]

As many respectable scholars have predicted the end for so long, a certain caution is in order before we, too, join the chorus. We cannot assume, as many do, that a changing environment will automatically spell the end of the community firm. What has changed, and what has not? In order to answer this question, we first need to establish a benchmark.

As we wrote in chapter 1, our three empirical areas of focus will be employment practices, corporate governance and management priorities, or ideology. In addition, we need to look at the boundaries and nature of community membership. In this chapter we will sketch key features or practices associated with the postwar 'classic model' of the community firm in these four areas. These will provide a benchmark for evaluating change.

Members, quasi-members and non-members

We start with membership. According to Japan's Commercial Code the company belongs to its shareholders, and they are its members. The common perception is different, however. Shareholders are not members, and

---

[1] Okamoto, 1965 [1987]: 136. Even earlier: 'For modern companies lifetime employment makes it difficult to adjust workforces with technological innovation. Henceforth the merits of maintaining managerial familism will come to outweigh the merits' (Hazama, 1960: 123).

neither are customers and trading partners. They do not 'eat from the same rice bowl'.[2] Non-regular employees are generally not viewed as full members, either, even though in firms in industries like retail and catering, they may constitute the bulk of the workforce. They are generally employed in hierarchical, status-based relationships with regular employees, which see them relegated to quasi-member status.

Full members are limited to regular employees. Pre-eminent among these are managers, as senior employees. Ideally, they join the company following graduation, and after lengthy internal careers they move into the top posts.[3] In terms of interest representation, they are not the agents of shareholders. *Because of this*, they can represent the community firm as its pre-eminent members.

In the postwar classic model, both non-manual and manual employees are full members, and distinctions between them are minimized (Inagami, 1981, 1985; Koike, 1988). Historically, the compression of wage differentials was preceded by the abolition of manual–non-manual status differences, the product of a burgeoning labour movement in the early postwar years.

Women, on the other hand, are seldom accorded full membership, even if they are regular employees. They are not necessarily excluded on the grounds of gender *per se*, but on the grounds of mobility, or potential mobility – the belief that they will not continue working long-term.[4] Real or potential mobility, however, reflects a strongly gendered division of household labour. Regular female employees occupy an ambiguous position nearer to short-term employees – traditionally temporary workers and day labourers, and nowadays part-time and contract workers, as well as foreign workers – than regular male employees. They tend to be seen as quasi-members.[5]

---

[2] Things are not always so clear-cut. As we shall see in chapter 6, movement of employees between companies in the same enterprise group is common, as well as close relations with subcontractors. In such cases, boundaries can be blurred.

[3] From their communities of practice perspective, Lave and Wenger describe a process of learning while moving from peripheral to full participation: '(L)earners inevitably participate in communities of practitioners and . . . the mastery of knowledge and skill requires newcomers to move toward full participation in the sociocultural practices of a community' (1991: 29).

[4] Frequent movement of members impedes community formation, and one requirement of full membership is long-term commitment and tenure. The consequences of exclusion, however, deter women from making long-term commitments – the process is self-reinforcing.

[5] Around the time the Equal Employment Opportunity Law was passed in 1985, many large companies introduced differentiated *sogo* (comprehensive/management) and *ippan* (general/clerical) tracks into their recruiting. Males and a limited number of females were recruited for the *sogo* track and the majority of women for the *ippan* track, which limited

The common perception, then, is of several categories of employee: managers, who are the pre-eminent members; regular male employees, including manual workers, who are full members; most regular female employees as quasi-members; and non-regular employees either as quasi-members or non-members. Thus there are at least three strata and categories of membership in the Japanese community company. As different categories of membership confer different rights and privileges, in some respects this is similar to Atkinson's (1985) 'flexible firm' model.

An important constituent of the community firm is the collective organization representing employee views – the enterprise-based union or employee association – at least as far as it plays an active role in constructing co-operative industrial relations. Where it plays no role, or an adversarial one, however, it is not considered part of the community. The employee shareholding association, a major shareholder in many large companies, is a latent constituent.[6]

And finally, there are employees' families. As we saw in chapter 1, community companies have tended to reach out to incorporate members' families, calling on the unpaid support of managers' wives, giving them adjunct-member status.[7] The gender bias of corporate communities can be seen here as well.

Significant changes to community firms can occur through alterations to community boundaries, membership status and means of integrating members. These, in turn, are influenced by employment relations or practices, corporate governance, and management priorities.

Employment practices

Underlying employment relations is a fundamental premise, of mutual support or compatibility between long-term living security for members on the one hand, and increasing corporate value through long-term skill development on the other.[8] Both are critical, but one does not necessarily

---

the place of work (*ippan* track employees were not subject to postings outside their home region) as well as promotion opportunities. This practice formalized common views of regular female employees and job tenure, and paradoxically discrimination.

[6] It is latent because there are few instances of the association actually exercising voice to influence management decisions. The overwhelming majority (95%) of listed companies have an employee shareholding association. According to a survey by the Tokyo Stock Exchange in March 2001 (TSE, 2002), 51% of employees belonged to their company's association, owning an average ¥1.4 million worth of shares. Employee shareholding associations are among the top ten shareholders in about half of listed companies. For the company, they are a passive, stable shareholder (cf. Michino, 1995).

[7] Cf. Whyte, 1956: part 7; Kanter, 1977: 104–26.

[8] Corporate value is not the same as shareholder value. It encompasses value for various stakeholders.

lead to the other. A number of practices have been institutionalized which embody these principles – lifetime employment (or more precisely, employment opportunities until retirement), *nenko* or seniority-based wages and promotion, and on-job-training (OJT) combined with career development. Let us look at these briefly in turn.

Lifetime employment

Lifetime employment – or long-term, stable employment – is an evolutionary product of management innovations in the 1910s–1920s, wartime controls in the late 1930s–early 1940s, union pressure after the war, and subsequent management innovations.[9] It evolved mainly through custom rather than direct legislation.[10] The Supreme Court, however, laid down certain conditions in various rulings as regards large-scale or retrenchment layoffs (*seiri kaiko*): Were they necessary? Were other means exhausted first? Was the selection of those to be laid off fair and appropriate? Was the procedure used appropriate (consulting the union, explaining to employees)? (Sugeno, 2002a, 2002b). While based on custom, then, long-term employment practices have been supported by judicial precedents which prevented managers from arbitrarily dismissing employees. In addition, labour policy in postwar Japan promoted long-term employment in various ways.[11]

If the legal environment was conducive to the institutionalization of lifetime employment, so was the economic environment. A long period of economic growth facilitated the establishment of the mutually supporting relationship between employment security and long-term value creation. As part of the attempt to rebuild Japan after the Second World War, improve productivity and overcome labour–management conflict, the Japan Productivity Centre was created in 1955 under the guidance of economists and social policy scholars such as Nakayama and Okochi (cf. Nitta, 1998). Initially its three principles of employment stability, joint consultation and fair distribution were created for macro-economic policy, but they gradually diffused within companies during the high growth period. In terms of the macro-economy too, co-operative industrial relations preceded the advent of full employment, and based on these a mechanism of 'moderate' wage increases was institutionalized.

---

[9] See, for instance, Gordon, 1985.   [10] Cf. Araki, 2001, 2002.

[11] Sugeno, 2002a; Inagami, 1998: 17f. Examples include establishment of the Employment Insurance Law, introduced in 1974 in the wake of the first oil crisis, and subsequent amendments such as the Employment Stability Fund System, Employment Development Services and Re-employment Allowances for Continuously Insured Older Persons.

The consolidation of lifetime employment was not simply the product of a supportive environment, a certain economic rationality, or management fear of upsetting industrial relations. Employers themselves considered it normatively desirable. Without reference to the norms of core members of the community firm – senior managers – we cannot fully account for the hesitation over employment adjustment and voluntary retirement schemes, attempts to secure jobs for middle-aged white-collar workers until retirement through secondment ('loan') or transfer, or assistance in job placement for those taking voluntary redundancy. Thus long-term employment is more than a statistical artefact.[12] Significantly, however, such norms are not extended to quasi-members or non-members, who face the brunt of employment adjustment when it is carried out.

On the other hand, long-term employment will crumble unless employees also consider it desirable. Employee career orientations, especially those of talented employees, are thus critically important.

Nenko *wages*

Nenko is a problematic word. 'Seniority' does not capture its complexity. It is made up of two Chinese characters, one of which refers to age, and the other to merit or achievement. It is not clear whether their combination means achievement which comes with age, automatically, or age plus achievement. The former interpretation assumes that there is a positive relationship between age and job ability, hence rewarding age and tenure is economically rational. The latter sees wages as partly based on personal attributes of age and tenure, and partly on evaluated ability and achievements. If *nenko* is suppressed, in the first interpretation it is because the relationship between age and job ability no longer holds; in the latter it is because the person-related elements – age and tenure – are being suppressed. When people talk about the collapse of *nenko*, as they have done for decades, they usually mean less *nen* (age and/or tenure) and more *ko* (merit).[13] This does not necessarily affect the age–wage curve, in which an upward slope is often taken by labour economists as evidence of seniority-based wages.

That is not all. *Nenko* wages also refer, implicitly, to a (male) bread-winner wage which varies according to life stage. Living costs generally begin to decline when breadwinners reach their mid-50s, and wages also decline around this age. According to this interpretation, providing it still

---

[12] Cf. OECD, 1984, 1997; Auer, 2000; Auer and Cazes, 2003; Streeck, 1996.

[13] Using a definition of *nenko* wages based strictly on age and tenure, for instance, Magota (1978) analysed the 1976 Wage Census and declared that, apart from university graduates, *nenko* wages had virtually collapsed.

supports living costs, a *downward sloping* age–wage curve can also represent a *nenko* wage. This, of course, is the very opposite of the rising curve assumption. Thus there is ample room for confusion, and we must be clear about which interpretation we are using. In the context of long-term living security, whose compatibility with long-term skill development forms the fundamental premise of employment relations, the living wage interpretation or dimension should not be ignored.

A further feature of the wage system is the suppression of differences within and between peer cohorts of community members, a product of postwar 'egalitarianism' and uniform management. As a result of recruiting practices, cohorts are relatively homogeneous in terms of age and education background, and differences in abilities are not reflected significantly in wages, even if they are apparent. And the annual earnings differential between corporate directors and new recruits is also kept small; until recently it was around ten times, a low figure by international comparison.

Nenko *promotion*

Differences in promotion of a given peer group of university graduates are minimized for a number of years at the beginning of careers, even if performance differs. With promotion to lower management ranks, length of tenure is considered alongside ability and performance, and promotion of younger employees over older employees in the same work unit is avoided.

Employees are rotated every few years to progressively more difficult work. They might have greater potential, but chances to use it are limited early on, while those with more seniority, having been posted to more difficult jobs, will have more opportunities. Thus ability differences of younger workers often remain latent until the opportunity for expression arises over a prolonged period of time. This is *nenko* promotion. On the one hand, performance and competition are built into the system through employees not wanting to fall behind their peers. On the other, it appears almost as an escalator system; once on the escalator – initial positions are determined by age, tenure, education and gender – relative positions hardly change.

When redundancies or layoffs occur, we might expect older workers to get laid off last, since age and tenure are supposedly valued in *nenko*. In fact, in case after case since the 1970s it is the older workers who are laid off first, whether voluntarily or involuntarily. This is similar in some respects to senior civil servants stepping down to make way for the front runners of a younger peer group. Wage costs are kept down, promotion tracks are cleared, and rejuvenation takes place, allowing the *nenko* mechanism to continue functioning. In the private sector not only directors but middle managers make way for younger cohorts through retirement, secondment or transfer in order of seniority (Inagami, 2003).

Long-term skill development

On the other side of the fundamental premise of employment relations is long-term skill development, which combines on-the-job training (OJT) and career development through job assignments. The former involves seniors and colleagues teaching employees the job through daily work. Human relations are critical for this, including a good balance between co-operation and competition, weighted towards trust-based interpersonal relations. The role played by the foreman or supervisor is critical, not just as the lowest rung of management, but conversely as a group leader, representing the group's interests, both to the management and other work groups. The foreman must foster trust, his role is diffuse, and sometimes extends beyond the workplace.[14]

Ambiguous job boundaries promote OJT (Koike, 1977). Instead of workers being assigned to do a job requiring specific skills, to some extent jobs are built around workers. This may be seen as poor staffing management, but it can also promote osmotic learning. OJT assumes that there are experienced workers to learn from, and inexperienced workers to pass knowledge on to, otherwise workers can end up doing the same work, and the assumption of increasing ability and achievement with age breaks down. It can also break down when technological innovation undermines the role of established skills, or new skills are acquired through off-JT. In practice, OJT in the narrow sense of learning through daily workplace situations is complemented by periodic rotations, postings or promotion, by small group activities like quality control (QC) circles, and off-JT and self-improvement.

Under this regime, workers who leave are cut off from the system which nurtures their skills, which may then degenerate in proportion to their absence. It works strongly against women, for instance, who may wish to take extended leave from work to raise children.[15]

---

[14] A long tradition of shopfloor studies includes Matsushima, 1951; Ujihara, 1953; Okochi et al., 1959; Koike, 1977; Inagami, 1981; Roshi kankei chosa iinkai, 1981; Nitta, 1987; and Nakamura, 1996. Okamoto (1966) describes the transition from the bootstrap foreman with little formal education or authority (the *nenko* foreman) to the 'new foreman' – more highly educated and with more formal authority, who emerged in the wake of technological innovation in the steel industry in the late 1950s.

[15] When they re-enter the labour market, they are often forced to do so on a part-time basis. Degeneration of skills *per se* does not account for this change of status, but the long-term skill development system is one of the institutional supports of the community firm, absence from which adversely affects membership.

Skills are developed gradually, over the long term, and in the process 'co-operative competition' is promoted. In the early years differences in promotion are suppressed, and there are chances for a recovery from a slight slip, encouraging workers to try not to fall behind their peers. There is no *de facto* policy of 'letting the cream rise to the top' – everyone is assumed to possess some 'cream' which needs to be drawn out.[16]

Finally, the system may be contrasted with the German approach where, in addition to OJT within companies, employees acquire externally recognized qualifications, which are linked to a system of industry-based wage determination. If Germany is a jointly (employer–union) managed 'qualification society', Japan is an employer-led 'corporate society'.[17]

Management priorities and corporate governance

A further institutional support of the community firm, and the long-term security–value creation employment dynamic, is the selection of top management from internally promoted employees. Top managers who come through this path are seen as the pre-eminent members of the community firm. They have made their way up through company ranks, surviving long-term selection on the basis of ability, personality and interpersonal skills, while benefiting from long-term living security and absorbing the principles of long-term skill development and corporate value creation. The small number of directors recruited from the outside – from the main bank, for example – are expected to exhibit the same sensitivities.

For the majority who are internally promoted, elevation to director status comes after a number of years as a division or general manager. In fact, they retain many of these management functions, even when they become senior managing directors.[18] For such directors, leadership is about securing the continuation, development and prosperity of the company as an ongoing community. In practice, this is often linked to sales growth emphasis, and maintenance or expansion of market share, for which purpose employee effort is mobilized, often against rival community firms. Organic growth is favoured, and may be complemented by mutually agreed, but not hostile, mergers and acquisitions.

---

[16] The rising cream analogy was used by some British managers in Whittaker's (1990) study of innovation in British and Japanese factories.

[17] Streeck, 1989, 1996; Inagami, 1999.

[18] Executives of subsidiaries often come from the core ('parent') company of the enterprise group. From the perspective of shared group interests, they are insiders as well, and are expected to raise the corporate value of that subsidiary.

Shareholders are not community members, and their interests are not prioritized. In fact, a common view in Japan is that their interests are sacrificed in favour of employee interests. Whether companies are actually managed in the interests of both shareholders and employees (cf. Aoki, 1994), however, if the company prospers both employees and shareholders benefit. Historically, shareholders have not expressed dissatisfaction at stable dividend policies, which most listed companies pursue, or indeed the dividends themselves.

This is no doubt related to the structure of share ownership and company financing. Postwar economic growth took place largely on the basis of indirect financing, in which 'main banks' played an important funding and monitoring (and on occasion, bail-out) role. And capital liberalization in the 1960s spurred the practice of stable, reciprocal shareholding, in which shareholding is an expression of a business relationship, with prior commitments and responsibilities. In normal circumstances, shareholders were largely silent, and capital was patient.[19]

In practice, internally promoted senior managers had to balance industrial relations on the one hand, and relations with major stable shareholders on the other, ensuring that the former were co-operative and based on trust, and that the latter group trusted them to get on with management.

In terms of accountability, a distinctive dual supervisory system (supposedly) operated. The board members supervised representative directors, but also had executive functions. In turn, the directors were supervised by the auditors. In reality, the board of directors did little supervision of representative directors; representative directors actually decided who board members should be. Auditors were frequently former directors. Thus the supervisory system effectively reinforced the long-term development, corporate value expansion orientation of senior management.

While top management – representative directors – were not significantly constrained by either the board of directors or the auditors, however, their freedom of action was constrained by their responsibilities as senior members of the community company, and to various stakeholders, including those they had inherited their position from.

Contingent factors

In brief, top management, corporate financing and the system of corporate governance complemented the institutional features of the

---

[19] On the origins of patient capital, see Okazaki, 1994; on main banks, see Patrick and Aoki, 1995.

employment system, and together, they strengthened the community characteristics of large companies in postwar Japan. That they did so, however, depended on a number of conditions, or functional requirements, being met. If those conditions cease to be met, the community model may well be forced to change, or may collapse.

In terms of employment, the first requirement is that the age–ability/achievement curve does not deviate too significantly from the age–wage curve. In the long term there must be a balance between living security and skill development, between wages and contributions. It is often claimed that employees are overpaid in their early 20s and their 50s, but that their contributions exceed wages in between. This is difficult to verify in practice, but notionally if the area under the age–ability curve falls below that of the age–wage curve, the imbalance will generate irresistible pressures for change. Ageing workforces can increase the portion of the workforce notionally overpaid, for instance. In addition, competitive pressures may shorten the time frame over which a balance is required.

Next, even if employers value long-term employment practices, if employees themselves – particularly the most able – seek greater mobility, the practices will ultimately be unsustainable. This can often be seen in small firms. And while long-term, stable employment is a necessary condition in the classic model, it is not a sufficient one. If employees' career aspirations and vocational needs – promotion opportunities to management, challenging work, suitable specialist work – are not met, their motivation will fall, and skill development and value creation will be impaired. To prevent this from happening, new institutional devices must be developed periodically.[20]

Relatedly, social relations at the workplace must be conducive to skill development through OJT. OJT cannot function if there is chronic understaffing, or no young employees to teach, and it will be impeded in the absence of mutual support, or in an atmosphere which discourages teaching and improvement.

A sense of distributional fairness is vital, but this can change or be challenged. A minimum guarantee which rises with age plus ability or performance, with relatively small differentials, was considered fair under the classic model, but as the nature of work changes, and greater emphasis is placed on performance, how big a gap should there be between peers with the same educational background? And how much of the 'pie' should be allocated to dividends, retained, used for executive remuneration

---

[20] New institutional devices aimed at *maintaining* the model, therefore, must be distinguished from those aimed at significantly *modifying* or *dismantling* it.

or employee pay? Notions of fairness could be challenged, as pressure mounts to assign greater priority to shareholder interests. There is no *a priori* set of rules to determine distributional fairness, but changing these and/or a changing sense of fairness would have an impact on the model.

The most critical requirement is that talented employees aim for top management posts, and that those top managers emphasize long-term company prosperity. If either internalized careers or management priorities (ideologies) change significantly – through changing values or changing conditions for long-term prosperity – so will the classic model.

Co-operative, enterprise-based industrial relations are in a sense a functional requirement of the classic model. The union voice helps to ensure employment stability, 'pie' increase effort, distributional fairness and interest adjustment.[21] If industrial relations deteriorate, or conversely if the union ceases to function effectively, there may well be knock-on effects for the model.

Finally, a number of buffer mechanisms provide flexibility to offset rigidities arising from long-term employment. They include adjusting working hours, variable use of non-regular workers, subcontracting and outsourcing, internal redeployment, temporary layoffs (in which the employment relationship is maintained, unlike layoffs in the USA), and secondment to subsidiaries. Bonuses and wages can also serve as buffers; it is not rare for employees to forgo wage increases or even take cuts to maintain employment. If use of buffer mechanisms is inhibited, pressures for change will mount, but if they become too extensive, the normative influence of the model will be undermined.

This list of conditions, or functional requirements, is by no means exhaustive. The point is that if some of them change, the institutional features of the model itself will come under pressure, and may even collapse. Conversely, however, if they continue to function, there is a good chance that the model will continue, though perhaps with periodic modification. This assumes that it can continue to deliver competitive performance, a requirement which cannot be taken for granted, particularly in the exposed, competitive sector where the model is most fully developed.

---

[21] For typologies of enterprise unions, see for instance, Inagami and Ide, 1995; Sato and Umezawa, 1983; Lee, 2001.

3   Change and Continuity

From the mid-1980s there was a groundswell of opinion that the Japanese community firm and employment model had outlived its day, and that a thoroughgoing overhaul was necessary. This now appears to be the official Japanese government view; without deregulation of labour policy, diversification of employment patterns and greater labour mobility, Japan will be unable to regain its vitality in the twenty-first century. We will not debate the pros and cons of the community firm and labour mobility here (but see chapter 14). Instead we will examine which parts of the model described in chapter 2 have changed since 1975, which have not, and why, focusing in this chapter on lifetime employment, *nenko* wages and promotion and long-term skill formation. 1975 is chosen because it marks the definitive break of the postwar high growth period, during which the classic model was constructed. The robustness of the model was tested in the mid-1970s following the first oil crisis, in the mid-1980s post Plaza Accord yen appreciation, and even more seriously, since the late 1990s.

The analysis is based on a number of surveys, mostly carried out by research groups chaired by Inagami. The surveys will be briefly introduced as they appear. Before the analysis, some brief background information on changes in the labour force and labour law will be helpful.

Background

Employment structure changes, 1975–2000

Between 1975 and 2000 the labour force population increased by 27%, from 53.2 million to 67.7 million. The increase in females and middle-aged workers was particularly marked.[1] The number of gainfully employed (which includes employees, self-employed and family workers)

---

[1] Statistics in this sub-section come from reports of official surveys carried out at various points in time.

increased by 23%, from 52.2 million to 64.5 million. The number of employees increased by a massive 47%, from 36.5 million to 53.6 million, and employees as a proportion of gainfully employed increased from 70% to 83%. Correspondingly, the number of self-employed decreased by 22% from 9.4 million to 7.3 million, and family workers by 46%, from 6.3 million to 3.4 million. The decreases were particularly marked in the 1990s.

Among employees, part-timers trebled, from 3.5 million to 10.5 million. Female part-timers increased 3.8 times, from 2.0 million to 7.5 million.[2] The rise in part-timers and dispatched (agency) workers was pronounced in the late 1990s. In 2000, 74% of employees were classed as 'regular', 23% were 'part-timers', and 4% 'other' (Labour Force Survey figures).

The official unemployment rate rose from 2% in 1975 to 5% in 2000, again with a sharp increase in the 1990s. The increase was most pronounced among youth, followed by older workers, creating a U-shaped age–unemployment curve. Job opening rates basically moved in parallel with the economic cycle, and openings for those in their 60s were particularly scarce.

Average reported working hours decreased by 10%, from 172 hours per month to 155 hours. According to a different survey, weekly working hours decreased from 47 to 43 hours.[3]

The greatest occupational increase among employees was of professionals, engineers and technicians, rising by 148% from 3.0 million to almost 7.5 million. Sales workers increased by 72% (4.3 to 7.4 million) and clerical workers by 59% (7.8 to 12.3 million). Production and construction workers increased numerically (12.2 to 13.2 million), but fell proportionately, from 33% to 25%. Thus there was a 'white-collarization' of the labour force.

Finally, the number of foreign workers more than doubled over the period, from 0.8 million to 1.7 million, with a sharp increase in the 1980s. As a proportion of the total labour force, however, the proportion remains small.

Changes in labour law

In response to these changes in the employment structure, and partly to encourage them, in the decade from the mid-1980s a series of new laws

---

[2] Cf. Nitta, 1999. Part-timers here are defined as working less than 35 hours per week, in non-primary sectors.

[3] Both surveys show a decrease, but the second shows longer hours. The former surveys establishments with 30+ employees, while the latter surveys individual employees.

was passed, including the Equal Employment Opportunity Law (1985, revised 1997), Worker Dispatching Law (1985, revised 1999), Older Persons Employment Stabilization Law (1986, 1994), major overhauls of the Labour Standards Law in 1987 and 1998 focusing on working hours, changes to the Disabled Persons' Employment Promotion Law (1987), Immigration Law (1990), Childcare and Family Care Leave Law (1991, 1996), Part Time Work Law (1993), and so on. Many of these revisions promoted more flexible working practices, or attempted to expand working opportunities for women and other groups. At the same time, labour law shifted from promoting long-term employment to a more neutral stance.[4]

A number of recent enactments have actually promoted mobility, such as revisions to the Employment Insurance Law (1998), deregulation of private job placement services (Employment Security Law revision, 1999), re-employment assistance, compelling employers to move towards ending age discrimination in recruiting (Employment Measures Law revision, 2001), and employment legislation accompanying the Transfer of Undertakings Law (the Labour Contract Succession Law, 2000).

Thus the legal environment, consolidated in the 1970s to support the classic model, has undergone substantial change, with a number of underlying currents, but no clear destination.

The end of lifetime employment?

Debates over Japanese employment practices in the 1990s had a number of features. First, they were focused on white-collar workers rather than production workers.[5] There were various reasons for this. Although price competitiveness had declined, resulting in a shift to higher value added activity domestically and overall a shift in production abroad, in terms of quality Japanese manufacturing was still seen as highly competitive. Future competitiveness, however, was seen to lie with the creativity of white-collar workers and R&D capabilities to produce high value added goods and services. Yet substantial numbers of white-collar workers – baby boomers taken on in the high growth years – were seen to be past their peak in terms of working ability and performance, while drawing high salaries.

---

[4] Cf. Suwa, 1994; Sugeno, 2002a, b; Araki, 2002.
[5] At least in large companies. In small manufacturing firms, concern was long expressed over the shortage of young workers and skill transmission problems, which may indirectly affect large firms: cf. Inagami, 1989; Kawakita, 1990; Kamata, 1999; Yahata, 1999a, b.

Relatedly, there was a shift from seeing white-collar workers as support staff for the efficient production of manufactured goods, towards seeing them as (potential) creators of high value added goods and services. Management interest was formerly focused on the shopfloor, and the direct production process. This focus began to change in the 1990s, when the creativity of white-collar workers itself became a new focus of attention.

Next, managers began to rethink their employment practices in parallel with, or together with, corporate governance reforms. There were debates about employment practices in the 1970s and 1980s, but corporate governance reform in the 1990s led to greater emphasis on profitability and capital efficiency, which injected a new impetus and direction into the debates. We will examine these developments in chapters 5 and 6.

Finally, like production workers, industrial relations were largely absent from the debates. Many managers saw industrial relations as unproblematic. Both managers and unions stressed competitiveness and employment maintenance. In the deflationary 1990s wage demands were at a low level (and in 2002 and 2003 many enterprise unions in fact made no wage demands, or accepted cuts in return for employment maintenance). In part, too, the apparent stability of industrial relations reflected a shift from collective to individualized employment and industrial relations.[6]

Other factors were important in prompting a rethink of employment practices, of course, such as protracted economic stagnation, deflation in the late 1990s, and the government's espousal of neo-liberal policies, albeit inconsistently. The question is, did the rethink lead to significant changes in employment practices? In particular, did it lead to a decline in lifetime, or long-term, employment, as the rise in part-time workers, for instance, might suggest?

An international comparison of long-term employment

It has been claimed that the disappearance of 'jobs for life' is an international phenomenon, brought on by intensified global competition, deregulation, emphasis on shareholder interests, technological innovation and so on. The statistical evidence, however, is not so convincing.

According to OECD (1984, 1993, 1997) data, average tenure in the USA increased slightly between 1978 and 1996, from 7.1 to 7.4 years. In Germany it increased between 1984 and 1994 from 9.8 to 10.8 years. And in Japan, it increased between 1980 and 1995 from 9.3 to 11.3 years.

---

[6] Legislation passed in 2001 mandated new arbitration committees in each prefecture to facilitate individual conflict resolution. On individualization as an international phenomenon, see Deery and Mitchell, 1999.

In the decade from the mid-1980s average tenure decreased slightly in the USA, remained the same in the UK, and increased in Germany, France, the Netherlands, Austria, Canada, Finland and Japan (OECD, 1997: 137–45). Even allowing for an ageing effect, which, other things being equal, would increase average tenures (hence static tenures would indicate some weakening), at an aggregate level, the end of 'jobs for life' thesis appears overstated.

Even more recently, according to Auer and Cazes (2000, 2003), average tenure over sixteen countries increased slightly between 1992 and 2000, from 10.2 to 10.4 years. The proportion of employees with 10+ years of tenure increased from 40.7% to 41.1%, but those with less than one year of tenure also increased, from 14.9% to 16.8%. Of those sixteen countries, five (the USA, Denmark, Germany, Finland and Ireland) recorded tenure declines, one (Greece) recorded no change, and the other ten all recorded increases. Job turnover rates of younger workers increased in several countries, but this was due less to changes in employment relations than new job creation. And while the proportion of non-regular employees increased in some countries, it declined in others. In other words, it would be hasty to extrapolate the (modest) decline in tenure of male white-collar workers in the USA into an international trend.[7]

Long-term employment in Japan

Then what about Japan? Let us first consider some statistical evidence from the *Basic Statistical Survey on Wage Structure*.[8] A number of statistics may be used, including average tenure, separation rates and 'standard' workers. We will mainly use the first of these, with data from five-yearly intervals between 1980 and 2000 (see figures in the Appendix).

Employment tenure for males rose from 10.8 years in 1980 to 12.5 years in 1990 and 13.3 years in 2000. Tenure of older workers in particular showed a large increase, while younger age bands showed little change, or a decrease. The overall increase reflects the increase in older workers. Tenure for females in all age bands over 30 increased, with little change for those in their 20s. Overall, there was a clear increase

---

[7] A distillation of research in the USA suggests there may have been a modest decline in long-term employment of male workers, but for female workers there has been an increase. For production workers there has been little overall change, while for white-collar workers, large-scale restructuring in the 1980s caused some decline, but not an emphatic end to long-term employment, as suggested for instance by Cappelli (1999a). In fact average tenure in large companies appeared to increase again in the 1990s, as did the proportion with 10+ years of tenure (Allen et al., 1999).

[8] As the name suggests, this survey focuses on wages rather than employment, but it is the only survey with a national sample which gives reliable statistics on tenure. It is used for the OECD *Employment Outlook*, and provides an unusually detailed picture.

in tenure for females. In large companies (1000+ employees) tenure of men in their 50s increased, while for men in their 30s, 40s and early 60s, it decreased from the mid-1990s. For women in their early 30s up, it increased.[9]

In general, then, tenure of older men and for women aged 30 or more increased, while for younger men and women it decreased somewhat.[10] The increase in tenure for older workers is noteworthy because one would expect these workers to lose their jobs first in an employer-led assault on lifetime employment. Although in the case of males the increase was halted in the 1990s, media reports of the collapse of lifetime employment for this group appear to be exaggerated.

More specifically, tenure of older male production workers in large manufacturing companies increased, as it did for university graduates in the same companies. Although average tenures are shorter, the trend for respective age groups in small manufacturers was similar. In the financial sector, however, tenure for male university graduates changed little. In the service sector in general, tenure of older male university graduates increased until the mid-1990s and then declined, while for other age bands, there was no marked change. There was no marked change for women aged up to 55 over the twenty years.

Gender gap

We have noted the ambiguous status of women in terms of community membership. Although the average tenure of women is increasing, there is still a substantial gap with men. According to a Ministry of Labour survey (Rodosho, 1995) of university graduates recruited by large companies, eight out of ten men and only three out of ten women remained with their company at age 30. Various reasons were given. Only 2% of companies said they had a company 'practice' of women quitting at marriage or childbirth, but 70% said that was how things tended to work out (80% in construction and 88% in financial services!).

In spite – or *because* – of the enforcement of the Equal Employment Opportunity Law in 1986 and its revision in 1999, many companies have

[9] In the remainder of Part 1, 'large company' means 1,000+ employees, and where a distinction is made, 'very large' means 5,000+ employees.
[10] Reasons for increased job changing among younger workers – one in two high school graduates quit their first job within three years – include changing work orientations which place priority on freedom, enjoyment and satisfaction of short-term needs, as well as changing school-to-work transition paths, and slow institutional response to change. Many schools have run 'one student per company' placement schemes, which did not necessarily take individual preferences into account, and this has been a factor in higher severance rates.

introduced multiple employment tracks, which are heavily gendered. Men are largely assigned to 'comprehensive' (management feeding) tracks with nationwide assignments, while women are most commonly assigned to 'general' (largely clerical) tracks with local assignments, even if they have the same educational qualifications. Technically it is possible to change from one track to the other, but in practice it does not happen often.[11]

In a survey of corporate headquarter white-collar workers (JRK, 2000a), 54% of women said their current work required less than one year to master, compared with 15% of men.[12] This suggests endemic under-utilization of female employees. The same employees were asked about career aspirations. One in six men aspired to become a director in their current company, but almost no women did. A quarter of men wanted to become a manager in their company, and only 5% of women did. And 7% versus 14% wanted to move to another company. These findings suggest that the gendered characteristics of the classic model, too, are highly resistant to change.

Retirement and employment of older workers

Even in large companies, tenure of men in their 50s increased between 1980 and 2000. Employment opportunities of those in their 60s has now become a critical issue, however. This is because, for men, the basic pension portion of the public pension is being raised in steps from 60 to 65 between 2000 and 2013. If current retirement ages are not extended, or new employment opportunities found, a major 'institutional gap' will result in large-scale unemployment of men in their 60s. The number wanting to work is very high, and the proportion actually working is, with Sweden, the highest amongst the OECD countries. Prospects of finding jobs in the external labour market are bleak, however. The job opening rate for men aged 60–64 deteriorated markedly, from 0.25 in 1990 to 0.06 in 2000, and unemployment for this age group rose to twice the national average.

Revision of the Employment Measures Law in 2001 banned age discrimination in job advertising, recruiting and re-employment, but there were numerous exceptions, creating doubts that the law would have much

---

[11] Fifty three per cent of very large (5000+ employees) companies and 41% of large companies reported such tracks in Rodosho (MOL), 1999.

[12] JRK is an abbreviation of *Jinji romu kanri kenkyukai* (Research group on personnel and labour management), a group of twenty-eight researchers commissioned by the Ministry of Labour to carry out a series of studies, under the overall chairmanship of Inagami. Of the sub-groups, JRK 2000a, b were also chaired by Inagami, and JRK 1999 by Imano.

real impact.[13] Labour unions have belatedly started to seek employment opportunities for this group, by negotiating re-employment, for instance. In one survey (Kosei rodosho, 2000), 91% of very large companies had a mandatory retirement age (MRA), mostly 60. Half had a means to extend work, or a re-employment system, and 15% more planned to introduce one, but in most cases (57%) this was limited to those deemed necessary by the company, or those meeting its criteria (26%), and in most cases there was an upper limit of 65.[14] When older workers *are* re-employed, working conditions do not change much, but wages and posts do. In the same survey, 42% of companies reported wage drops of 40% or more, and a further 21% reported drops of 30–40%. Management posts were almost always relinquished.

Conversely, a majority of companies reported mechanisms to encourage job changing *before* the MRA, including early retirement schemes (58%), transfer schemes (35%) and job-changing assistance (26%). Such schemes, especially early retirement (in practice little different from voluntary redundancy), proliferated in the late 1990s. Two-thirds of large companies had them in 1998.

On the one hand, then, companies have started to introduce re-employment schemes for workers aged 60 or more to fill the institutional gap left by the raising of the pension age. On the other hand, they are encouraging workers to leave before they turn 60. Even in the latter case, though, the most common mechanism is for workers to be seconded to companies in the same enterprise group, and if they are transferred permanently, it is mostly to those companies. Thus rather than collapsing, it could be argued that the 'lifetime employment sphere' has been extended from individual companies to enterprise groups.[15] The larger the company and enterprise group, the more this has been institutionalized.

Career orientations and views of lifetime employment

Lifetime employment cannot be maintained without the support of employees. According to the earlier survey (JRK, 2000a), 40% of large company headquarter middle (section) managers wanted to stay with their current company in a management position, and 18% hoped to become a director. A further 13% wanted to use their abilities as

[13] In theory, anti-ageist legislation should lead to the abolition of mandatory retirement systems (Seike, 1998). Instead of increasing employment opportunities for older workers, however, the resulting instability could have the reverse effect (cf. Sugeno, 2002a: 97).
[14] Only one in ten companies said they basically re-employed all applicants. One in five re-employed 70% or more, but half said they re-employed 30% or less.
[15] Cf. Inagami, 1989; Nagano, 1989; Kawakita et al., 1997.

specialists within their companies. Internal career orientations, it would appear, are still quite strong. For male employees, the respective figures were 24%, 16% and 22%, but only 5% of female employees wanted to stay with their current company in a management position. Twenty one per cent wanted to stay on as a specialist, but the same proportion wanted to change company.

We can get a sense of changes over time from a large-scale panel survey carried out in 1985–6, and 1998 (Rodosho, 1987; JRK, 1999). The proportion of potential job changers (those actively looking for a new job plus those who would consider changing jobs if one with better conditions offered itself) increased among employees in their late 20s to late 40s, and decreased among employees in their early 20s and in their 50s. The desire to become a manager weakened, and the desire to become a specialist strengthened. This suggests a qualitative change in internal career orientations, but by no means a collapse.

In the same survey, companies in principle offering employment until retirement fell from 75% to 62%. Those not necessarily employing until retirement but seeking places for older workers in subsidiaries and affiliates rose from 17% to 22%, and those conducting personnel management on the premise that workers would change jobs increased from 2% to 7%. Thus the premise of lifetime employment weakened on the company side, notably in large firms. The premise weakened across all job types, but more for rank-and-file employees than managers.[16]

On the employee side, too, those *expecting* to be able to work in their current company until retirement fell from 42% to 32%, while those expecting to move to a subsidiary or affiliate rose from 21% to 27%. Employee thinking, then, was basically in line with company thinking, but employees were even less optimistic about prospects for lifetime employment.

Finally, the proportion of companies anticipating increased spontaneous employee turnover increased – from 37% to 53% for males in their 20s, and from 22% to 36% for females in their 20s. For males aged 45 or over, however, expectations of increased turnover decreased.

In conclusion, tenure statistics show little evidence of drastic change in lifetime employment. At least until 2000, tenure of young workers

---

[16] Respondents – senior personnel managers – were also asked for their views on future turnover of specific kinds of workers, namely (a) male (university) graduates in their 30s; (b) female graduates in their 30s; (c) male graduates in their early 50s; and (d) male graduates in their late 50s. The dominant view was that there would be no change (47%, 46%, 63% and 58% respectively). However, more thought that the separation rate of (a) would increase than decrease, by a 22% margin. Conversely, more thought that the separation rate of (b) would decrease than increase, by a 6% margin, and likewise for (d), by a 5% margin. Views on the turnover of (c) were balanced.

was stable, or declined slightly, while that of females and older workers increased, giving an overall increase. Both managers and employees foresaw a weakening of lifetime employment, but internal career progression had not crumbled. Fewer employees now aspire to become managers, and more aspire to become specialists.

Changes to *nenko*

We now turn our attention to *nenko* wages and promotion. As we have seen, the meaning of *nenko* is not straightforward. Here we will examine scheduled (without overtime) earnings of different age groups, using the *Basic Statistical Survey on Wage Structure*, from 1975 to 2000. If we find the age–wage profile steeply inclined to the right, with relatively little spread for a given peer group with the same education, we can say that it has *nenko* characteristics. Figure 3.1 shows:

1. From an index of 1.0 for 20–24-year-old male university graduates (3.1.1), the curve slopes upwards and peaks at the 50–54 age group. In 1980 the peak was 3.2 times the 20–24-year-old level, but it fell in the 1990s to 2.7 in 2000. For those in large companies (3.1.2), the 50–54 peak was 3.5 in 1980 and 3.0 in 2000. Thus there has been a modest flattening of the *nenko* curve for male graduates, but it is still steeper and higher than that of males overall, and clearly shows *nenko* features.

2. Taking 18–19-year-old high school graduates as the 1.0 index for women (3.1.3), even at its highest, in 1985 for 55–59-year-olds, the peak was only 1.69. In 2000 the peak for 50–54-year-olds, was 1.44. The *nenko* principle is weak in women's earnings. It is somewhat stronger for female university graduates in large companies (3.1.4) where, with 20–24-year-olds as the index, the level for 45–49-year-olds dropped successively from 2.3 in 1975 to 2.0 in 1995, before rising marginally to 2.03 in 2000. For 50–54-year-olds, however, it rose in the 1990s, from 2.2 to 2.5.

3. For male production workers in large manufacturing firms (3.1.5), with 18–19-year-olds as the index, the peak consistently came at the 50–54 age group, and the level remained stable over the period, at 2.2 in both 1980 and 2000. For those in small (10–99 employees) manufacturers (3.1.6), the peak age group in 1975 was 35–39 at 1.7. Both the age group and the ratio rose steadily to 1.92 for 50–54-year-olds in 1995, before edging down to 1.87 in 2000, indicating a modest strengthening of *nenko*.

In brief, from age–wage statistics at least, there is little evidence of a collapse in *nenko*, although the curve for male university graduates in large companies has been flattened somewhat.

3.1.1 All industries, all sizes, male university graduates
(20-24=100)

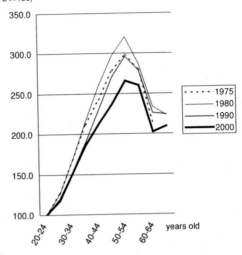

3.1.2 All industries, large companies, male university graduates
(20-24=100)

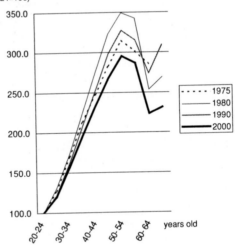

Figure 3.1 Changes in earnings profiles
Source: Rodosho/Kosei rodosho, *Chingin kozo kihon tokei chosa,*
respective years.

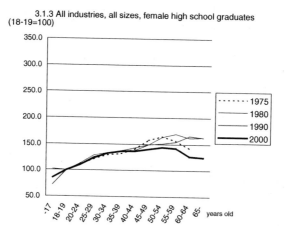

3.1.3 All industries, all sizes, female high school graduates
(18-19=100)

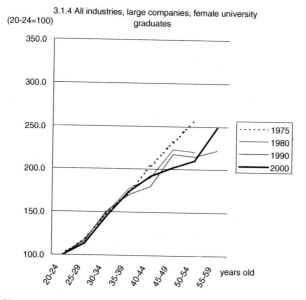

3.1.4 All industries, large companies, female university
(20-24=100) graduates

Figure 3.1 (*cont.*)

Wage differences

From average wages, we now shift our attention to wage spreads between 'standard employee'[17] peers with the same level of education. We look at scheduled earnings of male graduates aged 30, 40 and 50 for the years

[17] 'Standard employees' are employees recruited straight from school or university, who have not changed company – 'lifetime employees'.

3.1.5 Manufacturing, large companies male production workers

(18-19=100)

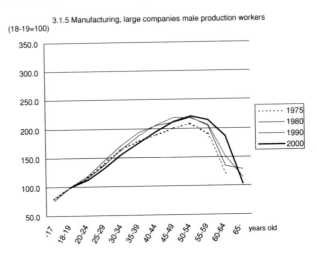

3.1.6 Manufacturing, small companies, male production workers

(18-19=100)

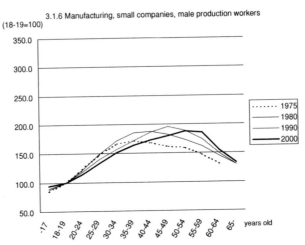

Figure 3.1 (*cont.*)

1982, 1990 and 2000. Table 3.1.1 gives figures for the end points of the first and ninth deciles. It shows that except for financial services, the spread for 30-year-olds shrank between 1982 and 1990, with no marked subsequent change in 2000. For 40-year-olds there was no marked change over the first period, but an increase in the second period in all industries. For 50-year-olds there was an increase over the first period, and a further increase over the second. Thus there was no increase for younger employees, but an increase for older employees, and the older the age group, the earlier the spread started to increase. Interestingly, too, the spread

Table 3.1.1 *Scheduled earnings spread of 'standard' workers 1: male university graduates, 1982, 1990, 2000*

	1982		1990		2000	
(1) 30-year-olds	1st decile	9th decile	1st decile	9th decile	1st decile	9th decile
Manufacturing	82.5	124.6	83.3	122.2	85.3	124.1
Wholesale, retail	81.9	136.6	80.6	131.1	84	130.6
Finance, insurance	74.6	132.2	72.3	149.2	72.8	142.6
Services	78.0	129.1	80.3	129.2	83.9	129.6
All industries	80.7	134.6	80.5	131.4	83.7	132.6
(2) 40-year-olds						
Manufacturing	78.6	127.4	77.6	128.4	77.0	141.1
Wholesale, retail	75.8	129.7	74.1	124.3	73.3	129.8
Finance, insurance	77.0	132.4	69.0	139.2	68.8	150.7
Services	84.0	122.7	76.8	133.6	71.5	137.4
All industries	76.8	128.7	75.1	132.1	74.9	142.4
(3) 50-year-olds						
Manufacturing	75.0	122.7	74.8	128.4	73.9	137.4
Wholesale, retail	71.2	120.3	79.3	128.9	72.3	140.7
Finance, insurance	79.3	118.7	73.5	139	69.0	140.2
Services	79.6	124.9	78.2	123.0	81.9	133.4
All industries	77.0	122.7	76.0	130.2	74.0	141.1

Note: First decile refers to the point at the end of the first decile.
Ninth decile refers to the point at the end of the ninth decile.
Source: Rodosho/Kosei rodosho, *Chingin kozo kihon tokei chosa*, respective years.

increased for older workers through a rise in the ninth decile point rather than a fall in the first decile point. For male university graduates, then, this *nenko* feature of wages has been weakened. Whether the spread exceeds a range considered distributionally fair is something we will look at in chapter 4.

For male high school graduate production workers there was little change over the twenty-year period (table 3.1.2). For female high school graduates the spread appeared to increase in the 1990s, but the trend is not clear.

From nenko *to ability/performance?*

What do companies and employees think about *nenko* wages? At both points in the above panel data, a majority of companies said they would increase the ability component of the base wage, but the proportion

Table 3.1.2 *Scheduled earnings spread of 'standard' workers 2: female high school graduates; male high school graduate production workers, 1982, 1990, 2000*

	1982		1990		2000	
(1) 30-year-olds	1st decile	9th decile	1st decile	9th decile	1st decile	9th decile
Female h.s. graduates (all industries)	79.7	127.3	79.5	134.9	80.0	127.6
Male h.s. grads, production (manufacturing)	84.5	120.6	82.6	123.2	82.4	124.6
(2) 40-year-olds						
Female h.s. graduates (all industries)	68.6	132.1	74.6	136.3	71.3	129.7
Male h.s. grads, production (manufacturing)	83.5	124.9	83.1	121.3	79.8	122.4
(3) 50-year-olds						
Female h.s. graduates (all industries)	73.0	122.9	74.9	124.7	72.6	137.0
Male h.s. grads, production (manufacturing)	84.3	137.8	81.0	135.1	79.7	135.3

Note: As for table 3.1.1
Source: As for table 3.1.1

increased from 72% in 1985–6, to 86% in 1998 (Rodosho, 1987: 124; JRK, 1999: 157). There is nothing new about the desire to suppress *nenko* and increase ability or performance, but the desire has become even stronger.

As for employees, in JRK (2000a), less than 10% thought on the one hand that there was no *nenko* in their wages, nor should there be, and on the other that *nenko* in wages should be maintained (without modification). Roughly half thought that *nenko* wages should be modified, and a third thought they should be fundamentally reformed to reflect ability and performance. Thus both employers and employees are in favour of giving ability or performance greater weighting in wages. As the above analysis suggests, however, this may not drastically alter the upward age–wage slope until age 50–54, even if rises become more conditional.

Nenko *and accelerated promotion*

The proportion of male workers not wanting to fall behind peers in promotion fell from 71% in 1985–6 to 54% in 1998, and the proportion of females fell from 56% to 42%. The proportion of males who thought promotion should be based on performance rose from 77% to 84%, and those who felt peers should basically be promoted together halved, from 18% to 9%.[18]

In 1985–6, 31% of companies said they would actively implement early executive selection, and 67% said they would do it sometimes. In 1998 the figures were 39% and 58% respectively. In very large companies active selectors rose from 28% to 52%. In the JRK survey (2000a: 174), too, managers were asked about early selection, defined as promotion from one peer cohort to a management post before the first of the cohort above. Roughly 10% said it happened quite often, 50% sometimes, 30% seldom, and 10% never. In brief, in practice, as well as in the thinking of managers and employees, age and length of tenure considerations in promotion appear to be weakening.

Long-term skill formation and the workplace

Living security – manifest through lifetime employment and *nenko* – must be complemented by contributions to corporate value through long-term skill formation or human resource development. The institutional supports of this are on-job-training (OJT) and career development. If skills aren't developed with age, and contributions fall significantly below the age–wage curve, the basis for long-term employment will be undermined. Is there any evidence of this happening?

Work ethic and ability curves

In the panel survey, the proportion of employees wanting to raise their knowledge and skill levels changed little, from 93% in 1985–6 (95% for men, 86% for women) to 94% in 1998 (95% and 92%). The main reason for wanting to raise knowledge and skill levels was to use them in work (53% to 57%). Slightly less than 10% gave job changing/becoming

---

[18] One factor in this change is a decrease in peers who can actually be promoted, due to a lack of posts (JIL, 2002: 216–20).

Table 3.2 *Skill levels and age: university graduates (%)*

	A	B	C	D	E	F	N.A.	(A+C+E+F)
Office workers	13.6	8.7	31.4	20.0	8.6	4.1	13.6	(57.7)
Sales and marketing	9.7	6.8	33.8	20.0	6.8	2.8	20.1	(53.1)
R&D, engineering	6.1	13.5	24.3	21.6	6.2	1.9	26.4	(38.5)

Note: The average age for the three groups was 35.7, 35.4 and 35.4 respectively.
Source: JRK survey, Nihon rodo kenkyu kiko, 2000: 20.

independent as the main reason at both points. The proportion wanting to 'work harder than others to do good work' was also virtually unchanged (78% and 76%).[19]

These findings point to a continued strong work ethic, but does this result in rising ability and performance with age? Large company planning department heads were asked which age–ability curves (figure 3.2) best fitted office, sales and research and development and engineering (R, D&E) employees. The results are given in table 3.2.

Of the various profiles, A, C, E and F may be considered compatible with long-term employment. The sum of these choices gives 58%, 53% and 39% for the three job types respectively. Profile B shows a drop after a certain age, and is technically incompatible with long-term employment. It was chosen by 9%, 7% and 14% respectively. According to this survey, then, abilities generally rise with age for office and sales workers, but not necessarily R, D&E workers. (Many of these, however, become managers after a certain age, or are assigned to different work.) We will look at this issue further in chapter 4, when we discuss 'creative' work.

OJT and the workplace

A primary mechanism of skill formation in the classic model is on-job-training (OJT).[20] In JRK (2000a), 88% of headquarter middle (section) managers and 74% of employees (82% of males and 61% of females) said they could raise their skill levels through their work. Most thought

---

[19] Rodosho, 1987: 150, 176; JRK, 1999: 200, 215. A similar result was found in JRK, 2000a: 26.

[20] Three-quarters of respondents in a MWLH survey (2002) thought that skill development had been the responsibility of the company, and 69% thought it would continue to be so, a modest reflection of the increasing emphasis companies have been placing on individual employee responsibility for skill development. Planned OJT (based on a written plan setting out who provides the training, for how long and in what steps) was reported by 42% of companies (72% of companies with 300+ employees), and off-JT by 65% (91%).

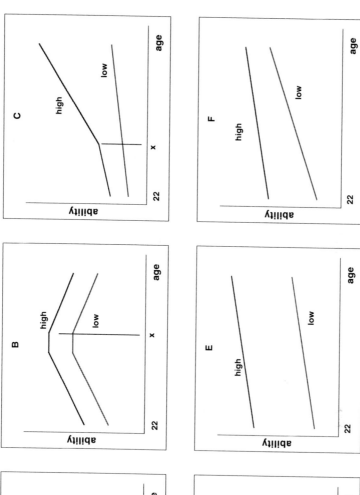
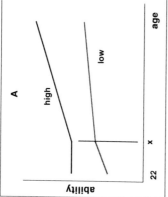
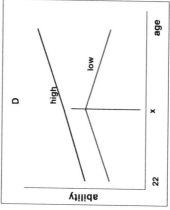

Figure 3.2 Age–ability curves

Table 3.3 *Workplace atmosphere according to white-collar workers (at large company headquarters, %)*

	Section managers	Male employees	Female employees
Everyone can utilize their abilities	88.3	69.2	53.9
Mutual support in work	86.3	75.2	74.7
Educating and training juniors	85.0	67.9	60.2
Raise overall workplace performance	72.7	64.4	54.9
Can consult on non-work-related matters	54.3	48.6	46.1
'Luke warm'	33.6	43.6	51.5
Employees compete with each other over results	12.7	11.4	6.4
Restrained interpersonal relations	10.3	23.6	19.8

Note: Figures are for those answering 'There is such an atmosphere.'
Source: As for table 3.2.

their current work suited them, that they had to study to do their work, and that it required specialist knowledge.

The workplace environment is critical for the effective functioning of OJT. As table 3.3 shows, the majority of middle managers and employees reported a co-operative and mutually supportive atmosphere conducive to raising skill levels, although female employees were less inclined to think their skills could actually be used to contribute to overall performance. With this caveat, as far as surveys can discern, the majority of workplaces are conducive to OJT and skill formation.

Thus, there appears to have been no marked decline in the work ethic necessary for skill development on the one hand, and work environments are seen as conducive to nurturing skills on the other. Most middle managers and white-collar headquarter employees believe they can raise their abilities through their work, but there are marked gender differences.

Company consciousness

In the panel survey, the proportion of employees who thought they were 'living like a company man' was identical in both 1985–6 and 1998 (31%; men had decreased from 35% to 34%, and women had increased from 14% to 17%). The proportion gradually rose with age and tenure at both points. Those who thought it 'natural to sacrifice one's private life for the sake of the company to some extent' fell slightly, from 47% (men 52%, women 27%) to 43% (men 46%, women 31%). Interestingly, the proportion of women rose in both questions, suggesting more women are becoming 'company men'.

Employees who agreed that company postings involving separation from family (*tanshin funin*) were acceptable – unavoidable – if it was for the sake of the company edged up from 47% (48% and 41%) to 48% (51%, 38%). The proportion often doing company work at home was virtually unchanged at 19% (21% of men, and 10% of women: Rodosho, 1987: 146, 148–50; cf. JRK, 1999: 200). In a period of change and uncertainty, then, company man appears to live on, while community companies continue to permeate their members' private lives.

White-collar employees still frequently socialize with their colleagues,[21] although the proportion of employees who said they 'pursue hobbies, study or social activities away from work and company people' increased slightly over the thirteen years, from 54% to 58%.

Surprisingly, perhaps, satisfaction with company, work, status and workplace relations all *increased*. Over the thirteen-year interval, those very or reasonably satisfied with their company increased from 56 to 61%, and those satisfied with their work rose from 61% to 71%. Satisfaction with status in the workplace rose from 57% to 70%, and satisfaction with interpersonal relations at the workplace rose from 60% to 70%. Even satisfaction with wages, perennially lower than the other items, rose from 34% to 44%!

The greater the satisfaction with status and interpersonal relations in the workplace, the greater the satisfaction with the company. Satisfaction with the sub-group, in other words, is associated with that of the larger group. The workplace community does not function in opposition to the community company, but concentrically, in support of it.

Finally, while merely suggestive since the figures come from different surveys, the proportion of employees who did *not* consider their relation with the company to be simply that of employer–employee increased slightly, from 59% to 63%.[22] The employment relationship still appears to be a diffuse one, of status rather than contract, for white-collar workers in large companies. Sixty four per cent of section managers and 62% of employees thought companies should offer living security for employees over the long term (JRK, 2000a: 47).

Concluding comments

In this chapter we began to investigate the empirical reality of the classic model, and how much change there was between 1975 and 2000. There was little statistical evidence of the collapse of lifetime employment. In

[21] JRK 2000a: 42. Although slightly dated, a survey of white-collar employees of large companies in the Tokyo region put the average frequency of 'after 5' socializing at 2.3 times per week: Rodosho, 1991.
[22] JPC, 1988; JRK, 2000a: 26–7.

some sectors it weakened, in others it strengthened. *Attitudes* towards lifetime employment, however, have changed – weakened – somewhat. The employment of women is changing, but gradually.

The *nenko* principle – taken here as an upward sloping earnings curve with a small spread around an age mean – is strongest for male university graduates in large companies, and weakens with decreasing company size, and for production workers and women. Between 1975 and 2000 the top age group's earnings relative to 20–24-year-olds among white-collar university graduates in large companies shrank, and the peer spread increased, indicating a weakening of *nenko*. Among production workers in small companies, however, it strengthened. Thus *nenko* has not died, either, but attitudes supporting it have also weakened, with acceptance of greater emphasis on ability or performance, and less on age and tenure.

While there are some concerns over the age–ability curve, in general it is considered to be upward sloping over time. The work ethic is still strong. The principal means of developing skills is through OJT, which requires a favourable workplace environment. Most white-collar employees of large firms feel they can raise their skills through work, and that interpersonal relations are conducive to this, although somewhat fewer women share these views.

Company man lives, too. With declining attitudinal support for lifetime employment and *nenko*, however, and an increasing specialist or professional orientation, there has been a qualitative change amongst such employees. Satisfaction with company, work and workplace rose during the 1990s, and there was little evidence of employees abandoning a diffuse status-based view of employment, with a moral dimension, in favour of a contractual view.

At this broad level of analysis, therefore, the model appears to be reflected in reality, even today. Of course this could be problematic, if it fails to provide solutions for emerging issues faced by Japanese companies. This is an issue we will return to.

4   Company Professionals and Creative Work

For the classic model to survive, skill development which increases corporate value cannot fall below the age–wage curve in the long term. As we saw in chapter 3, there are problems in this regard, but to date none of them appears fatal. However, we need to look more closely at this proposition in the light of the changing nature of competition facing Japanese companies. Japanese companies are being pushed relentlessly in the direction of higher value added, knowledge-based, aesthetically creative ('smart') products and services, and need an employment system which can deliver these. Can the classic model methods of long-term skill development also nurture creative work? Is high value added, white-collar creative work compatible with classic model employment practices?

Chapter 4 examines these questions, looking first at the changing nature of value creation, and the rise of 'company (or organization) professionals'. Managers in many countries have struggled to devise personnel systems capable of motivating and rewarding such employees, and Japan is no exception. In the 1990s leading companies refined their human resource management (HRM) systems for this purpose. We will examine Hitachi's response in Part 2; here we will focus on creative work itself, and those who do it. For this we will look at evidence from a questionnaire about creative work carried out in the mid-1990s.

Company professionals

Until the mid-1980s in the manufacturing sector, the focus of Japanese managers' concern was in their factories, especially their production departments. This was where competitiveness was seen to lie. Indirect white-collar employees were viewed as support staff, whose job it was to raise the efficiency of manufacturing, but not as sources of value added in their own right. And as long as factories were highly competitive, they could pull the whole company along, and the system was not fundamentally questioned.[1]

At the macro-level, also, finance was considered the handmaiden of industry.[2] Banks were shielded from tough international competition by a barrage of regulatory obstacles, and grew on the backs of manufacturers, for which they were the main bank and/or silent shareholders. As long as their manufacturing clients remained competitive, they did not need to expend much effort in developing new financial products.

With the bursting of the bubble economy, however, questions began to be asked about both macro (finance-for-industry) and micro (white-collar-as-factory-support) assumptions. Information technology giant Fujitsu, for instance, in collaboration with its labour union, sent four missions to the USA and Europe to study HRM of research, development and engineering (R, D&E) workers. The result was a determination to change the company's system of HRM. In 1991 the president of the union proposed to Fujitsu's president: 'The structure of value added is moving from assembly to knowledge production and mind work. Our members support ability-based appraisal. We need to devise a system focusing less on the number of hours worked, and more on the quality of that work.' The union presented a list of twenty-seven proposals regarding 'smart' work for researchers and engineers at a central joint consultation meeting the following February. Noteworthy was the view that the HRM system needed to be built around the quality of work rather than working hours, and behind this view, that a fundamental change was occurring in the nature of value creation.

The company subsequently started to work on a system overhaul to 'create a mood of challenge and professional consciousness'. In March 1994 the new system was introduced, featuring management by objectives, as well as a system of 'discretionary working', virtually without restriction in terms of working hours.[3] The proportion of professional/

---

[1] White-collar workers remained peripheral to most researchers' interest, too. Even in 'white-collarization' research, the main focus was on blue-collar workers. (White-collarization referred not just to harmonization of blue-collar and white-collar employment conditions, but white-collar-like skills and career development for blue-collar workers; cf. Koike, 1981, 1988; Inagami, 1981.)

[2] Or in Veblen's (1904) terms, mechanical process assumed priority over the business principle; cf. also Gerschenkron, 1962. In Britain the balance was quite different; cf. Ingham, 1984; Collins, 1991.

[3] 'Discretionary working' was legally recognized in 1987, but for a limited number of job types such as R&D workers, system development engineers, reporters, editors, designers, lawyers, accountants, architects and financial analysts. In April 2000 a new 'management planning' type – for 'duties of planning, investigation and analysis of matters regarding management of the enterprise' – was legalized. Companies introducing the new system were required to establish a joint committee, and to gain the consent of workers placed on the system.

specialist track employees had increased from 10.2% in 1973 to 33.9% in 1993, and was expected to rise further. Hence 'the future of the company depends on the vitality and contributions of these workers'. This marked the birth of performance-based HRM at Fujitsu.[4] Both management and the union realized that the future of the company henceforth depended on the creativity of company professionals. This applied not just to R, D&E workers, but to 'support staff' as well, who were now expected to become sources of value added contributions themselves.

This shift, however, is far from straightforward. Despite increased use of the word 'professional', it is not self-evident what a 'company professional' is, or should be. In the USA, sociologists began writing about 'problems' of professional workers employed in corporate R&D labs in the 1950s. They were deemed to have different, more 'cosmopolitan' values than other employees, to be more concerned with freedom to pursue their own technical interests, and with recognition from peers outside their organization than climbing up a corporate hierarchy in pursuit of a 'local', managerial career.[5] Dual ladders were developed to address their orientations, but these led to problems of their own.

Japanese companies began to introduce professional tracks from the 1960s, not so much to deal with alienated R, D&E workers as to address promotion bottlenecks, as well as to encourage the development of advanced technical skills. Japanese R, D&E workers were seen to have both 'cosmopolitan' as well as 'local' characteristics, and were dubbed 'organizational professionals'.[6] In the 1990s the concept was extended to other white-collar workers such as corporate planners in companies like Fujitsu.

It is useful here to recall Goldthorpe et al.'s (1968a, b, 1969) 'affluent worker' research in the UK, which identified a number of 'orientations to work' based on the ordering of workers' goals and aspirations. In addition to instrumental, solidaristic and bureaucratic orientations, they identified

---

[4] *Rosei jiho*, 2002: 33. Fujitsu revised its system in 2001. Originally it was limited to management and specialist grade employees, but in 1998 it was extended to all employees. With the initial system, it was found that quarterly appraisals strongly linked to bonuses encouraged the setting of short-term objectives and short-term behaviour. The revised system was designed to encourage setting higher goals, and emphasized not just results, but the process for achieving the results, including teamwork. Rather than a standard system company-wide, it was adapted flexibly to the needs of each business unit.

[5] On 'cosmopolitan' and 'local' values and orientations, see Gouldner, 1957–58.

[6] Westney, 1992. Shapira, 1995 and McCormick, 2000, report on a comparative study of US, UK, German and Japanese R&D workers in which the Japanese workers showed a strong commitment to professional associations and an orientation towards developing technical skills and autonomy, while at the same time showing commitment to their employing organizations and careers inside them.

Table 4.1 *Typology of orientations to work*

	Instrumental	Bureaucratic	Solidaristic	Professional
Central life interest	private life	work	work, private	work
Purpose	means	end/goal	means	end/goal
Time necessary for skill formation	rather short	medium	long	long
Dependence on individual for results	weak	medium	medium	strong
Work–private life separation	clear	vague	vague	vague
Internal promotion orientation	weak	strong	weak	medium

Note: In the solidaristic orientation, work is a means to an end, but commitment to the workplace community or labour union is strong.

a fourth type, a 'professional' orientation, but did not describe it in any detail. If we were to fill in the missing details, we would get the last column of table 4.1.

The professionals described in this column are those depicted by Kanter and Heckscher, who emerged from restructured US bureaucratic corporations in the 1980s. Their central life interest remains work, as in the bureaucratic orientation to work. Work is an end in itself, with substantial intrinsic rewards. The period for gaining necessary skills is long, however, and reliance on individual performance increases. Work and private life are not sharply distinguished, but unlike the traditional company man, the professional is less oriented towards internal progression up a corporate hierarchy and associated status. In this respect the professional orientation to work falls between the bureaucratic and instrumental orientations.

This type of worker has become more prevalent in Japanese companies, and more critical for corporate value creation. Can classic model practices educate, motivate and utilize the skills of such workers?

Creative work survey

To answer this question, we turn to a survey carried out by Inagami and colleagues in the mid-1990s. The survey focused on creative work and workers, who overlap to a considerable extent with the company professionals we have just described. One questionnaire was sent by post in December 1995–January 1996 to the senior personnel manager, who was asked to distribute one copy to a manager in a department with a high proportion of creative workers and work (according to the first definition below), and one copy to a manager in a department with a low proportion of creative workers and work. 'Creative department' responses were predominantly from functions such as R&D, planning, editing and design, while 'routine department' responses were predominantly from functions like accounting, personnel and general affairs. A second questionnaire was distributed to employees of those departments.[7]

The questionnaire used the word 'creative' in two senses. First, the cover stated: 'What we mean by creative work, workplaces or people is (a) the nature of the work is not fixed and has a high discretionary content; (b) performance of the work can differ greatly according to the individual; and (c) the output can have a major influence on the company.' As well as this 'essential' definition, it was also used more loosely, as in 'What kind of things prevent you from doing your work creatively?' This recognizes that even in sections where much of the work is predominantly routine, there is scope for creative work and improvisation.

Creative workers, working and workplaces

Managers were asked what proportion of their subordinates was engaged in creative work (according to the essential definition). In planning departments the average was 38%, in design and editing it was 42%, and in R&D it was 27%. The average in 'creative departments' was 32%, and in 'routine departments' it was 23%. Interestingly, employees themselves gave lower figures – 23% in creative departments and 20% in routine departments.

Creative workers in creative departments:[8] (1) were aged 33–34 on average; (2) were mostly males – 96% of engineers and system engineers, 81% of designers and planners, 80% of other specialists; (3) were highly educated – over a third of engineers, system engineers and other specialists had postgraduate qualifications; (4) were as likely to be recruited fresh from university as other groups; and (5) had worked at their present company for ten years on average, the same as other groups. They were

[7] The questionnaire was commissioned by the Ministry of Labour and carried out through the Sanwa Research Institute by the 'Knowledge-Intensive Work Committee'. Members were T. Inagami (chair), K. Ido, T. Kawakita, A. Sato and T. Shimoda. The report appeared as Rodosho, 1996. The survey issues were first clarified through interviews with personnel department heads as well as group interviews. One thousand companies were selected from the Teikoku Data Bank database in addition to the companies originally interviewed, and 237 MOL monitor companies. The managers' response rate was 27.5% and the employees' response rate was 53.5%.
[8] Engineers, system engineers, designers, planners and other specialists; n = 577.

Table 4.2 *Attributes of creative workers (%)*

	Department managers		Employees	
	CD (n = 368)	RD (n = 350)	CD (n = 1384)	RD (n = 525)
Strong sense of curiosity	72.0	54.0	78.4[1]	73.3
Challenge risky work	52.4	39.4	42.1	40.0
Trusted by superiors/colleagues	47.6	45.1	41.2	40.0
Wide external personal network	46.7	41.7	55.9[2]	57.7
Meticulous about work	43.8	40.6	42.0	41.1
Good sense of balance	39.4	41.7	53.1[3]	55.6
Carries on, come what may	30.4	30.6	28.9	29.7
One outstanding skill	23.9	23.1	38.2	33.7
Performance oriented (not seniority)	22.6	21.4	36.6	37.7

Note: CD = creative department; RD = routine department. Figures are for the 'strongly applies' choice
Source: 'Survey on Knowledge Intensive Work'.

distinctive in terms of education levels, but not in terms of recruitment and job tenure, a finding which contradicts some fashionable views in Japan in the 1990s.[9]

Respondents were asked about the characteristics of creative workers. Table 4.2 lists the top characterizations out of twenty-nine choices. It shows that managers of both creative and routine departments had similar views – strong sense of curiosity, challenging approach to work, wide personal networks, meticulous, balanced, etc. Conversely, they did not link them to certain elite universities, and they did not think they were strongly promotion-oriented, or markedly loyal. Thus they were different from the stereotypical 'company man'. The views of managers and employees were fairly congruent, but employees rated personal networks and balance higher, and felt even more strongly that creativity was not linked to university background, promotion orientation, loyalty or seniority.

Nonetheless, they were deemed to possess a strong work ethic. Sixty-one per cent of employees in creative departments and 52% in routine

[9] The Japan Federation of Employers' Associations (Nikkeiren, 1995; cf. also Nikkeiren and Kanto keieisha kyokai, 1996), for example, proposed a 'portfolio' of employment types consisting of a 'long-term skill accumulation' type, a 'highly specialized skill' type and a 'flexible' type. The second, specialist type was conceived as having relatively high levels of inter-firm mobility. In terms of career profiles, however, creative workers in the survey reported here would actually come within the first, long-term skill accumulation type, which Nikkeiren envisaged as based on 'traditional lifetime employment'.

Table 4.3 *Characteristics of work in department*

	Creative departments		Routine departments	
	Managers	Employees	Managers	Employees
Strong links with other departments, outside	58.4	58.9	36.0	41.1
Multiple tasks, themes	47.8	50.0	20.6	26.1
Developing new areas	43.2	45.5	1.4	2.5
Highly specialized	35.9	32.9	13.7	15.2
Dynamic/fluid organization	30.4	24.6	5.1	6.5
Extemporaneous work style	27.4	24.0	8.9	10.9
Freedom in hours, etc.	22.8	23.8	5.4	11.8
Experience in related work	21.5	17.5	10.9	9.3
Much work is individual	16.8	16.1	16.0	21.1
Work similar to other companies	13.3	20.3	12.0	18.3
Most workers are young	10.6	19.0	9.7	15.8
Fluid member composition	5.4	5.6	1.4	3.0

Note: Figures are for 'very relevant'.
Source: As for table 4.2.

departments thought they had a passion for work, and 87% and 82% thought they were passionate about certain kinds of work. And while loyalty *per se* was not considered important, three-quarters thought that creative workers had loyalty or affinity for their company.

The majority of managers had made some attempt to gather creative workers in their department, largely by drawing them from other departments in the same company, but sometimes through mid-career hiring. Roughly 15% reported internal job posting systems. Managers of creative departments appeared to have greater influence over personnel decisions than managers of routine departments. They were more likely to try to strengthen links with specific universities and labs (20% versus 5%), and construct external networks to secure creative workers (16% versus 9%), but few reported using internships, re-employing former employees, headhunting, employing foreign workers or using non-regular workers.

Managers were asked to rate twelve features about their departments and work as 'very relevant', 'somewhat relevant' or 'not relevant.' The results are summarized in table 4.3. Here the differences between creative departments and routine departments were more pronounced than between managers and employees. Creative department managers and employees reported stronger links with other departments, suppliers and customers; multiple tasks, projects or themes; developing new areas;

highly specialized work; project teams and so on.[10] Again, contrary to some common views, they were not linked with higher turnover, younger workers or individual working. And interestingly, neither managers nor employees felt that creative work required skills which were general rather than company-specific.

Working hours and practices in creative departments were more flexible than in routine departments. Fifty-eight per cent of creative departments had flex-time, for instance, versus 48% of routine departments, and 32% versus 19% said it was often used. Three-quarters of managers in creative departments allowed outside business visits without reporting in to the office before or after, and 27% said the system was often used, versus 64% and only 8% in routine departments. Working from home was not widespread, either as a policy or in practice. When asked about the scope to do research or study not relevant to immediate work needs but potentially useful in the future, 7% of employees in creative departments said they had considerable freedom, and 35% some freedom, compared with 2% and 21% in routine departments. Employees in creative departments also had more budgetary discretion, and more discretion over phone calls for private use.

But there were limits to such discretion. Managers were asked what was not permitted, even by high performers. Failure to meet deadlines topped the list (82% and 78%), followed by failure to report (69% and 69%), failure to carry out instructions, bad attitude to customers and bad attitude in general, doing other work in company time, and so on. These all scored around 60%, but being unsociable and variable in application to work scored only 20%.

Creativity-supporting environments

What kind of environment fosters or hinders creative working? There were few clear differences between managers in creative and routine departments with regards physical environments.[11] There were differences, however, in views about the mood or atmosphere of their workplaces (table 4.4). Most managers thought their workplaces were co-operative, with good communication and 'after 5' socializing, but creative departments scored much higher on understanding by top management, mutual

---

[10] Almost half the employees in creative departments were involved in project work, compared with a quarter in routine departments. In both types of departments teams averaged ten members. A quarter of teams were active for less than six months, 30% for less than a year, and 10% for no fixed period.

[11] New facilities or equipment were considered important by 48% and 43% respectively; LAN and other communication means, 36% and 25%; spacious facilities, 23% and 23%; partitioned workplaces 20% and 16%; and sufficient budget, 9% and 4%.

Table 4.4 *Workplace 'atmosphere' (managers' views, %)*

	CD	RD
There is a co-operative atmosphere	82.9	85.1
There is smooth up–down communication	64.4	63.4
Top corporate managers are understanding	45.4	27.4
Superiors and subordinates often go for a drink	45.1	43.1
There is mutual stimulation	40.8	26.6
Various members offer ideas	39.9	18.6
Authority is delegated to employees	35.9	27.7
There is acceptance of risk	31.3	12.0
Meetings are unnecessarily long and/or frequent	25.0	31.1
There are opportunities for self cultivation/recharging batteries	25.0	19.1
Postings reflect employee wishes	20.7	18.9
The appraisal system is transparent and fair	16.0	20.3
Proposals opposed at the top managers' meeting can survive	10.1	2.9
Performance-based pay differentials are large	5.2	3.7

Note: CD = creative department; RD = routine department
Source: As for table 4.2.

stimulation, ideas put forward by various people rather than a select few, and risk acceptance. Both types of department, however, scored low on scope for self-cultivation or 'recharging batteries', career paths respecting individual wishes, and fair appraisal, indicating some dissatisfaction with current manning or work distribution and HRM practices.

Managers and employees were asked about obstacles to creative work (up to five choices; table 4.5). There were some interesting differences between managers and employees; for employees the biggest obstacles were an atmosphere of risk aversion, no chance for self-cultivation or recharging batteries, lack of delegated authority and a frenetic pace of work. The first and third of these are two sides of the same coin, and by and large managers shared this view. The second and fourth are related, too, however, and were felt more acutely by employees. Related issues of insufficient support staff and long and frequent meetings were also felt more acutely by employees, particularly of creative departments. When coupled with findings below on when and where workers were most creative, these findings give rise for thought.

Employees felt it was not necessarily a lack of mutual stimulation or friendly competition that impedes creative work, but insufficient scope for self-cultivation or recharging batteries, as well as company or supervisors who did not accept risk or delegate authority, hours and pace of work, and progress checks that reduce freedom. By contrast, while there were complaints about low pay, lack of performance-based pay differentials,

Table 4.5 *Impediments to creative work*

	Department managers		Employees	
	CD	RD	CD	RD
Atmosphere of risk aversion	57.1	53.1	49.6 (1)	35.8 (2)
Little mutual stimulation or friendly rivalry	38.3	33.4	25.4	23.4
No opportunities for self-cultivation/ recharging batteries	34.8	34.3	37.6 (2)	39.6 (1)
Little communication with other departments	32.3	25.4	28.5 (5)	28.0 (5)
Lack of diversity of members	31.8	28.3	16.5	17.3
Authority is not delegated to employees	31.0	32.3	30.6 (3)	35.0 (3)
Uninspiring superiors	26.1	19.1	24.5	22.5
Top corporate managers are not understanding	25.5	17.4	21.3	17.5
Postings don't reflect employee's wishes	19.0	22.9	17.8	24.0
Necessary IT equipment not available	18.5	15.7	19.5	14.1
Too much work, frenetic pace of work	17.7	23.4	30.4 (4)	31.0 (4)
Budget restrictions, insufficient budget	17.1	9.1	19.5	15.2
Lack of support staff	14.7	14.9	20.3	19.6
No atmosphere of co-operation	14.1	13.7	18.4	17.7
Long, frequent meetings	12.5	7.4	18.3	13.3
Pyramid-type organization structure	12.0	9.7	15.5	17.1
Performance-based pay differentials too small	11.7	10.6	10.1	8.0
Appraisal system is not transparent or fair	11.1	14.9	12.1	16.6
Lack of company education/training	5.7	8.9	6.1	10.9
Lack of latest equipment	5.2	4.6	4.6	6.3
Poor physical working environment	5.2	2.9	8.7	7.0
Low wages	4.9	3.7	8.6	9.3
Unequal opportunities for work	4.6	9.1	7.2	15.8
Restrictions on side work, other activities	1.1	1.7	1.7	1.1
Performance-based pay differentials too large	0.3	0.6	0.1	0.8

Note: CD = creative department; RD = routine department
Source: As for table 4.2.

lack of company-sponsored education and training, appraisal procedure, lack of equal work opportunities and poor physical work environment, these were not considered major impediments, either by managers or employees. There is little support here for claims that creative work would be stimulated by reforming the appraisal system or greater performance-based pay differentials.

Table 4.6 *Skill development for creative work* (%)

	Department managers		Employees	
	CD	RD	CD	RD
In-company				
Development through daily work	66.0	60.0	76.1	72.4
Planned in-company rotation/postings	55.2	66.0	20.6	23.6
Self-study for qualifications	38.9	47.1	24.6	33.4
In-company specialist training	35.6	34.0	27.3	28.7
Small group activities, research groups	26.1	24.6	18.5	19.5
Production, sales, etc. workplace experience	26.1	19.7	23.1	13.7
Company-wide training	10.1	12.3	9.1	19.5
External				
Industry-based information exchange	56.5	47.1	31.6	22.9
Networking with external experts	45.9	33.7	31.2	17.1
Participation in inter-industry exchange forums	35.6	34.2	21.2	16.4
Joint development with other companies	25.2	9.9	13.7	4.0
Training/education at other institutions	22.3	22.9	11.3	14.3
Experience abroad	18.4	16.2	7.7	4.6
Study at domestic/foreign universities	16.3	11.6	6.9	3.8
Exchange through secondment	13.6	23.2	6.1	4.8

Note: CD = creative department; RD = routine department
Source: As for table 4.2.

Managers rated lack of diversity the fifth most serious obstacle for creative work. We noted earlier that managers in creative departments were active in creating networks to secure creative workers, but it was not clear how actively they used these to create diversity. If classic model practices favour homogeneity over diversity, this is a potential problem, and we shall return to it later in the book.

Relatedly, what did employees want of their managers? In creative departments priorities were the ability to work with other departments (50%), fostering abilities of subordinates and young workers (43%), trustworthiness (36%), trusting employees and delegating work (34%), and attractive personalities (31%). Priorities were reasonably similar in routine departments, except that delegating work was replaced by high skill levels.

In other words, employees saw impediments to creative work as rooted in the company organization and management systems. If their managers were better at interacting with other departments, trusted their

Table 4.7 *Rewards for extraordinary results (current situation and preferred means, %)*

	Current situation (managers)		Preferred means (employees)	
	CD	RD	CD	RD
Increased bonus	69.3	68.3	40.2 (1)	42.3
Assignment to more important work	44.6	36.9	28.6 (3)	27.6
Award	42.4	31.4	7.4	8.8
Promotion	22.6	23.7	31.1 (2)	33.7
No special consideration	15.5	18.6	2.5	3.0
External publicity	16.0	9.1	8.5	4.2
Opportunities for education	13.0	7.4	7.0	6.3
Raise in base pay	9.5	6.0	25.3 (4)	26.5
Assignment to preferred work	9.8	2.9	14.7	14.7
Flexible working time	9.0	3.1	11.7	9.0
Special leave	1.6	1.1	8.3	8.2

Note: CD = creative department; RD = routine department
Source: As for table 4.2.

subordinates and nurtured their skills, and allowed for risk taking, they felt they could work more creatively.

Finally, we should note two other findings. First, employees were asked whether their ideas or those of their team had been taken up by the company. Just under half (42%) of those in creative departments and 15% of those in routine departments said ideas had been taken up which had an important influence on company performance, 48% and 39% ideas which had had an important influence on efficiency, and 27% and 4% reported patents arising from work.

Second, employees were asked whether they had their inspiration or problem solving insights (1) in the company or outside it; (2) while working or not working; (3) alone or with others; and (4) when relaxed or under pressure. Irrespective of department, roughly 60% responded out of the company, 60% away from work, and 70–80% when they were alone and when they were relaxed. In other words, inspiration or breakthroughs came away from the fray of daily work. Placed beside complaints about few opportunities to recharge batteries, frenetic pace of work and so on, this suggests employees felt they were not given sufficient opportunities to do creative work. This does not mean that they gained little stimulation from work, however; when asked what people were helpful for gaining insights, the most common responses were workplace superiors or colleagues, and people in other departments in the same company.

We conclude that working environments are not sufficiently conducive to creative working for organizational and management reasons, pointing to the need, perhaps, for greater professionalization of management itself (in the sense of improved skills to diagnose and deal with such issues), but these are not necessarily linked intrinsically to the classic model.

Appraisal, pay and the age–skill profile curve

Let us now turn to the compatability of creative work and workers with classic model employment practices, looking first at skill development, age–skill/ability curves and then remuneration.

As table 4.6 shows, both managers and employees agreed that the most common in-house means of training/education was through daily work (OJT). Thereafter, however, their views diverged sharply. Managers ranked planned rotation close behind OJT – higher in routine departments – but this view was not shared by employees. In fact, apart from self-study and specialist training, they saw relatively little other in-house training taking place.[12]

As for training and education outside the company, both managers and employees ranked information exchange through industry bodies, networking with external experts and participation in inter-industry forums highest. Again, employees gave lower scores, but significantly both managers and employees of creative departments rated external education and training conducive to building networks more extensive than those of routine departments (as opposed to studying for external qualifications, where the opposite was the case).

With this kind of education and training, how do abilities change with age? Managers were asked about the 'most creative work' and later about ability to perform that work with age. They were asked to choose from six age–ability profile curves (similar, but not identical, to figure 3.2). Combined creative and routine department managers gave the following ratings: constant skill rise with age, 10%; flat then rising, 17%; rising then flat, 30%; an inverse U, 17%; completely flat, 4%; and random, 10%. Thus almost 60% of managers saw some form of positive correlation between age and ability, though not necessarily a smooth, direct one, while 20% saw a decline after a certain age.

If anything, creative department managers had a harsher view of the age–ability relationship. In sales, marketing and advertising, and R&D, over 20% opted for the reverse U, roughly equal to the constant rise and

---

[12] This suggests caution is needed when building a picture of training based solely on managers' accounts; cf. Whittaker, 1990a.

flat-then-rise choices combined. On the other hand, in personnel, general affairs, advertising and financial accounting, where there was judged to be more routine work, constant rise and flat-then-rise choices totalled 30%.

Managers who chose flat-then-rise, rise-then-flat and reverse U profiles were asked to identify the age of the turning point. The flat-then-rise turning point averaged 31–32 years old; the rise-then-flat averaged 43; and the reverse U averaged 41–42, with only small differences between creative and routine departments. A composite profile suggests a pronounced expansion of skills in the 30s followed by a gradual levelling off, if not decline, from the early 40s.

Employee views were rather different. Engineers and systems engineers, planning and design staff and other specialists were three times more likely to choose a constant rise than managers, half as likely to choose flat-then-rise, more likely to choose rise-then-flat, and somewhat less likely to choose the reverse U. In brief, they had a more optimistic view of the age–skill profile curve than managers. This tendency was even more pronounced for office workers, and sales and marketing staff. Estimations of turning points, however, were not very different, and around 15% of specialists thought that creative abilities declined after a certain age.

Asked what they wanted to do if or when they passed their skills peak, a fifth chose 'take what comes', followed by 'become a manager in the same department' (18%), 'learn a new skill and change jobs' (14%), 'become a manager in another department of the same company' (12%), and trailing at 5%, 'set up my own business'. Employees in creative departments were much more likely to want to become managers in the same department or company, and less likely to want to learn a new skill and change jobs, again suggesting the need for caution about associating creative work with mobile workers.[13] The range of responses was most pronounced for

---

[13] The image of highly creative, mobile workers probably comes from IT sector engineers and analysts and fund managers working for foreign financial institutions. Research by Imano et al. (2000) casts doubt on the stereotypical picture of IT engineers, particularly in larger companies (cf. also Yahata, 1999a: 140; Sato, 2001: 219). The image is closer to reality in foreign financial institutions, which largely recruit specialists from other foreign financial institutions (Nissei kiso kenkyusho, 2000). It is not clear at this stage whether Japanese financial institutions will converge towards these practices or not. Goh (2000: 105–6) suggests that there are separate commercial bank and investment bank models in the USA. If so, the changes may depend on the extent to which commercial-oriented Japanese financial institutions become more investment-oriented. As for foreign *manufacturers* in Japan (pharmaceutical and chemical firms are prevalent), many adopt 'localized' employment practices, with the notable difference that the arrival of a new president from the home country is often followed by headhunting of other senior personnel, frequently from other foreign manufacturers.

those in their late 20s (with 7.8% opting for setting up their own business), followed by a sharp convergence towards staying in the same company after 30. This was most pronounced in R&D, new product development and new business development.

Given these rather mixed views on the relationship between abilities or skills and age, how did the respondents think they should be remunerated? And how were they actually remunerated? First, managers were asked about wage differentials. Taking the average annual income of a male university graduate peer cohort in their early 40s as the index (100), the lowest paid of the cohort was said to be earning 86.0 on average in creative departments, and the highest paid 115.6. In routine departments the spread was 83.4 to 116.0. In other words, there was a range of plus–minus 15% around the mean. The ideal spread for these managers was wider – 79.0 to 129.2 for creative department managers and 77.9 to 125.4 for routine department managers. In other words, they wanted to increase the spread, mainly by increasing the ceiling. Many managers considered the ideal spread to be 80 to 130.[14] Thus the current reality, as well as the ideal, points to a kind of egalitarianism with respect to 'pie' distribution, especially if we also consider the normal distribution of the curve.

But what about employees who produce extraordinary results? This has become a controversial issue in Japan following some well-publicized examples of (former) employees suing their company – including Hitachi in 2002 – over patent payments.[15] Table 4.7 shows that within one year of producing extraordinary results, such high performers were mainly given extra bonus, followed by assignment to more important work, and an award. Trailing by a considerable margin was promotion. Less than 20% of managers said they were given no special consideration, primarily because the company had no mechanism for this, or it was handled within the normal appraisal procedure.

What the employees wanted was different. They wanted recognition in the bonus, and assignment to more important work, but they also wanted promotion and a rise in base pay. They did not want awards or external recognition. These preferences crossed departmental boundaries, and suggest a weaker attachment to *nenko* principles than managers.[16]

[14] These findings are very similar to those of Rodosho (1995: 173), which found an actual spread of 83.5 to 121.0, and an ideal spread of 79.0 to 129.1.
[15] The most widely publicized case is that of Nakamura versus Nichia, over income derived from Nakamura's development of blue light-emitting diodes (LEDs). Shimadzu researcher Tanaka Koichi, by contrast, received little payment or recognition prior to being awarded the Nobel Prize in 2002, but expressed little dissatisfaction.
[16] Quite possibly this is even more pronounced for high performers themselves; in 2003–4 growing alarm was being expressed in Japan about poaching of high performing R, D&E employees and managers, by Korean and other Asian companies.

Conversely, when a project did not produce the expected results, according to employees, there were no particular repercussions, or it tended to be swept under the carpet. This might indicate loose management, or an inadequate basis for strictly evaluating performance.

Regarding appraisal, over a third thought the current system was reasonable, but around 60% thought it had problems. Criticisms were, in order of frequency, that it was unclear what was being appraised, the outcome was not made known, there was no chance to respond to the outcome, results of the evaluation were not reflected in pay, the appraisal was relative rather than set against absolute criteria, the ability of the appraiser was questionable, and appraisal itself was unfair. (Differences between creative and routine departments were not great.) These criticisms point to faults in the appraisal systems, problems of reflecting the results in pay, and questions of fairness.

Employees were asked what two things their superior emphasized most in appraisals, and what two things they *wanted* to be emphasized most. Employees of both types of departments felt that professional or specialist skills, management or organizing abilities, and short-term results were emphasized most. While maintaining the first two emphases, they wanted greater emphasis on long-term results – a future orientation rather than focus on the present. This is a significant finding, as it runs counter to the perception of increasingly short-term horizons, especially on the part of creative workers. As their second choice, too, creative department employees wanted long-term results to be stressed, while routine department employees favoured personality and fitting in. Both groups wanted more emphasis on potential, and there was negligible support for emphasizing the *nenko* pillars of age, tenure and education background.

Employees, it seemed, wanted the classic model of employment relations to be modified rather than abandoned, evolution rather than revolution, away from *nenko* towards evaluating professional skills or abilities, but in the long term rather than the short term. While there were internal tensions in the HRM system, therefore, there did not appear to be fundamental contradictions.

Conclusions: employment, creative professionals and organizations

In the 1990s, the productivity of white-collar employees came under increasing scrutiny. The number of specialists, or 'company professionals', was rising, and they were now expected to make high value added contributions of their own. But were classic model employment practices compatible with the expectations now being placed on them? We investigated this question through the findings of a survey of creative workers and work, characterized by: (a) high levels of discretion over non-routine work; and (b) potentially wide variations in performance, depending on the individual; (c) the outcome of which may have a large impact on company performance. Some of the main findings are as follows.

'Creative workers' were distinctive in terms of education, but in terms of job tenure, they were little different from employees doing routine work. Unlike stereotypical 'company men', they were not particularly concerned about promotion, security or loyalty, but they did have a strong work ethic, and a sense of affinity or loyalty towards their company. Their perceptions were long term, as can be seen in their views of appraisal, where there was considerable dissatisfaction. They wanted greater emphasis on professional skills, but they also wanted performance to be measured over the long term, including potential.

Workplaces were seen as co-operative, and communication was good. Creative workers often worked in flexible, relatively autonomous project teams, with substantial external networks, in principle conducive to raising skill levels. Two thirds of managers thought there was a positive relationship between age and ability to do creative work, and only a minority – 10–20% – felt that ability declined significantly after a certain age. Long-term employment, therefore, would appear to remain a viable option, especially when we consider that employees are often moved to new kinds of work, anyway, when specialist performance starts to decline.

Concerning fairness, too, current remuneration policies were not considered a major impediment for creative work. There was widespread support for a modest widening of wage differentials, mainly by raising the ceiling for high performers, but within certain bounds.

Thus there appeared to be no fundamental contradiction between creative work and classic model employment practices, although increasing prominence of creative work is likely to intensify a weakening of *nenko* principles, lead to greater openness of workplaces, flexible organization, discretion in working hours and practices, and so on.

The survey did highlight, however, some serious obstacles to working creatively, which were related more to the organization of work and management than to employment practices. Many workers felt there was an atmosphere of risk aversion, and of a lack of delegation of authority. They also felt there were no opportunities for self-cultivation and recharging batteries, that the pace of work was frenetic, and relatedly that there was a lack of support staff and meetings were long and frequent. Perhaps this was the reason the majority felt they were most creative when out of the company, away from work, when they were alone and relaxed.

Unless such issues are addressed – through redesigning work and reforming management structures and processes – they could lead to deteriorating performance, with repercussions for the community firm. The costs of forgone creativity, however, are impossible to calculate, while the benefits of squeezing a bit more work in, of reducing staff just a little more, are tangible. The temptation is to opt for the latter, especially in times of recession and intense competition.

The survey also suggests that related issues must be tackled for the effective introduction of flexible working hour practices, including clarification of goals and evaluation of standards of work, clarifying indices of managers' work, improving work management ability of employees, increasing the amount of self-contained work and reducing the frequency of meetings.[17]

Thus there are a range of issues which need to be addressed to promote the creativity and professionalization of white-collar work. If anything, they point to the need for greater professionalization of management – in the 'company professional', creative worker sense.

[17] Cf. also Sato, 2001: 129.

5   Corporate Governance and Managers' Ideologies

In chapters 1 and 2 we noted the importance of managers' priorities, or ideologies, in determining the future of the community firm. In this chapter we turn to these, in the context of the global tide of corporate governance reform, which started in the 1980s in the USA and UK, and subsequently swept developed and developing countries alike. With it came a greater emphasis on shareholder interests. Despite a growing interest in varieties of capitalism,[1] it was in fact the 'neo-American' variety which made most of the running under economic globalization and corporate governance reform, at least until the collapse of the IT bubble and wave of corporate scandals in the USA at the turn of the century.

What happened when this tide hit Japan? What corporate governance reforms did Japanese managers themselves initiate? After briefly reviewing developments at the macro-level, we turn to a large-scale survey of executive directors of listed companies conducted by JTUC and chaired by Inagami in January and February 1999. The survey offers insights into the thinking of Japan's top managers about corporate governance reform at that point. It also allows us to explore the relationship between views on corporate governance and managers' responsibilities on the one hand, and changing employment and industrial relations on the other. Through this, we will gain a better picture of change and continuity in managers' priorities or ideologies, and the consequences.

By exploring corporate governance, too, we will be able to consider how changes in financial markets as well as competitive conditions in product markets are influencing community firms. As we have suggested, the viability of the classic model depends on more than the internal integrity of the model itself, but on competitive performance and its adaptability to a changing environment. In chapters 5 and 6, as well as in Part 2, we broaden our focus to consider such influences.

---

[1] Cf. Albert, 1991; Dore, 2000. Also Berger and Dore, 1996; Katz and Darbishire, 2000; Freeman, 1998, 2000; Hall and Soskice, 2001; Whitby, 1999.

The corporate governance reform boom

Three models of corporate governance

The corporate governance reform movement began in the USA in the 1980s, spread to the UK in the late 1980s, and thence to continental Europe and Asia in the 1990s. This movement brought a renewed emphasis on shareholder interests, rooted (in industrialized countries) in the rising share of pension funds, insurance companies and other institutional investors in share ownership, their increasing influence on stock markets, and behind these developments, industrial maturity and demographic ageing. Corporate scandals triggered the movement to raise capital efficiency and shareholder value through corporate governance reforms.

The movement gave rise to a number of influential reports, such as the Millstein Report (1998) and the OECD Principles of Corporate Governance (1999), but there is no universally accepted definition of corporate governance, as can be seen by a cursory glance at the various codes and principles which the boom produced.[2] Even in the USA, the diversity can be seen, for instance, in reports by the American Law Institute (1992), TIAA-CREF (1997), the Business Roundtable (1997) and CalPERS (1998).

In the UK, too, the Hampel Report (1998: 7, 12–13) noted that the earlier Cadbury (1992) and Greenbury (1995) Reports placed heavy emphasis on accountability to shareholders, but gave little space to directors' responsibilities for business prosperity. Further, it argued that good stakeholder relations are crucial for increasing shareholder value over the long term, and that there is no single, globally applicable, model of corporate governance.

The Blair government subsequently published a green paper on Company Law reform (DTI, 1998a), followed by a Strategic Framework which proposed several models of corporate governance for consideration (Company Law Review Steering Group, 1999). Extrapolated features of these models – the 'classic model', the 'enlightened shareholder value model' and the 'pluralist model' – are shown in table 5.1.

The classic model (not to be confused with the classic model of the community firm and employment practices used in this book) sees the company as the property of its shareholders, and executives as their agents whose primary duty is to secure maximum gains for the owners in the immediate, short term. If shareholder expectations are not

---

[2] Cf. DTI, 1998b; http://www.ecgi.org.codes/

Table 5.1 *Three models of corporate governance*

	Shareholder value maximization	Interest in long-term corporate prosperity	Short-term orientation	Stakeholder orientation	Unitarism
Classic model					
Exit type	●	✗	●	✗	●
Voice type	●/○	●	○/△	△	●
Enlightened shareholder Value model	○	●	✗	○	✗
Pluralist model	✗	●	✗	●	✗

Note: Stakeholder orientation implies balancing responsibilities to (or claims of) multiple parties – stakeholders – including employees and customers, as well as shareholders. Unitarism refers to a 'one size fits all' approach (cf. The Business Roundtable, 1997; Millstein Report, 1998).
● strongly associated with
○ moderately associated with
△ weakly associated with
✗ not associated with
Source: Extrapolated from DTI, 1998a.

met, the shareholders either exit through selling the shares (exit type), or they express voice and push for changes which will secure their proprietary interests (voice type). In the enlightened shareholder value model emphasis is placed on business prosperity to maximize shareholder value in the medium to long term. Establishing and maintaining good stakeholder relations is seen as critical to securing business prosperity. In the pluralist model the primary objective is business prosperity for the benefit of the various stakeholders. Objectives and means of achieving prosperity may be diverse. Thus the models express fundamental differences in views over the role of top management.[3]

The past decade has seen an increase in shareholder activism (classic model, voice type) in many countries, but shareholder activism itself has

---

[3] According to this typology, the views expressed in the Cadbury Report (1992), for instance, would belong to the classic model, exit type, while those of CalPERS (1998) would belong to the classic model, voice type. The American Law Institute (1992), The Business Roundtable (1997), TIAA-CREF (1997), Hampel Report (1998) and OECD (1999) would belong to the enlightened shareholder value model. The German KonTraG (Gesetz zur Kontrolle und Transparenz im Unternehmensbereich, 1998, at http://www.ecgi.org/codes/all-codes.htm) and Kommission Mitbestimmung (Bertelsman Stiftung und Böckler Stiftung hrsg, 1998) as well as Japan's Keizai Doyukai (1998) and Nikkeiren (1998) would belong to the pluralist model.

also come to encompass a growth of interest in socially responsible and ethical investment. As well, the enlightened shareholder value model has become more prominent.[4]

Debates over the reform of Japanese corporate governance

In Japan the Japan Committee for Economic Development (JCED) and Japan Federation of Employers' Associations (JFEA) produced influential reports on corporate governance (Keizai Doyukai, 1998; Nikkeiren, 1998) which can be described as pluralist. JCED is an organization of self-styled progressive executives which has aimed at creating a 'reformed capitalist' model since its inception in 1946. It translated the Hampel Report and debated an appropriate form of corporate governance for Japan in its 1998 *Enterprise White Paper*.

It argued, first, for emphasizing capital efficiency, through strict self-discipline, transparent, bold and speedy decision-making, concentration on high profit activities, rapid restructuring, changing priorities in management indicators, improving investor relations, and shareholder emphasis. Second it advocated reform of perfunctory annual shareholder meetings, boards of directors and auditor boards. Third, however, it argued that there was no one best model of corporate governance and that trying to impose one for the sake of appearances was meaningless. And fourth, it argued that companies should strive to become good corporate citizens, by 'actively addressing environmental issues, concern for customers, and creating and maintaining good industrial relations' (Keizai Doyukai, 1998: 5). It declared that emphasis on capital efficiency could not be justified in the absence of good corporate citizenship. This stance places it in the pluralist model camp.[5]

In the second report, JFEA's International Special Committee[6] argued that it is simplistic to think that US and UK corporate governance practices constitute a global standard which all other countries must aspire to. It recognized that shareholder emphasis would strengthen, but argued that this was not – should not be – incompatible with valuing

---

[4] The UK Strategic Framework, for instance, argues that pressures on managers to maximize shareholder interests in the short term frequently impede investment for value creation in the longer term, and also that theories which view executives primarily as agents of shareholders are unrealistic for modern companies.

[5] JCED's reports have not been consistent. The recommendation of its Corporate Management Committee (Keizai Doyukai, 2002) are, on balance, closer to 'Americanization', while its 2003 Enterprise White Paper is pluralist (see chapter 14).

[6] The Committee was chaired by Tateishi Nobuo, then Chairman of Omron Corporation, and a member of the OECD's Millstein Committee.

employees. It warned, moreover, that excessive emphasis on direct capital markets would increase the gulf between haves and have nots, creating social divisions and unrest (Nikkeiren, 1998: 5). The report criticized a 'one size fits all' approach, and argued that reconstructing corporate governance in Japan did not imply rejecting everything Japanese. Positive aspects such as respect for employees and management from a long-term perspective should be retained. This report, too, can be interpreted as advocating a pluralist approach.

Also worth noting are the Japan Corporate Governance Forum (2001) and the Pension Fund Association (Kosei NKR, 2001). The former advocated the adoption of American corporate governance practices, such as those subsequently incorporated into the revised Commercial Code (see below). The guidelines of the Pension Fund Association suggest that the companies fund managers invest in 'should be managed to maximize the interests of shareholders'. Boards of directors 'should be comprised of members able to make appropriate management decisions as agents of shareholders, an appropriate number of whom should be external to and independent from the company in question'. Both bodies' reports are close to the voice type of the classic model.[7]

In March 2002, moreover, the Japan Association of Corporate Directors was formed, headed by the chairman of the Japan Corporate Governance Forum, Miyauchi Yoshihiko. Its aim is to promote 'healthy' boards from a corporate governance perspective; in substance it marked the establishment of an American practice-oriented directors' organization, but this may not go uncontested (see chapter 14).

Overhaul of the Commercial Code

On 22 May 2002, revisions to the Commercial Code were approved by the House of Representatives. They followed a number of other reforms to the Code in the previous five years, such as the recognition of stock options in 1997, recognition of share buy-backs in 1998, stock swaps in 1999 and transfers of undertakings in 2001, as well as removal of the prohibition of owning own-company stocks. In 2002 the green light was given for electronic notification of shareholder annual general meetings (AGMs), and the shareholder representative litigation system was revised, reducing liability for corporate managers.[8]

---

[7] In 2003 the Pension Fund Association announced that it would vote against the re-election of management, and payment of their retirement allowances, if a company had three straight years of losses with no dividend payments.

[8] Iwahara (2000) characterizes changes to the Commercial Code in recent years as follows: (1) the changes since 1997 represent the fourth major set of reforms, after those of the

Although the Commercial Code has undergone frequent revision, the 2002 changes were unusually far-reaching. For the first time since 1950 it became possible to reform boards of directors and auditors. Listed companies were presented with a choice. If a company chooses the committee system, (1) the executive and supervisory functions are separated – the former are carried out by executive and representative executive officers and the latter by the board of directors (thus the board of auditors is abolished); (2) three new committees for appointments, remuneration and auditing are created under the board, which now makes the decisions to appoint or remove executive and representative executive officers; (3) each of these committees must have at least three directors, the majority of whom must be external to the company. By introducing the option of US- (or UK-)inspired boards in this way, the revised Commercial Code represents a radical departure from the past.[9]

Whether they choose to follow this option or not, however, is left up to companies themselves. A critical question, therefore, is how many companies choose this option, and which ones. The Japan Association of Corporate Auditors, which will be directly influenced by the outcome, carried out a survey of members in April 2002. The results showed that only four companies (0.4%) were planning to use the new option, as opposed to 525 (49%) which planned to continue the current system, and 450 (42%) which had not yet decided (and no response from 9%: Nihon kansayaku kyokai, 2002). As the new option was radically different from both existing law and practice, and the law had not yet been passed, the size of the 'don't know' category was understandable. By mid 2003, only thirty-six listed companies had adopted the new system, including Sony (not surprisingly), Toshiba, and Hitachi and eighteen of its group companies. We will look at Hitachi's adoption of the new system in chapter 10.

Meiji period, the late 1920s–early 1930s, and after the Second World War; (2) unlike past reforms which were bureaucrat-led, the current reforms have been promoted by business, or the business-backed ruling party; (3) as in the past, the current reforms have a backdrop of deep economic malaise; (4) a major objective of the reforms has been to address declining share and land prices, and the crisis of financial institutions; (5) they are ambivalent about 'Japanese system' features such as the main bank system, reciprocal shareholding and *keiretsu* transactions; (6) they have placed heavy ideological emphasis on efficiency, competitiveness and the market; (7) but while emphasizing shareholder interests generally, the actual contents of reform do not always reflect this (for instance reducing the range of issues subject to shareholder approval, and increasing the scope of management discretion); (8) with a backdrop of coping with economic crisis, the reforms are incomplete and not necessarily consistent; (9) they represent a process of Americanization of company law, eroding the former German basis; (10) they have spurred a shift among non-profit organizations to for-profit status.

[9] Contents aside, the *procedure* for reforming corporate law in Japan and the UK provide a sharp contrast, particularly in terms of the extent of consultation.

Corporate governance and managers' ideologies

As we have seen, leading executive and business organizations in Japan have espoused pluralist views, while others have called for the Americanization of Japanese corporate governance. Our interest, however, is primarily in the views of individual directors rather than business organizations. How do they see – want to see – corporate governance in Japan changing or not changing from the model we presented in chapter 2? To answer this question we will draw on a survey of executive directors (*jomu* level and above) of listed companies, conducted in January and February 1999,[10] supplemented in the next section by a survey of corporate planning heads.

Directors' backgrounds and decision-making

Three-quarters of executive directors whose responses are used in the analysis were internally promoted, a figure corresponding to the findings of other surveys. Half the remainder came from 'parent' or other enterprise group companies, and may be considered 'semi insiders'.[11] Almost half replied that at their company 'many auditors have had experience as directors'. Here we can see internal career ladders extending to the top posts, spanning regular employees, managers and directors.

In fact, the executive directors had a lot in common with employees, in respect to both work and remuneration. Three-quarters retained operational responsibilities when they became directors. Often their work did not change much at all. And the majority said a significant portion of their pay came from these operational responsibilities.

Executive directors earned an average of 9.2 times the salary of a new university graduate employee, and presidents and chairmen earned 11.3 times. This figure is much lower than in the USA and UK, and 'fat cat' accusations are correspondingly rarer.[12]

[10] The 'RIALS top manager survey' was conducted by the 'Corporation and Society Research Group' of JTUC's Research Institute for Advancement of Living Standards (RIALS), and chaired by T. Inagami. The findings are reported in Inagami and Rengo soken, 2000. The survey covered executive directors of 1,307 companies listed on the first section of the Tokyo Stock Exchange. There were 1,211 (15.1%) valid responses. Where there was more than one response from a company, that of the most senior-ranked respondent was chosen, yielding information on 731 (55.9%) companies.

[11] Relatedly, 58% of the directors had concurrent director or auditor appointments at an average of 3.6 companies. Most (90%) were part-time appointments, and most (83%) were at group companies, at which they worked an average of 2.8 days per month. Seventy per cent were not paid. This shows the extent of co-directorships within enterprise groups.

[12] In the USA the AFL-CIO launched a campaign against executive greed with an Executive Pay Watch site (http://www.paywatch.org) in 1997. For the UK, see for instance the Greenbury Report, 1995; Machin, 1996; and Conyon and Murphy, 2000.

Four-fifths agreed that 'corporate strategy and other important decisions are substantially made in the executive directors' committee, and the board authorizes or confirms those decisions'. The former met once a week on average, while board meetings were held once a month. In addition, 86% agreed that directors' appointments from the vice-president level down were strongly influenced by the views of the president. Only 16% thought that appointments of presidents themselves were strongly influenced by major shareholders such as the main bank or life insurance companies.

In these respects, reality closely matched the model sketched in chapter 2. But what are the prospects for change, of the development, for instance, of an executive labour market?

Prospects for change

Only one in eight directors thought that in five years' time 'the president and other key executives will not be chosen from those employed long term in my company (or group), but the majority will be recruited externally, according to their management skills from the shareholders' perspective' (cf. table 5.3). Only a quarter of their companies had appointed external directors in the past three years, while another 17% were considering it. It appears unlikely that there will be a drastic reduction in the ratio of internally promoted executives in the medium-term future.

It is quite possible, however, that there will be some diversification in executive career paths. As we shall see in chapter 6, a number of leading companies are attempting to create group-wide executive development structures; this may lead to an increase in 'quasi-insiders'.

Second, regarding work and remuneration of executives, in three-quarters of companies representative executive directors (excluding the president and chairman) held operating responsibilities, but only half thought this was desirable. While only 4% had introduced the corporate officer system (separating these corporate officers from directors without operating responsibilities) in the past two to three years, 38% were considering introducing it. The separation of strategic from operating responsibilities indicates a weakening of the employee-like work characteristics of top management. In parallel, remuneration systems were also being separated from those of employees, and being linked to performance. It is difficult to predict at this stage what impact these changes will have, and specifically whether they will lead to a weakening of the employee representative orientation of top management in the community firm.

Third, a majority (61%) favoured a shakeup of boards, to make them places of more active debate. And only 18% thought it was desirable for auditors to be drawn from retiring directors. Two-thirds agreed that: 'In order to prevent corporate scandals, the authority of corporate auditors should be strengthened, and at the same time they should become more specialized and independent.' If indeed both boards of directors and auditors are strengthened in this way, the result will be a strengthening of the dual supervisory system, so that it begins to play the role originally envisaged for it, rather than its dissolution.

Shareholders

Another crucial dimension of corporate governance is relations with shareholders. How closely do these match the model in chapter 2, and what are the prospects for change?

Almost all (98%) companies had stable shareholders. These included the main bank (79%), employee shareholding association (75%) and key customers or trading partners (62%). Stable shareholders owned an average of 54% of shares. Some 39% of companies held shares reciprocally with almost all stable shareholders. Moreover, 80% of respondents agreed that 'normally, the views of major shareholders are not expressed in management', suggesting that stable shareholders are mostly silent. Only 11% thought that 'major shareholders have become forthright about exercising voting rights at recent shareholder AGMs'.

Almost three-quarters agreed that 'while the AGM is said to be a formality, that does not mean the interests of stable shareholders are ignored'. Just over three-quarters also agreed that 'rather than linking dividends to performance, emphasis is placed on dividend stability'. This suggests an implicit contract in which stable shareholders are provided with stable dividends, in return for funds, in keeping with the model in chapter 2.[13]

Managers' ideologies

What are the prospects for changing relations with shareholders, specifically of shareholders assuming greater prominence in managers' priorities? First, let us look at managers' ideologies, followed in the next section by capital efficiency.

Only a very small proportion (9%) of respondents agreed with the statement 'the company is the property of the shareholders, and employees are simply a factor of production', while 86% agreed that 'stakeholders are not limited to shareholders, and management must appropriately reflect multiple interests'. Almost as many (84%) agreed that 'the purpose

---

[13] In the past five years, however, companies had increasingly turned to bonds as a source of finance. The main sources were bank loans (66%), convertible bonds (45%) and normal bonds (30%).

Table 5.2 *Cross-tabulation of basic views of the company (%)*

	a	b	c	d
(a) Disagree with statement 1 (n = 483)	×	90.7	43.7	87.6
(b) Agree with statement 2 (n = 627)	69.9	×	46.4	87.1
(c) Agree with statement 3 (n = 365)	57.8	79.7	×	79.7
(d) Agree with statement 4 (n = 615)	68.8	88.8	47.3	×

Statement 1: 'The company is the property of the shareholders, and employees are simply a factor of production.'
Statement 2: 'Stakeholders are not limited to shareholders, and management must appropriately reflect multiple interests.'
Statement 3: 'The basic job of company executives is to improve the efficiency of capital, contributing to the maximization of shareholder interests.'
Statement 4: 'The purpose of management need not be the same for everyone. Priorities should be determined according to the individual characteristics of companies, and managed accordingly.'
Source: RIALS top manager survey.

of management need not be the same for everyone. Priorities should be determined according to the individual characteristics of companies, and managed on that basis.' These findings suggest strong support for a pluralist model of governance among Japanese executives. However, half also agreed with the textbook-like statement 'the basic job of company executives is to improve the efficiency of capital, contributing to the maximization of shareholder interests'. This apparent contradiction is one that directors have had to live with, as there has been a divergence between their responsibilities in law and in practice, but the latent tension may have intensified in recent years.

According to table 5.2, two-thirds of directors (483 out of 731) did *not* agree that 'the company is the property of the shareholders, and employees are simply a factor of production'. Of those 91% agreed that 'stakeholders are not limited to shareholders, and management must appropriately reflect multiple interests'. However, 44% also agreed that 'the basic job of company executives is to improve the efficiency of capital, contributing to the maximization of shareholder interests'. Of the four propositions in table 5.2, (a) and (c) are basically incompatible, while there is more compatibility between (b) and (d), and indeed (a).

We can relate this table to the three models of corporate governance. In one calculation, we interpret those who support (c) as well as (b) and (d) to be close to the enlightened shareholder value model. Advocates represent 40% of the total. Of the remaining 60%, roughly 10%

agree with Statement 1, supporting the classic (shareholder primacy) model. The remaining 50% espouse a pluralist position. Thus the classic model: enlightened shareholder value model: pluralist model ratio is 1:4:5.

By another calculation (a) plus (b) and/or (d) indicate support for the pluralist model. Sixty per cent fall in this category, and with the same 10% supporting the classic model, the ratio becomes 1:3:6. This calculation places more weight on continuity rather than change, while the first calculation suggests a somewhat greater movement from a pluralist model towards an enlightened shareholder value model. Just how prevalent the enlightened shareholder model becomes will depend on a range of factors, including the business environment, the financial environment and state of the stock market, as well as perceptions of US corporate governance practice.

Capital efficiency

A complementary picture emerges from a survey of heads of corporate planning departments – the JRK management strategy survey, carried out in 1999 (JRK, 2000b; see chapter 6 for details). The survey suggests a variety of factors lie behind changing corporate governance practices and perceptions, including changing competitive environments and new accounting standards.

According to the corporate planning heads, the management indicator most stressed in the past was sales (47%), followed by operating profit (27%), sales profit (10%) and net profit (5%). In future, however, they predicted greatest stress on operating profit (31%), net profit (21%) and sales profit (14%), with sales plummeting to 12%. Sixty per cent agreed that in the coming five years 'as a corporate performance indicator ROE will be given greater priority than sales or market share', while only 5% disagreed. With the growing emphasis on capital efficiency, the finance and accounting functions are likely to become more influential.

Stable and reciprocal shareholding

Specific financial priorities, according to the same survey, included greater asset fluidity (58%), securing stable shareholders (51%), dissolving 'inefficient' reciprocal shareholding (44%), amortizing own-company shares (31%), switching from bank loans to corporate bonds (26%) and share issues (14%). With the imminent introduction of new accounting standards, it is not surprising that managers were attempting to dispose of non-performing assets, increase asset fluidity, and to raise returns on equity through amortizing their own shares.

However, even in the context of strengthening capital market influence – or perhaps because of it – importance was attached to continuing relations with main banks, and stable shareholders such as key trading partners, suppliers and employee shareholding associations.

One-third of respondents said their company did not own shares on a reciprocal basis. Of the remaining two-thirds, 21% said they had reduced the proportion in the past three years, 66% reported little change and 13% reported an increase. Almost half said that the current rate was appropriate, but 45% thought it should be reduced in future.[14] The main reasons for wanting to reduce current levels were improving asset efficiency and consolidated ROE, and conforming to 'global standards'. Global standards may be in vogue, but conversely when one thinks of the share-buying spree many companies engaged in in the late 1980s, as well as current difficulties with non-performing assets, the desire to eliminate 'inefficient' reciprocal shareholding may be seen as a corrective to past vogues.

Investor relations and institutional investor interest

In the 1990s communication with institutional investors became a prominent issue. According to the corporate planning heads, many large companies started regular meetings with institutional investors to report on performance. On average these were held twice a year, and were attended by analysts and fund managers from securities companies, investment funds, financial research institutions, insurance companies and banks on the investor side, and the chairman, president and responsible directors on the company side. The interest of analysts and fund managers focused on the company's strategy (86%), detailed product information (64%) and operating profit (61%). Significantly, very little interest was expressed in reforming the board of directors or board of auditors (2%) or corporate social responsibility (1%), and none was expressed in reforming the Japanese employment system!

Stakeholder priorities

The shift in management priorities from sales to profit appears to represent a fundamental shift towards capital efficiency. But does this mean

---

[14] In the RIALS top management survey a majority (61%) of executive directors thought that current levels would be maintained in the next five years, 23% thought they would be reduced, and 13% thought they would be increased.

prioritizing shareholder interests above those of other stakeholders, notably employees? Respondents were asked the following question: 'Reflecting your company's management priorities, what would happen if your company's performance were (a) significantly better, or (b) significantly worse than average medium–long-term performance? For significantly better performance, they chose: increase employee pay/bonus (84%), increase the dividend to shareholders (79%) and increase director remuneration (44%). For significantly worse performance they chose: reduce employee pay/bonus (84%), reduce director remuneration (84%), and with a considerable gap, reduce/forgo the dividend to shareholders (61%). This suggests that Japanese managers do not simply prioritize employee interests at the expense of shareholders. It also suggests that directors draw the short straw; they are the last to benefit when times are good, but have their remuneration cut when times are bad (commonly by more than employees).

Reforming the director system

From this survey, too, then, we can discern elements of both continuity and change in corporate governance. Relating to our earlier discussion of directors, the JRK survey also revealed that over half (54%) of the companies had begun to reduce the number of directors. A number of related measures were also being introduced or contemplated, including fixed-term directorships (60%), increasing remuneration differentials of directors according to performance (47%), reforming the executive director committee (45%), revising or abolishing the corporate adviser system (37%), introducing the corporate officer system (35%), external directors (34%) and stock options (24%).[15] Companies were also trying to rejuvenate management by appointing younger corporate officers.

Corporate governance, employment and industrial relations

In chapters 3 and 4 we considered changes to employment practices. In this section we return to these, and consider what kind of impact changing corporate governance practices is likely to have on employment practices, and additionally on industrial relations. Again we draw on the same surveys.

---

[15] Similar responses were given in the RIALS top manager survey.

Table 5.3 *Management, employment and industrial relations in five years'*
time (%)

The president's remuneration will be over 50 times that of a normal employee	−78.4
There will be a significant increase in female directors and auditors	−63.3
The union will significantly increase its purchase of company shares	−58.4
An MBA will be desirable for promotion to director status	−55.4
Stock options/market-indexed bonuses will comprise over half of directors' pay	−48.7
Short-term employment will be common, even for core employees	−46.9
There will be a significant increase in non-Japanese directors and auditors	−45.9
It will be common for outstanding executives (from the shareholders' perspective) to be recruited externally	−40.2
Many executives will view the union as an irrelevance	−24.6
Large-scale layoffs will be possible without internal or external ructions	−18.2
There will be an annual pay spread of 50–200 around a mean of 100 for 40-year-old employees	0
Skill development will be considered a matter for the individual employee	1.9
There will be a move from collective to individualized employment and working conditions	10.3
A holding company will be formed within the enterprise group	12.3
Employee pay will vary with division/job type (multiple pay systems)	39.4
ROE will replace turnover/market share as the top management priority	62.8
Promotions will be decided principally by performance; age, tenure will be irrelevant	64.8

Note: The question asked was: 'Do you think the following will happen in your company in
five years' time?' Figures are the sum of 'conceivable' + 'already the case' − 'inconceivable'.
Some statements have been shortened.
Source: As for table 5.2.

Changes in employment practices

In five years' time, only one in eight executive directors envisaged 'short-
term employment will become common for core employees' in their company, while 59% did not see this happening (table 5.3). Only one in five
thought that 'it will be possible to lay off considerable numbers of employees without ructions within the company or in the broader society', while
42% disagreed. On this evidence, long-term employment is not about to
crumble.

As for *nenko*, over half (57%) thought that in five years' time in their
company 'promotions will be decided by performance, without reference
to age or tenure', while a mere 6% did not see this happening. Opinion
was divided over whether 'given the same education and years of service, there will be an annual pay spread of 50–200 around a mean of
100 for 40-year-old employees' – 34% agreed, and 35% disagreed. This
range would be considerably more than the normative views of employees
themselves. These responses also reinforce our earlier finding, that the

value attached to the *nenko* principle is weakening, but there will be limits for performance-based pay.

On balance, executive directors foresaw increasing individualization of employment and working conditions; 36% thought that in five years' time 'employment and work conditions will be determined mostly individually, by the company and individual employees, rather than collectively, by management and the union', while 28% disagreed. Half thought that 'employee pay will vary with division and/or job type; there will be multiple pay systems', and only 15% disagreed.[16] Opinion was divided over whether the locus of responsibility for skill development would be with the individual or with the company.[17]

Unions and industrial relations

'Individualization' of employment and working conditions suggests a decline in collective industrial relations. What will happen to labour unions, and what will their functions be? In five years' time only 16% of executives thought that 'many executives will view the union as an irrelevance' in their company, while 46% disagreed. In JRK (2000b), however, corporate planning heads thought that the most likely developments in the near future would be: increased need to deal with grievances over individual pay and evaluations; increased weight of individualized employment relations between company and employee; and decreasing importance of the labour union.[18] These scenarios elicited 'likely' responses of about 10%, and 'possible' responses of 50–70%, suggesting that even if executives do not see unions as an irrelevance, there may well be a diminution of their role in a shift from collective to individualized industrial relations.[19] While there are few instances of direct attempts to undermine unions, then, it does appear that many will struggle to retain a significant influence in the employment relationship and conditions of work, despite in some instances government legislation encouraging this.

---

[16] An impetus for this is operating divisions in the core company becoming more tightly integrated with subsidiaries in the same business area, resulting in remuneration, and even HRM, differentiation within the core company (see chapters 11, 12).

[17] These findings are supported by those of the JRK survey (2000b: 175), which additionally highlighted measures to extend the scope of exempt working, to rejuvenate management, to increase external hires and contract workers, and rein in non-statutory welfare costs.

[18] There was at least one union at 78.0% of the companies, and no union at 21.9%. Unions were less common in services (53.9%), wholesale (66.7%) and construction (68.3%).

[19] Individualization does not automatically undermine collective industrial relations. The new discretionary system legalized in April 2000 expanded the scope for individualization of working practices, but its actual introduction has to be carried out through a company or establishment-based joint committee. Unions or employee representative associations were thus given a role. For the UK, cf. Brown *et al.*, 1998.

Basic views of the company, employment and industrial relations

Table 5.4 explores the relationship between basic views of the company and management's role on the one hand, and future employment and industrial relations on the other. One might expect that those who see managers as agents of shareholders would favour reforms strengthening the role of the market, away from classic model employment practices, but this is not necessarily the case. Interestingly, there is relatively little difference between the three groups on many individual issues, and overall. Group A directors appear to be somewhat more reformist. They foresee slightly more emphasis on performance and promotion, and greater individualization. They also foresee a more marginal role for unions, and a slightly greater emphasis on ROE as the top management priority. But they do not foresee a more marked rise in short-term employment, for instance, and overall the similarities are more notable than the contrasts.

These findings are supported by Sato (2000), who looked at emphasis on share price, ROE and EVA (economic value added) as performance indicators, and produced a typology of fundamental reformers (n = 182), modifiers (n = 217) and status quo maintainers (n = 285). He found that fundamental reformers were more positive about dissolving non-performing reciprocal shareholding, moving from indirect to direct finance and securing stable shareholders. They were also more positive about reforming the director system and executive remuneration. But there was little difference in priorities attached to shareholder, manager and employee interests. Fundamental reformers were slightly less positive than status quo maintainers about maintaining lifetime employment, and gave somewhat more weight to individualization of employment relations, but there were few differences over the reform of individual HRM measures.

Fujimoto's (2000) typology, too, based on implementation of six investor relations criteria or activities,[20] did not produce clear-cut differences over stakeholder priorities and lifetime employment. The active implementers were somewhat more likely to be reformers in other areas, but the differences were not marked.

This suggests that views of corporate governance and views of employment and industrial relations are in many respects independent of each

---

[20] The activities were: information using American accounting standards; fullness of information provision to analysts, institutional investors and credit raters; improving management and financial information provision to general investors; declaring ROE and dividend targets; changes to corporate accounting standards; and holding of regular investors' meetings.

Table 5.4 Basic views of the company and future of employment, industrial relations (%)

Basic view of the company	The role of managers is to maximize shareholder value through improving capital efficiency (A: n = 365)	Disagree with 'The company is the property of the shareholders; employees are a factor of production' (B-1: n = 483)	Stakeholders are not limited to shareholders; managers should reflect their various views (B-2: n = 627)
Short-term employment even for core employees*	−43.0	−45.6	−48.7
Large-scale layoffs possible without ructions*	−12.4	−21.1	−18.2
Promotions decided by performance*	71.5	64.6	64.9
Skill development as a matter for the individual*	4.4	0.1	1.6
Collective to individualized employment relations*	17.0	6.7	9.3
Multiple pay systems (by division, job type)*	44.6	40.2	39.7
Executives will see union as irrelevant*	−21.0	−26.4	−23.2
ROE will replace turnover as top management priority*	67.6	60.4	63.8
Employee representative auditors**	−18.9	−11.8	−15.0
Union voice in management as a shareholder**	−33.1	−28.5	−28.6

Note: * In five years' time 'conceivable' + 'already the case' − 'inconceivable'
** Desirable − undesirable
See table 5.3 for fuller wording.
Source: As for table 5.2.

other. This in turn suggests that change (and stability) in employment and industrial relations will proceed in the directions discussed in chapters 3 and 4, irrespective of corporate governance reforms. The relationship between attitudes to corporate governance and employment and industrial relations may change over time as managers attempt to establish institutional and attitudinal congruity, but this is not a foregone conclusion.

Concluding comments

The 1990s were a decade of shareholder capitalism and corporate governance reform. The tide began in the USA in the 1980s, quickly spread to the UK, thence to continental Europe and Asia. In Japan, corporate governance in the community firm has been pluralist, and influential executive and employer organization reports have advocated pluralist positions. Others, though, have advocated variants of the enlightened shareholder or classic models. In May 2002, moreover, Japan's Commercial Code was fundamentally revised, allowing for the 'Americanization' of the board of directors. Would this result in significant changes to corporate governance practices?

To date most companies have stayed relatively close to the pluralist ideal type we presented, which features emphasis on the continuity and development of the community firm; internal career structures and multiple functions of executives; 'silent', stable shareholders and reciprocal shareholding, the main bank system and indirect finance, and long-term, trust-based stakeholder relations with employees, customers and suppliers; and the dual insider supervisory system.

In the past few years, however, there have been a number of developments which may accelerate nascent change. One of these is the introduction of the corporate officer system and the separation of corporate officers' and directors' functions. This weakens the employee features of directors' work, and possibly remuneration. This is part and parcel of a move towards faster decision-making by a smaller group of top managers. Directors themselves have become uneasy about the effectiveness of the dual supervisory system, and have begun to take steps to strengthen it. Even without 'Americanization' of boards, then, changes to corporate governance institutions are taking place.

In addition, there has been expansion of investor relations activities, and the emergence of consolidated management which places emphasis on capital efficiency. One in three executive directors already espouses views close to the enlightened shareholder value model, and it is possible that this proportion will grow in the future to become as influential as the pluralist model.

As for employment and industrial relations, the RIALS top management survey reinforces earlier findings that stable employment will not crumble in the near future, but *nenko* will exert less, and performance will exert more, influence on promotion. Wage differentials will rise somewhat, employment and work conditions will become more individualized, remuneration systems may become more diversified within single companies, and there is likely to be more emphasis on self-responsibility in skill and career development. Labour unions which are unable to keep up with these developments will lose influence.

The survey also suggests, however, that directors' views on corporate governance on the one hand, and employment and industrial relations on the other, are loosely coupled. This might be expected during a time of transition, but it does caution against assuming changing corporate governance views will precipitate far-reaching changes in employment and industrial relations. Conversely, however, changes in the latter are likely to occur irrespective of views of corporate governance.

6   Consolidated Management and Quasi Internal Labour Markets

In chapter 5 we found that links between managers' ideologies and corporate governance views on the one hand, and employment and industrial relations on the other, were rather loose. This picture is partial, however, as we have not yet examined an important area of management which is related both to corporate governance and to employment. This extends beyond the boundaries of individual companies, to encompass enterprise groups.

Through extending our horizons we will see that community companies have been sustained by the evolution of quasi internal labour markets,[1] encompassing companies within the enterprise group. Historically these developed around the practices of secondment (*shukko*) and transfer (*tenseki*). The extent of these practices differs according to industry; two extremes are the 'city bank pattern' and the 'department store pattern'. In the former, secondments and transfers begin at age 47–48, and almost no one reaches 60 at the city banks. In major department stores, by contrast, there are relatively few secondments and transfers, and most regular employees stay until they are 60.[2]

Recent changes to financial disclosure requirements, however, have triggered a growth in consolidated management, which is linked to the increasing emphasis on capital efficiency and profitability on a group-wide basis.[3] We explore this development and its implications through the JRK

---

[1] By 'quasi internal labour markets' we mean an internal labour market which historically has spread beyond an individual company's boundaries, group-wide, through secondments and transfers. Technically it is not a market, since allocation is largely through placement rather than the market mechanism. In cases like Matsushita Electric and Toray, there are few fundamental differences between employment and working conditions in the core company and those of major subsidiaries, and terms used to describe movement of workers between companies are similar to those used internally.

[2] Nihonteki koyo seido kenkyukai, 1994: 75.

[3] The new rules, introduced in March 2000, require consolidated accounts for 50%+-owned subsidiaries, and 49–20% under certain conditions conducive to a dominating influence by the core company, and importance of the subsidiary. Consolidated management aims to maximize performance of companies subject to consolidated accounting as a whole.

management strategy survey of corporate planning heads, carried out in February–March 1999.[4]

Consolidated management will potentially have a major impact on the evolution – or dissolution – of quasi internal labour markets. We will look at developments in two companies – Nippon Steel Corporation and Toray Industries, which illustrate the extent to which managers have attempted to sustain their community companies in the face of increasing adversity, and offer a prognosis for future developments, hinting again at change and continuity in managerial ideologies.

Consolidated management, group HRM and industrial relations

The medium-term plan boom

Consolidated management is the response to a number of dilemmas Japanese companies faced in the late 1990s, not least of which was the imminent introduction of new accounting standards from March 2000. The number of subsidiaries subject to consolidated accounting was increased, market-to-market (market-price rather than book-price) accounting was introduced, and lump-sum retirement funds were moved on-balance. In the past, as long as the balance sheet of the core company was healthy, it did not matter too much if subsidiaries were in the red, especially if their share of group turnover was low. This changed with the introduction of the new accounting standards. With more subsidiaries in the consolidated figures, and with market value listings, if subsidiaries were in the red or had non-performing assets, there was an immediate impact on financial performance, with potential negative consequences in financial markets, as well as reputation.

Other factors prompting reforms were new demands from capital markets, deregulation and globalization, resulting in intensified competition, market maturation and prolonged economic stagnation within Japan. Consolidated management could no longer be ignored until the annual accounts were produced. The result was a wave of medium-term management plans quite different from those in the past.[5]

---

[4] The survey was sent to 2,370 private sector companies with over 1,000 employees, with 690 (29.1%) valid responses. The sector composition of the valid responses was: manufacturing 39.9%, services 16.7%, finance and insurance 10.6%, construction 8.7%, transport and communication 8.1%, retail 8.0% and others 8.0%. Half were core companies of enterprise groups. The findings of the working group were published as JRK, 2000b.

[5] According to a MOL survey of unquoted companies in November 2000, 62% of large companies with subsidiaries (requiring consolidated accounts) had a group strategy or

Towards consolidated management – 'one set' reforms

The medium-term plans set out strategies for reform which many large companies were embarking on. Between 1997 and 1999 over 80% of JRK survey companies implemented or were considering strengthening consolidated management, reducing the number of directors and speeding up decision-making, and creating a 'small headquarters', in addition to other measures such as assigning individual management responsibilities, restructuring subsidiaries and affiliates, strengthening the finance function, and co-ordinating business operations group-wide (table 6.1).

There are strong intrinsic links between these reforms. Strengthening of consolidated management is frequently coupled with moves to speed up decision-making by a smaller, select number of top executives. This, in turn, is associated with a reduction in the number of directors, introduction of the corporate officer system, and separation of top management and operating responsibilities. Top management responsibilities include creating group-wide strategy, clarifying missions and responsibilities of subsidiaries and restructuring of unprofitable operations on a group-wide basis. With the clarification of its mission, the headquarters is streamlined, but the finance function is strengthened. It becomes, *de jure* or *de facto*, a holding company, with strengthened supervisory and support functions, and with greater emphasis on capital efficiency. Together, these constitute a 'set' of reforms aimed at establishing enterprise group-wide consolidated management.

Authority of subsidiaries and 'in-house subsidiaries'

Consolidated management and related management reforms have seen a flurry of activity in redrafting corporate boundaries, creating and consolidating real or 'virtual' (in-house) subsidiaries.[6] Between 1997 and 1999, 12% of JRK survey companies had created 'in-house subsidiaries', and a further 24% were planning to do so. Forty-seven per cent had created subsidiaries, and a further 41% were planning to do so. Most in-house subsidiaries were for existing business activities, but others had been created for new activities.

Whether they retain operations in-house as 'virtual companies' or spin them out as subsidiaries, questions of independence must be addressed.

---

group medium-term plan, and a further 24% were preparing one. The main reasons for having or preparing one were new accounting standards (51%), intensifying international competition (41%), market sector maturation (37%) and prolonged economic stagnation (36%). Almost all of the strategies/plans had been drawn up since 1998.

6 Reasons for favouring the creation of 'in-house subsidiaries' (virtual companies) over spinning out subsidiaries are not always clear. In some cases it is a kind of trial.

Table 6.1 *Management reforms in the past three years (plans and implementation, %)*

	Implemented (A)	Considering (B)	Not considering	N.A.	(A) + (B)
Slimmed top management, faster decision-making	49.6	31.3	15.7	3.5	80.9 (2)
Restructuring of subsidiaries and affiliates	36.4	32.8	26.7	4.2	69.2 (5)
Devolving, clarifying management responsibilities	29.4	44.5	22.0	4.1	73.9 (4)
'Small headquarters'	26.5	54.1	16.4	3.0	80.6 (3)
Strengthening consolidated management	26.5	56.5	12.8	4.2	83.0 (1)
Strengthening finance function	22.3	42.8	31.2	3.8	65.1
Co-ordinating operations group-wide	16.8	39.7	38.3	5.2	56.5
Strengthening profit centre status of R&D	13.3	37.1	43.2	6.4	50.4
Making in-house companies	10.4	32.5	52.9	4.2	42.9
Removing directors' line responsibilities	4.5	19.6	70.7	5.2	24.1
Reconsidering executive selection	4.3	21.3	69.1	5.2	25.7

Note: Statements have been shortened.
Source: JRK, 2000b: 165.

Authority given to representative in-house subsidiaries ranged from recruiting 42% (73% in legal subsidiaries), labour conditions 32% (56%) and investment 30% (28%), to industrial relations negotiations 23% (45%), raising funds 16% (31%) and appointing directors 10% (9%). Not surprisingly, legal subsidiaries were given more discretion, but when it came to director appointments, raising funds and investment decisions, even they had to gain the approval of the 'parent' company. Conversely, over 40% of in-house subsidiaries had autonomy in recruiting, and over 30% in determining labour conditions, pointing to growing divergence of recruiting, employment and labour conditions within individual companies. This runs counter to the postwar trend of unifying conditions within clearly defined corporate boundaries.

Respondents (corporate planning heads) were also asked about setting wage and conditions standards. For in-house subsidiaries responses were: 'even if they are better than the parent company, labour conditions should reflect their performance' (28%); 'conditions should be determined according to industry standards rather than those of the parent company' (24%); and 'labour conditions within the enterprise group should be as close as possible' (23%). Trailing by a considerable margin was 'even if it performs better, the conditions of the in-house subsidiary should not be better than those of the parent company' (4%). For legal subsidiaries, the responses were: performance-based labour conditions 31%; industry-based conditions 38%; group-wide standards 13%; and no better than the parent 12%. In other words, both types should determine labour conditions, but according to their performance, with reference to other companies in the same industry, and not according to those of the parent company.

These findings, too, suggest divergence rather than standardization of labour conditions across group companies, as well as within them. This is based on the belief that benchmarks should be competitor companies outside the group, and setting of wages and conditions should reflect this competition. This can be interpreted as the penetration of market forces inside enterprise groups and core companies (cf. Cappelli, 1999a, on this trend in the USA).

Maturation of group-based HRM

In an apparent contradiction to the marketization trend, there are also signs of the emergence of group-wide HRM. First, 'total labour cost management' has attracted growing interest. Forty-one per cent of respondents reported an overall group target for labour costs.[7] Seventeen per

---

[7] The proportion was particularly high in retailing (66%). The most common means of setting the target was as a proportion of sales (53%), followed by last year's performance

cent reported a target for group-wide or consolidated-base employee numbers, and a further 36% were considering one. Only a small minority (7%) had an executive development plan for consolidated companies, but 39% were considering one. One in five (19%) had a group-wide or consolidated company pension scheme (15% were considering one), and 13% reported recruiting and assignment by the core company for consolidated companies (28% were considering this). It appears from these figures that group-wide HRM, while still in its infancy, will develop in the coming years. We will return to the apparent contradiction between growing market-based divergence and nascent group-wide HRM later in the chapter.

With regards group-wide industrial relations, the vast majority (68%) of corporate planning heads felt that industrial relations and labour contracts were a matter for individual companies, and that collective bargaining and joint consultation should be carried out in individual companies.[8] Thus from the companies' perspective at least, industrial relations should be confined to individual companies, in contrast to some aspects of HRM.

Even within individual companies, moreover, the creation of in-house subsidiaries is sometimes accompanied by a decentralization of industrial relations. These constraints potentially affect unions' ability to respond to consolidated management, even when it has serious implications for their members.

Quasi internal labour markets – development and prospects

In order to understand the development of group-wide HRM, the apparent contradiction with increasing diversity as consolidated management is implemented, and how potential industrial relations limitations play out in reality, we need to know when and how group labour markets were formed, and how they have evolved. To do this we will trace the historical development of secondment (*shukko*) and transfer (*tenseki*) practices, since these laid the basis for quasi internal labour markets.

---

plus productivity increase rate (37%), labour share of turnover (31%), trends in other companies in the same industry (29%), and last year's performance plus cost of living increase (17%).

[8] Over half (57%) reported union federations or consultative bodies, while 36% reported no such organization. Only one in eight, however, considered it desirable to have an overall, federal collective contract on basic working conditions, and one in six thought that group-wide discussions were desirable. Only 1% approved of group-wide collective bargaining, 7% of observers from subsidiaries at core company consultations, and 10% of observers from the core company at subsidiary consultations.

The earliest reported cases of secondment and transfer, and related collective agreements, date from the late 1940s and early 1950s, with rapid diffusion in the 1960s.[9] With various nuances, although the company could order workers to be seconded, the will of the individuals concerned was important. In most cases secondment was to subsidiaries. Pay and welfare levels were virtually guaranteed, and the period of secondment was counted in years of service calculations. Work was determined by the receiving company. By and large the system as it evolved in the 1960s is still used today.

In many instances secondment was for technical guidance or associated with the transfer of work, but there were also many instances of secondment and subsequent transfer as a result of rationalization. The high growth years, not to mention the subsequent recession years, were a time of concerted technological innovation, and resulted in surplus labour. Secondment and transfers were thus used in both a positive, strategic sense, as well as defensively, but from the mid-1960s emphasis shifted to the latter.

Nippon Steel Corporation[10]

At Nippon Steel Corporation the first written record of secondment dates back to the company's predecessor Yahata Steel. Article 46 of the Employment Regulations, 16 August 1948, stipulates: 'As part of their work employees may be required to undertake business trips or secondment outside of the company.' 'Outside the company' apparently referred to public offices, assignments abroad related to technology licensing and collaboration, and long-term business assignments. Until the 1960s, however, external secondment was largely confined to managers, and was limited in both Yahata Steel and Fuji Steel, which merged to become

---

[9] Cf. Rodo horei kyokai, 1964. A survey on personnel movements by the Kansai Employers' Association in late 1961 also indicates growing interest in the issue.
  At Hitachi, secondments began in the early 1950s, to government agencies, organizations and some related companies for management guidance. They spread in the 1960s with the transfer of work, production guidance, back-up and work volume adjustment, and began to include union members. A collective agreement was signed in 1964 which recognized the practice, and in which management promised early information, no downgrading of labour conditions, and specification of the period as far as possible. It seems that transfers (involving a change of employer) grew subsequently, as some secondees stayed at the company they were seconded to (corporate planning manager, personal correspondence). The union history reveals frustration with what it saw as a fundamentally different motivation behind secondment in the 1960s – 'rationalization'. In breech of the collective agreement, moreover, the union was sometimes not notified, and its safeguards over the purpose of secondment were sometimes flouted (Hitachi rodo undoshi hensan iinkai, 1980: 958–78).

[10] Based on correspondence and interview, senior HRM manager, 22 March 2002.

Nippon Steel Corporation in 1970. Around the time of the merger, in conjunction with integration and efficiency measures, some operations were hived off into separate companies, and workers were seconded to these. Even then, only 2% of employees – mostly white-collar – were working outside the company.

With the merger, regulations relating to secondment were revamped, creating the basis for the regulations in force today, with very little change over the years. Through the oil crises of the 1970s, extension of the retirement age in 1981 and the steel slump of the mid-1980s, the number of employees seconded to subsidiaries steadily rose. It leapt with the post-Plaza Accord yen rise. Steel became a 'structurally depressed' industry, and in the restructuring which followed the number of secondees more than doubled, to 6,100 (10%). By 1990 the number of employees at Nippon Steel had been reduced by over a third, while those on secondment had almost trebled. Blue-collar secondees now outnumbered white-collar secondees by a ratio of two to one.

Secondments became transfers. To facilitate the process the company, informally, promised that 'lifetime earnings' (until age 60, that is) would not suffer, and that those transferred would not be left without a job (within the group, until age 60). A vast amount of money was spent on secondments, transfers and early retirement by selling off shares and real estate.

Despite the fact that almost all secondments became transfers, the proportion of secondees to total employees continued to rise. In the face of the continued yen appreciation, severe competition from Korea, and domestic post-bubble recession, then-president Imai unveiled the company's third medium-term plan to the union in March 1994, declaring that the survival of the company depended on its success, and that the plan was premised on 'securing employment'. He pledged to maintain trust in industrial relations and called on all to work towards rebirth of the company.[11]

The plan consisted of three parts – one for the core steel business, one for engineering, and one for new businesses. The key steel plan called for a reduction in costs of at least ¥300 billion over three years, and for a new management system which would include a streamlined top management structure focusing on strategic issues to make faster decisions, as well as greater and clearer divisional autonomy, and a shared group strategy. The new management system envisaged a 40% reduction in the number of managers, and a 15% reduction in the number of engineers.

[11] *Rodo kumiai nyusu* No. 83, 1 April 1994.

The method of workforce reduction switched from secondment to direct transfer (change of employer). Through 11,900 transfers, the company strove to keep its principle of 'securing employment' in spite of severe financial pressure. An early retirement scheme was subsequently introduced, however, eliciting 1,600 responses. This, and a system of paid leave to prepare for job changing, opened up the path for voluntary redundancy, and effectively overrode the 'securing employment' principle, which had been extended to 'reaching retirement (at age 60) within the group'.

Table 6.2 shows the proportion of secondees to staff and production employees from the mid-1990s to 2001. In six years the number of employees fell by almost 40%, from 44,354 to 26,333. Still, at the end of 2001, almost 40% of those remaining were on secondment.

In future, however, the proportion will probably continue to fall. The company's policy was not clear at the point of writing, but as long as consolidated management is pursued it will be difficult to place workers at subsidiaries which don't need them, whether on secondment or transfer. These will only occur when the strategic needs of both parties mesh. This appears to be producing a new type of secondment – 'consolidated management secondment' – mostly of white-collar employees around the age of 40, some of who will return, fostering *mutual* exchange. This appears to encompass recent trends in executive development in some enterprise groups.

Second, in the face of a harsh competitive environment, the company appears committed to maintaining trust relations with the union and stimulating employee efforts to build international competitiveness. In the spring bargaining round of 2002, a two-year joint employment stability pact was signed.[12] But securing employment through 'consolidated management secondment' and intra-group transfers will not be easy. Transfers outside the group may well increase. At the same time, however, the strategic nature of transfers within the group, including executive development, will strengthen.

Third, as business conditions are so severe and the company's assets so strained, it is likely that pay will become tied to the job actually done by secondees, without the wage gap subsidy (between Nippon Steel and subsidiaries). Thus even if 'securing employment (within the group)' and the 'lifetime earnings guarantee' expressed from the first medium-term

---

[12] In making its case to members for the agreement, the union noted the history of the company's efforts to secure employment, and its own to contribute to business development as the basis of employment security, and argued that it would be even more vital in the face of new looming difficulties.

Table 6.2 *Employee and secondment trends in Nippon Steel Corporation, 1995–2001*

	Staff (*shumu*)				Technical				Total			
	Within NSC	Seconded	Total	Secondee/in house ratio (%)	Within NSC	Seconded	Total	Secondee/in house ratio (%)	Within NSC	Seconded	Total	Secondee/in house ratio (%)
1995	13,151	9,543	22,694	72.6	17,921	3,739	21,660	20.9	31,072	13,282	44,354	42.7
1996	11,731	3,868	15,599	33.0	15,852	9,213	25,065	58.1	27,583	13,081	40,664	47.4
1997	10,493	3,801	14,294	36.2	14,034	8,441	22,475	60.1	24,527	12,242	36,769	49.9
1998	9,521	3,604	13,125	37.9	13,039	6,536	19,575	50.1	22,560	10,140	32,700	44.9
1999	8,918	3,481	12,399	39.0	12,496	5,080	17,576	40.7	21,414	8,561	29,975	44.9
2000	8,301	3,514	11,815	42.3	11,515	4,359	15,874	37.9	19,816	7,873	27,689	40.0
2001	7,976	3,440	11,416	43.1	10,952	3,975	14,917	36.3	18,918	7,415	26,333	39.2

Note: Figures are for the end of the financial year. From 1998 the staff/technical distinction in the HRM system was abolished.
Source: Company materials.

Table 6.3 *Employee and secondment trends at Toray Industries, 1960–99*

	Employees (a)	Secondees (b)	Secondee ratio (b/a)
1960	24,542	194	0.8%
1965	30,366	705	2.3
1970	25,269	3,612	14.3
1975	23,326	3,935	16.9
1979	18,100	3,724	20.6
1985	17,698	5,065	28.6
1986	17,462	5,627	32.2
1987	17,096	6,014	35.2
1988	16,151	6,008	37.2
1989	15,392	5,332	37.6
1990	14,729	5,322	36.2
1991	14,540	4,493	30.9
1992	14,022	3,879	27.7
1995	13,530	3,381	25.0
1999	12,000	2,600	21.7

Note: 1960–75 secondees are calculated as the difference between registered employees and employees actually working at the company in March; 1976–9 includes secondees within and outside Japan; and 1986– figures are for absent registered employees.
Source: Toray kabushiki kaisha shashi henshu iinkai, 1977: 270; Nihon keieishi kenkyusho, 1997: 754, 978; interview 19 March 2002.

plan (1987) to the third (1994) are not formally abandoned, they might be progressively weakened.

Toray Industries[13]

The second case is the major synthetic fibre and materials producer Toray Industries (Toray). Secondment at Toray was first used in the late 1950s to strengthen newly formed subsidiaries. It first appears in a collective agreement in 1960, although significantly it was (and still is) referred to as 'rotation'. Directors over 50 and managers over 55 were usually transferred, whereas union members were seconded (until 60 at least) and not transferred.[14]

As table 6.3 shows, employment at Toray began to dip after peaking in 1965, as the company faced recession, while the number of secondees

---

[13] Based on correspondence and interview, senior personnel manager, 19 March 2002.
[14] As of March 2002 secondees were unambiguously Toray employees, paid exactly the same wages, working the host company's hours but where appropriate with a Toray supplement, and with appraisals discussed between the host and Toray's personnel department, within a Toray framework.

began to climb. In the turbulent 1970s, a Joint Committee to Overcome the Recession was formed, and met eleven times between 1975 and 1977. The union position was that labour adjustment should be carried out through secondment, natural attrition and a reduction in hiring, with no compulsory or voluntary redundancies. In 1978 a reduction of 5,000 on-site workers (over a quarter of the total workforce) was carried out – 2,530 through natural attrition (many of those leaving were females), 850 through 'special retirement', 460 to especially created companies[15] and 1,160 secondments to subsidiaries.

Large-scale movements continued as the company scaled down or closed faltering operations and started others. To facilitate these, a unified collective agreement covering Toray and two other group companies was signed in 1981. And in 1987 'federal management' was launched as the post-Plaza Accord yen appreciation undermined the competitiveness of Japan's synthetic fibre industry.[16]

As a result, the number of seconded employees reached a peak of 6,014 in 1987. The proportion seconded continued to rise until 1989, when it reached 37.6%, before steadily dropping in the 1990s to 21.7% in 1999 (table 6.3).

In 1999 there were seventy-six subsidiaries and affiliates in which Toray had at least a 20% equity stake and close relations. We can divide them into types: (1) independent recruiting, autonomous in labour conditions, with less than 10% of the workforce seconded from Toray (sixty-two companies, twenty-one with unions); (2) independent and autonomous, no secondees (three companies); (3) no independent recruiting, 90%+ Toray secondees, hence Toray-type labour conditions (eight companies); (4) those run by Toray secondees, with no independent recruiting (three companies, all joint ventures with foreign companies). Of these, only (3) is likely to change in the near future, towards greater independence in recruiting, and transfer of senior management. Overall there will be a shift from secondment to transfer which will result in divergent labour conditions, and in effect, the partial dissolution of 'federal management'.

This does not mean the dissolution of the quasi internal labour market itself, however, as there are parallel moves to *strengthen* federal management. In 1986 a 'subsidiary strategic personnel management system' was established, in which the presidents of subsidiaries submit personnel requests, including requests for specific people, to the head of Toray's

---

[15] A critical problem was older employees. Toray raised its mandatory retirement age to 60 in 1966, before most large companies, and subsequently created new companies to secure employment for them beyond the retirement age, as well as to absorb surplus workers in the mid-1970s. In 2002 there were ten such companies in the group.

[16] Cf. Nihon keieishi kenkyusho, 1997: 976, 979. On the unified collective agreement, cf. Inagami and Kawakita, 1988: 51–6, 104–5.

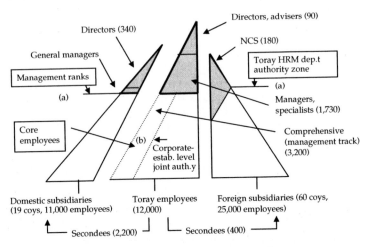

Figure 6.1 Core employee management in Toray Group
Notes:
  (a) Management ranks, subject to Toray headquarter HRM
  (b) Corporate-establishment (operating) joint authority
      (1) Toray general managers and above, subsidiary director level
          appointments subject to Toray president's approval.
      (2) Figures as of March, 1999
Source: Interview, personnel director.

personnel department, which sorts the requests and reports to the board of directors. With the board's approval, the personnel department then mediates with line managers. According to the personnel director:

The system has taken root . . . From 1992–97 I would say we had requests for 200–250 people per year, and met 70–80% of those requests. Recently the system has been used not just for requests, but increasingly as planned rotation to develop younger employees.[17]

Relatedly, there is a group-wide employee management system (cf. figure 6.1) which provides education and training for management and professional grade staff of Toray, department managers and above at domestic subsidiaries and 'national core staff' (NCS) at overseas subsidiaries. It includes an executive development programme, started in 1998, in which high fliers are selected for special training and assignments (with annual reviews of the list). In future the weight of secondments may well shift to such people, as in Nippon Steel's 'consolidated management secondee'.

[17] Personal correspondence, 29 June 2002.

On the one hand, therefore, there is a trend towards transfers (changing employer) and away from secondment, ultimately bringing a contraction of the quasi internal labour market. On the other, a nascent group-wide executive development programme is forming, and a maturation, or further stage of development of the quasi internal labour market. It is not clear at this stage how these two trends will intertwine and develop in the future, but it is clear that both are being spurred by consolidated management.

Concluding discussion

Community companies have been sustained by quasi internal labour markets, which developed around the practices of secondment and transfer, through which environmental turbulence and stresses were dissipated. Consolidated management, the changing balance of independence in subsidiaries (both legal and virtual) and the penetration of market forces could, by changing the dynamics of quasi internal labour markets, unleash new forces for change on community firms. In fact, if top managers were so inclined, they could deliberately use consolidated management to weaken the community aspects of their firms, as unions' ability to respond is apparently limited. Is this happening?

We looked in some detail at Nippon Steel and Toray, which have long experienced severe competition, and have extensive experience in restructuring. These cases suggest that secondment developed differently in different industries, depending on when and how they faced structural recession. They appear to have developed first in textiles, then in shipbuilding, followed by steel, and more recently in the consumer electronics and semiconductor industries. (This ordering also overlaps with the occurrence of trade friction. Internationalization of the economy and efforts to strengthen group competitiveness are a common thread.)

As for specific companies, in addition to the industry we must also consider managers' ideologies.[18] In both Nippon Steel and Toray there was an ideology supportive of long-term stable employment and co-operative enterprise-based industrial relations, in addition to policies of strengthening group growth and competitiveness. In Toray's case, problems in affiliates have been taken up at the group level and considered from the perspective of group management for many years. Toray's group structure is much less hierarchical than that of Nippon Steel, and was an important influence on the development of its secondment and transfer system.

---

[18] In an international comparison we would also have to consider the legal framework. Fair trade legislation is said to present an impediment to such practices in Korean chaebol: cf. Inagami, 2002.

It is hazardous to speculate on the basis of two cases, but some tentative predictions about quasi internal labour markets can be made. First, the trend from secondment to transfers is likely to accelerate. The practice of supplementing wages will decrease as intensified competition forces companies to pay wages at rates appropriate to the industry, and to set wages according to levels in the industry.

Second, under consolidated management the bargaining position of subsidiaries and affiliates is strengthened, and push-type secondment and transfers will become more difficult. This means that they are likely to spread beyond enterprise groups. Indeed, this has been one factor in the recent rise of early retirement and assisted job changing.[19]

Third, with the trend from secondment to transfers the notion of a 'lifetime earnings guarantee' will decline, pushed by the move from seniority-referenced wages to market-referenced job-type wages. In these respects, quasi internal labour markets will shrink, with a possible impact on classic model employment practices.

Fourth, nonetheless, consolidated management has spurred group-based HRM and the *maturation* of quasi internal labour markets. Significant in this respect is the recent trend towards group-wide executive development, created by the personnel planning sections of slimmed down core company headquarters. For the foreseeable future, both the shrinkage and maturation currents will develop in parallel.

At the group level management strategy is most developed, followed by HRM, and trailing far behind, industrial relations. If we also consider the simultaneous individualization of employment relations, restructuring – including transfers of undertaking and related legislation[20] – and so on, these structural developments pose a real threat to the raison d'être of labour unions. They are likely to accelerate qualitative changes in community companies, and raise the possibility of changing contours – 'thinner', more porous and flexible, but 'wider', perhaps.

---

[19] The proportion of large companies with early retirement schemes rose from 41.1% in 1991 to 58.2% in 2000, and the proportion offering mediation assistance in job transfers rose from 6.9% in 1994 to 26.4% in 2000 (Rodosho, *Koyo kanri chosa* [Employment Management Survey], respective years). Voluntary retirement schemes in the first half of 2002, moreover, surpassed those for the whole of 2001.

[20] Revision of the Commerical Code in 2000 simplified procedures to divide companies. The Labour Contract Succession Law was passed shortly after to prevent abuse (using division to get rid of unwanted workers). Nonetheless, with the changes, employees working 'mainly' in an operation prior to being hived off could be transferred without their consent (cf. Yamakawa, 2001).

7   Summing Up

The origin of Japan's community firms can be traced to the interwar years, perhaps even earlier, but interwar and postwar community firms were not the same. There was a shift from managerial familism to managerial welfarism (Hazama), or welfare corporatism (Dore). Our interest is in changes since Hazama and Dore's portrayal of community firms in the late 1960s and early 1970s, and whether another fundamental shift began in the late 1990s. Are the encroachment of market forces, and social and ideological change, destroying the community characteristics?

In the final chapter of Part 1 we briefly summarize our findings so far and offer just a few preliminary conclusions, saving our main evaluation for Part 3.

Foundations of the community company

In chapter 1 we examined what has been written about the norms, behaviour and institutions of the community company, in which an implicit 'contract' involving an exchange of loyalty and effort for security is integrated into management priorities, and engenders a sense of membership and the development of shared norms and 'we-consciousness'. This becomes a source of motivation, but it may also override individual interests.

In our selective review of Japanese management, we saw that for Tsuda, company-as-community was a feature of modern management, and Japanese management was simply one variation. He changed his position, however, and began to emphasize the distinctiveness of Japanese management, linked to Japan's cultural traditions. Others, too, popularized the view that community firms were a particularly Japanese phenomenon. We questioned this view, drawing attention to research in the USA and elsewhere. The community firm has distinctive features in Japan, but is not uniquely Japanese. But the same research depicted the erosion if not collapse of the community features of firms in those countries. Is Japan next in line?

Based on our review and related writing, we proposed a number of features of community firms. Some are relatively intangible. More directly tangible are employment practices, corporate governance, and managers' priorities, or ideologies, which we explored in subsequent chapters.

Classic model

First we constructed a benchmark for evaluating change and continuity in these areas. In the classic model core members are internally promoted managers and male regular employees, both white-collar and blue-collar. Female regular employees, by contrast, are considered quasi-members. Most non-regular employees are considered non-members. Shareholders, too, are considered non-members in popular perception, although legally they *are* the members.

Employment relations are based on a fundamental premise, of mutually supporting long-term living security for members on the one hand, and increasing corporate value through long-term skill development on the other. Key institutional features are 'lifetime' employment and *nenko* wages and promotion, and on-job-training (OJT) combined with career development. The viability of these institutions, and the fundamental premise, depends on a number of conditions – skills rising in parallel with wages, for instance, fulfilment of members' vocational needs, workplace relations conducive to skill development through OJT, a sense of distributional fairness, co-operative industrial relations . . . It also depends on a number of buffer mechanisms, which provide flexibility to offset rigidities in the model.

A further support of the community firm, and the long-term security–value creation employment dynamic, is the selection of top management from internally promoted employees. Top managers who rise in this way retain a number of employee features, absorb the implicit principles and emphasize corporate value creation. They are the key members of the community firm, and not the agents of shareholders, who are not considered community members. Shareholder interests are not ignored, but they are not prioritized. Relational financing, through indirect main banks and stable, reciprocal shareholding, promotes 'patient capital' and enables managers to focus on corporate value creation. The dual supervisory system, in practice, also enables top managers to focus on long-term corporate value creation.

Employment practices, corporate governance and managers' priorities or ideologies exhibit what Dore (2000) calls institutional interlock and motivational congruence, which we called the classic model.

Change and continuity in employment practices

In the third chapter we looked at evidence of change in employment practices over the period 1975–2000. Lifetime employment is far from dead, although attitudes supporting it have weakened. For some groups of employees, such as women, tenures have in fact increased. It might be argued that our cut-off point fails to capture the increased turbulence at the turn of the century, as more and more companies introduced early retirement schemes, assisted job changing and voluntary redundancies. This was the result of both supply and demand factors – especially the bulge of the ageing baby boom generation, and deflationary recession. If these conditions persist for long enough, they could weaken the normative influence of lifetime employment (and *nenko* principles), but on the other hand, the baby boomer bulge will eventually dissipate, and demand conditions are at least partly cyclical, so this turbulence might be temporary.

The rise in non-regular employment, surpassing the decline in family labour and self-employment, might also weaken the normative strength of lifetime employment (even if non-regular labour helps to stabilize lifetime employment). We don't deny that there is some change, particularly in attitudes, but there is little evidence to support media accounts of a wholesale collapse of lifetime employment.

Despite difficulties in pinning it down, we found that *nenko* has not disappeared, either, although attitudes supporting it have weakened even more than lifetime employment. The principle is strongest among full corporate community members – male graduate employees of large companies. In the 1980s and 1990s their age–wage curve became slightly less steep, and the wage spread of peers increased, suggesting an erosion of the *nenko* principle. On the other hand, it strengthened among male production workers of small firms.

With some qualifications, employee job performance and skills appear to rise with age. The work ethic is still strong, and the majority of workplaces still appear conducive to skill formation through OJT. 'Company man' has not died out, but with the weakening of attitudes supporting lifetime employment and *nenko*, and a strengthening of specialist career orientations, he has changed somewhat. (Company man is still predominantly a man, moreover; companies are still male-oriented in their institutions, practices and membership.) Employment relations still have a moral and status dimension. Satisfaction with company, work and workplace have, if anything, increased.

In other words, for better or for worse, these key employment practices do not appear to have unravelled at this level of analysis.

Creative work and professional orientations

That they have not unravelled does not mean they are compatible with new demands. In chapter 4 we looked at the changing nature of work, and hence changing skill requirements, in many large Japanese companies. There has been a marked rise in the importance of creative white-collar work, which involves individual discretion that may have a major influence on company performance. Are employment practices associated with the classic model compatible with such work by 'company professionals'?

According to the creative work survey, and contrary to popular views in Japan, creative workers do not change jobs frequently for challenging work and higher wages. They, too, have long-term employment orientations, and if not the loyalty of the traditional company man, then at least a strong sense of affiliation with their company. They are not strongly concerned about academic credentials, seniority or even promotion. They prefer performance-based remuneration with slightly larger spreads than at present. Their views of distributional fairness, then, appear to match changing management emphases. But this is not their primary concern. They are more concerned with work opportunities and their work environment.

Creative workers work in more open workplaces than routine workers, with frequent project-based interaction with customers, suppliers and other departments in their company. Workplace organization is more fluid, permitting flexible and self-motivated work patterns. There is greater acceptance of risk, and greater stimulation from fellow workers, than in routine departments.

The central life interest of such 'company professionals' is work, and boundaries between work and private lives are often blurred. It takes a long time to acquire their skills, but unlike traditional professionals such as lawyers or doctors, their careers are oriented towards internal progression, not as strongly as in a 'bureaucratic orientation', but stronger than an 'instrumental orientation' (to employ Goldthorpe et al.'s terms).

It is possible that, while the workplaces of creative workers are relatively open and their external networks are relatively wide, they are not open or wide enough. It may also be that while workplace culture is relatively dynamic, it does not sufficiently encourage creative participation or 'intrapreneurial' behaviour. Many employees felt there was an atmosphere of risk aversion, insufficient scope for self-cultivation or 'recharging batteries', that work was too frenetic and that insufficient authority was delegated. They got creative insights away from work. These findings point to organizational and management problems, but from the survey evidence, at least, there appears to be no fundamental contradiction between creative work and the classic model, or at least a modified version of it.

Corporate governance reforms and their influence

In chapter 5 we looked at managers' priorities or ideologies in the context of the tide of corporate governance reform which swept Japan in the late 1990s. In a milieu of economic globalization and intensification of competition, prolonged stagnation and corporate scandals, many large companies in Japan set about reforming corporate governance.

It is worth noting that although some shareholders or organizations, such as the Pension Fund Association, have become more restive, and there is a nascent movement for socially responsible investment, by and large the reforms were initiated by executives themselves. Some have become concerned about weak monitoring and boards, and feel that positive reform of the dual supervisory system is necessary. As of the mid-2003 AGM season, however, only thirty-six listed companies had adopted American-style governance institutions made possible by changes to the Commercial Code. (Interestingly, these included the three general electric companies Hitachi, Toshiba and Mitsubishi Electric, as well as eighteen Hitachi subsidiaries.) And as we shall see, some of those that have announced a switch are attempting to mould the institutions in ways compatible with community firm preservation. The majority of companies still favour reform within the existing dual supervision framework.

The overwhelming majority of listed companies continue to have stable shareholders. Many have reduced their levels of reciprocally held shares, and typically around a third say they will reduce these levels in future as well, but few think the practice is unnecessary. The most common reason for this practice continues to be 'to form stable, long-term relations' (Zaimusho, 2003). Likewise, the main bank system has not disappeared, even after a decade of turbulence among financial institutions.

Managers' careers are still primarily built on internal promotion, and hence they retain employee characteristics, even if they are given stock options, and their remuneration emphasizes performance. Quite a few companies have begun to appoint external directors, but this has not led to a fundamental change in the career paths or appointment of top managers.

Management performance indicators have changed. Sales growth and market share have become less important, and restoring profitability and raising capital efficiency have become more prominent. Through this top managers hope to ensure long-term corporate viability, as well as to become more attractive to shareholders, but this does not equate with maximizing shareholder returns.

In their drive to improve competitiveness, raise capital efficiency and make their companies more attractive to investors, top managers have been making smaller top management teams and headquarters, giving more autonomy to operating divisions, merging or restructuring non-core businesses, shifting emphasis from sales to operating profits, and improving investor relations. At the same time, however, they have attempted to avoid undermining employee interests and morale.

In *parallel* to corporate governance reforms, they have been addressing employment relations – making use of outsourcing and non-regular workers, fixing total labour costs and implementing performance management. To date, however, corporate governance reforms and employment reforms have been somewhat decoupled. This means that the drive to improve capital efficiency has not been pursued directly at employees' expense, but it also means that employment reforms are being implemented irrespective of corporate governance orientation.

Thus in corporate governance, as with employment practices, we see both change and continuity, but we do not see a fundamental break with the classic model. The 'enlightened shareholder value' model of corporate governance is probably becoming more influential, but only a small minority espouse the shareholder sovereignty ('classic') model.

Group management and quasi internal labour markets

Chapter 6 examined a complementary area of both management reform and employment practices. A key impetus for consolidated (group) management was the introduction of new accounting standards in 2000. In addition, deregulation and the intensification of competition have led to a rethinking of efficiency, value creation profitability group-wide.

In the late 1990s there was a boom of new-style medium-term plans. It had become difficult to ignore subsidiaries making losses. Managers were forced to focus management resources more determinedly. Group companies were divided into categories and assigned goals, including numerical performance targets. They were given authority to pursue those goals, but the goals themselves were strongly influenced by the core company, often as a holding company. Decentralization and centralization thus occurred simultaneously.

In the area of human resource management, these developments led to divergence rather than standardization, across enterprise groups as well as within core companies, based on the view that benchmarks should be competitor companies, and wages and conditions should reflect this competition. In this sense, market forces have increasingly penetrated enterprise groups and core companies.

Related to these developments, both a contraction and a deepening or maturation of quasi internal (group) labour markets took place. Quasi internal labour markets were formed through secondments and transfers, beginning in the late 1950s for technology and management support of subsidiaries, and subsequently extended to secure work opportunities for core company employees. After the bursting of the bubble, however, and particularly after the introduction of new consolidated accounting standards, these subsidiaries were required to become more independent and efficient. This strengthened their bargaining position, and resulted in a contraction of secondment (as well as the placement of some core company middle managers outside the group, and the introduction of early retirement schemes). This represents a shrinking of the quasi internal labour market, and an expansion of the external labour market. Simultaneously, however, group-wide HRM schemes were introduced, in part to develop future executives. This trend represents a deepening or maturation of quasi internal labour markets, and an expansion of boundaries for career rotation and training in higher echelons.

Seen in the cases of Nippon Steel Corporation and Toray Industries, these developments illustrate both the strains corporate communities have come under, as well as continued attempts by managers to combine efficiency imperatives with responsibilities as corporate community leaders.

Penetration of market forces on the one hand, and expanded 'internal labour markets' on the other, show there is not a single dynamic at work, dissolving community characteristics, for instance, though marketization.

Whither community firms?

Many of the features of community companies depend on long-term employment. This has come under strain, but has not collapsed. It is not surprising, then, that community firms persist. At an institutional level, we find modifications in both employment practices and corporate governance, but not outright negation of the classic model. At an attitudinal or ideological level, we also find changes, both on the part of employees and top managers, but these do not constitute outright rejection of the model, either. Thinking about distributional fairness has changed, but there is basic agreement on the direction of change (though not necessarily on the extent desirable), so this has not been particularly divisive.

We see the beginnings of divergence in wages and conditions of regular employees within some companies, but no fundamental schism has opened up which might undermine shared interests. Labour–management communication has not deteriorated significantly, either. In sum, the community firm has not given way before the onslaught of market forces. Nor do we find another type of community which might take the place of the community firm.

Boundaries may be getting 'thinner', more porous and more flexible, and perhaps wider for senior members. And internally we can see the rise of the 'company professional', with a 'professional orientation to work'. Company professionals may well bring qualitative changes to the community firm, but to date there is limited evidence of them leveraging their skills to job-hop like Bennett's 'new organization man' in the USA, outside of the financial sector. Financial companies may come to diverge from the classic model; we cannot say for certain without further case research. In Part 2 we turn not to this sector, but to manufacturing, and to a company which has long exemplified the classic model – Hitachi Ltd.

Part 2

Hitachi: 'Here, the Future'*

---

* 'Here, the Future' – an advertising slogan used by Hitachi in the late 1990s.

8   Hitachi: A Dancing Giant

Introduction

The viability of the community firm depends not just on the internal consistency of its institutions, and supporting ideology, but on its ability to respond to changing environments, and produce goods or services at profit. It assumes the community firm is compatible with competitiveness, or enhances it. But companies can fail for a variety of reasons not directly related to employment relations or community, such as management failure, technology shifts or disruptive technology (Christensen, 1997). And if there is no enterprise, there is no community.

As we progressed in Part 1, we broadened our focus from employment practices to corporate governance and management reforms in response to intensified global competition (in both product and financial markets), market maturation, rapid changes in technology, and legal reforms to accounting and governance practices. There are limitations to how far these can be explored through large-scale surveys, however. Competitive conditions differ widely by industry, and so do managers' responses. To present a 'grounded' picture of the community company features and developments we described in Part 1, as well as to deepen our understanding of the links between the changing competitive environment, managers' responses, and changes to the community firm, we turn in Part 2 to a detailed case study. We have chosen Hitachi Ltd, the largest of Japan's general electric manufacturers, with production operations ranging from chips and fridges to nuclear power stations. We focus particularly on the announcement in 1998 of the company's first loss for over half a century, the sense of crisis generated by this loss, and the reforms which followed.

On 3 September 1998, Hitachi's president, Dr Kanai, nervously clasped his hands as he sat in front of the nation's press at the Tokyo Stock Exchange to announce a projected loss of over $2 billion. The scene was perhaps not as dramatic as that of Yamaichi's president announcing his company's bankruptcy less than a year earlier, his tears broadcast around the world, but it was highly significant nonetheless. Japan's leading economic newspaper commented:

Japan's economic woes have now reached the major electric machine companies which support the nation's very economic foundations. The picture of this giant battleship Hitachi, losing its way, unable to take effective measures before this massive loss materialized, is the very picture of Japan today. (*Nikkei shinbun*, 4 September 1998)[1]

'Gigantic battleship' was an apt description. The consolidated turnover of Hitachi Ltd and its group of around 1,000 companies was equivalent to some 1.7% of Japan's GDP in 1997–8, making it third in *Fortune*'s global rankings of electric, electronics and computer businesses after GE and IBM. Size, moreover, was accompanied by a keen awareness on the part of Hitachi's top managers of 'special responsibilities'. When Dr Kanai declared: 'The inability of Japanese companies to aggressively lay off workers is a cross Japanese companies must bear'[2] and 'Jack Welch (of GE) was able to get out of computers and light bulbs. For us to get out of a business would involve firing people, and that can't be done easily in Japan',[3] he was particularly mindful of these responsibilities.

The electric, electronic and computer industries, however, are characterized by intense competition and a dizzying pace of technological innovation. Size can easily become a liability if not combined with agility. It was becoming increasingly difficult to compete with nimble, specialist competitors on a wide range of fronts, and the strain showed in steadily declining profits, which culminated in the 1998 loss.

These pressures were similar in many respects to those faced by US and UK companies in the late 1970s and 1980s, which led to the reforms described in Kanter's (1989) *When Giants Learn to Dance*, as well as the demise of company man and the community firm in those countries, described in chapter 1.[4] Hitachi's competitive strengths may have enabled the company to forestall these reforms for over a decade, but ultimately, it could not avoid them. In fact its competitive strengths may have made it more difficult to embark on the reforms prior to 1998. In 1998, however, a sense of crisis was generated not just within the company, but in the wider economy in the wake of the Asian Crisis, Japan's own financial crisis, and growing gloom in Japan's manufacturing heartlands.

---

[1] The consolidated loss projection was for ¥250 billion. The actual loss for the year, including special write-offs, was almost ¥340 billion.
[2] *Nikkei*, 14 February 1997.
[3] *Fortune*, 5 August 1996, F-1.
[4] Cf. also Gerstner's account of the transformation of IBM in *Even Elephants Can Dance* (2002).

Hitachi is particularly significant for the reasons just given – its size and diversification, its sense of 'special responsibilities', and its presence in the turbulent information and electronics industries. In addition, Dore's (1973) *British Factory – Japanese Factory* vividly describes classic model employment practices and community at two of Hitachi's factories as the institutional finishing touches were being made to them in the late 1960s. This provides us with a concrete benchmark to consider long-term changes with, in addition to changes from the late 1990s.

This is not a 'Japanese factory revisited' account, however. Our study took us to different parts of the organization. For one thing, heavy electric and consumer electric goods production are no longer as central as they were in the 1960s.[5] And while over half of Hitachi's employees in the late 1960s were production workers, by the late 1990s the proportion had dropped to under 30%, and it was the white-collar workers and indirect departments which were the target of most HRM reform efforts. Moreover, the critical management reform decisions which we wanted to find out about were being made in corporate-level committees, not on or near the shopfloor.[6] Thus our interviews took place at various levels of the Hitachi, and in Hitachi Group companies and the Hitachi Workers Union, but were weighted towards office and corporate Hitachi rather than the shopfloor.[7]

Fortuitously (for us), Hitachi was one of the first companies to announce its adoption of the US-style committee system of corporate governance, along with eighteen listed subsidiaries, in 2003. We are thus able to explore the reasons for its *apparent* conversion to a shareholder-favouring system, and implications for employment practices and community.

Obviously no single company or group can be taken as representative of Japan; Hitachi's sheer size makes it unrepresentative of the vast numbers

---

[5] In 1970 electric power and industrial systems (for which Dore's Furusato Works was the key factory) contributed 41% of corporate turnover; by 1995 this had dropped to 32%. Consumer electric goods (cf. Dore's Taga Factory) had dropped from 29% to 10%. Information and electronics, by contrast, had surged from 20% to 50% (unconsolidated figures).

[6] Fruin's (1997) study of Toshiba's Yanagicho Works is more consciously in the mould of Dore's earlier study. It incisively analyses the strengths of Toshiba's 'knowledge works', but offers no clue as to why, like Hitachi, Toshiba should be forced in 1998 to announce far-reaching organization reforms, including transforming operating divisions into separate companies and the headquarters into a holding company, selling units with poor prospects, and changing corporate governance institutions.

[7] Around 150 interviews were carried out between 1996 and 2004. Most were of individuals, but small group focus interviews to gauge shopfloor (and office and lab) reactions to the reforms were also carried out. We were interested not just in the *contents* of the reforms, but the *process* as well.

of small businesses for a start, and few other companies or enterprise groups span such a broad range of markets and industries. Many of these are characterized by rapid technological innovation, which is felt more acutely than in many other firms. In these senses it is an extreme case.

Nonetheless, the problems faced by Hitachi, the debates over what to do about them, and in particular management reforms, are broadly familiar to many other large Japanese companies. The reforms we describe in chapters 10 and 11 resonate with the survey findings of chapters 5 and 6. There is a sense, moreover, in which we can say 'if Hitachi changes, Japan will change'. This is quite different from Sony, for example, of which we might say 'if Sony doesn't change, Japan won't change'.

Our objective of an in-depth view, and the sheer size and complexity of Hitachi, prevent us from presenting more than a single case study. For the same reasons we do not attempt a full comparative view, although we do include comparative references, particularly to GE and its reforms under Jack Welch.

Ultimately, the fate of Hitachi as a community company depends on the success of Hitachi as a business enterprise. Our case study, therefore, looks at Hitachi in its business context, not in isolation from it. The organization of Part 2 reflects this perspective. In the remainder of this chapter we sketch the rise of Hitachi, in order to understand what made it a giant in the first place. We end the chapter with a conceptual model, which we use in chapter 9 to explore Hitachi's growing problems, and its attempted response to them, particularly up to 1998. Chapter 10 looks at the organization and governance reforms between 1998 and 2004, and chapter 11 looks at changing human resource management (HRM). Chapter 12 looks at the impact of these reforms on industrial relations, and vice versa, and chapter 13 concludes the case study by exploring the significance of the reforms, in terms of their own objectives, in a comparative sense, and in terms of the survival, evolution or disappearance of the 'classic model'. We maintain our content focus on employment practices, corporate governance and managers' priorities or ideologies, without mechanically mirroring the structure of Part 1.

Entrepreneurship in a growth economy

Hitachi traces its founding not to 1908, when Odaira Namihei started a repair shop to fix motors at Kuhara Mining's Hitachi mine, nor to 1912, when he began to assert his independence by calling his workshops Hitachi Manufacturing (the current name in Japanese), nor even to 1920, when Hitachi Manufacturing became formally independent from Kuhara Mining as Hitachi Manufacturing Ltd. Its founding is traced to

1910, when Odaira succeeded in making three five-horsepower electric motors. It was his dream that Japan should develop its own technological capabilities, and not have to rely on foreign imports, and it is this dream which gave birth to today's giant Hitachi.

Odaira and his team were self-consciously ambitious and unorthodox. They shrugged off criticism from Kuhara, their first customer, that their work was inferior to GE imports, and that they had better stick to repairs, and also problems with their 10,000-horsepower turbine and controller for the Tone river, which they had audaciously bid for in 1914 when the First World War prevented their supply from Germany. Seizing the window of opportunity provided by the war, they began making new products, including copper wire, and tooling for their manufacture, moving the business closer to Odaira's dream of self-sufficiency. By 1918 the company had its own research section (with one machine – an electromagnetic oscillograph). Undeterred by a fire in 1919 which gutted much of the Hitachi Works, and with it machines and work in progress, they made the business formally independent in 1920.[8]

During the interwar years Hitachi grew phenomenally, both organically and by acquisition. Between 1922 and 1927, Hitachi built 12–15% of the country's new turbines, hydroelectric power generators and transformers. It expanded into transportation equipment – including rolling stock and ships – and consumer products, receiving another major boost when the Great Kanto Earthquake destroyed competitor factories in Tokyo in 1923. And between 1939 and 1945 it built and acquired thirteen new factories, including the Taga Works, which spearheaded postwar consumer goods, and Riken Vacuum Industry, which provided base technology for electronics. Emphasis continued to be placed on research; in 1934 the research department of the Hitachi Works became a research centre, and in 1942 the pivotal Central Research Laboratory (CRL), which spawned later corporate research labs, was established in western Tokyo to 'create new technologies for the coming ten to twenty years, as well as pursue development work for our current business'.[9]

War of course played an important part in this phenomenal growth, but it ultimately led to decline and destruction. At the Hitachi Works military goods accounted for only 16% of output in 1940; by 1942 this had risen to 38%, and by the end of the war it reached 95%. Long before this, however, materials were running short, and many of the skilled craftsmen had been conscripted. In June and July 1945, the Hitachi Works and other

[8] Historical information here draws on *Hitachi seisakusho shi* (History of Hitachi Ltd), Vols. 1–4, and *Hitachi kojo 75 nenshi* (Hitachi Works 75-Year History).
[9] Odaira's words, cited in a CRL brochure.

key factories were reduced to rubble by US B29 bombers. As the war drew to a close Hitachi's first attempt to become a general electric company – and Japan's first attempt to become a major industrial power – lay in ruins.

More travails awaited. Odaira and fifteen directors were purged under the Occupation.[10] Hitachi was designated a holding company and ordered to hand over shares of its subsidiaries. There were plans to split the company itself in three (or six – there were various plans), but as Occupation priorities shifted, it was instead ordered to dispose of nineteen of its thirty-five factories (mostly non-core ones). Struggling to rise again under new management, and dedicated to 'peaceful industry', the company was dealt a further blow by the severe deflationary policies of 1949–50, when it became embroiled in a major industrial relations dispute (about which more later).

Special procurements for the Korean War which broke out in 1950, however, breathed new life into Japanese industry, and Hitachi. Implementation of the government's first five-year plan from 1951 brought a surge in hydroelectric power development, Hitachi's forte. By the end of the decade the thrust of energy development had shifted to thermal power, at which domestic producers, and particularly Hitachi, were at a disadvantage,[11] but by then Japan had entered its remarkable high growth period, and there was more than enough work in other areas, such as industrial machinery. Hitachi worked to full capacity to fill orders for new factory plant and machinery, and for rolling stock, including the new *shinkansen* bullet train, scheduled to be completed in time for the Tokyo Olympics in 1964. The heavy electric segment accounted for around 40% of Hitachi's production in the 1950s, and industrial machinery about 30% in the 1960s.

Household appliances and consumer electrics grew into a major segment, too, starting with the 'home electrification boom' of 1955–6. Hitachi was a latecomer in electric appliances, and had to construct a nationwide sales organization from scratch, but its motor and compressor technology made entry relatively easy. By the end of the 1950s, transistor radios and TVs had been added to refrigerators and electric fans. With the addition of several new factories in the 1960s and early 1970s, consumer goods became the leading segment. As profits from the heavy electric segments had nurtured consumer goods, though, profits from

10 Odaira's exclusion was lifted in 1951, and he was made Adviser to Hitachi, but died shortly after.
11 Hitachi entered into licence agreements with foreign companies, including GE and Babcock and Wilcox to try to close the technology gap in thermal, and then nuclear, power equipment.

the latter nurtured electronics and computers. Hitachi benefited from its tie-up with RCA in the 1950s and early 1960s, but it simultaneously ploughed a significant portion of its own R&D budget into developing its own technology in these areas.[12]

At the same time as this rapid organic expansion into new areas, Hitachi was spinning out non-core activities to develop independently. Some of these, such as Hitachi Cable, Hitachi Metal and Hitachi Chemical, grew with the Japanese economy into major companies in their own right, while others serviced core Hitachi operations. Spinouts rather than acquisitions, therefore, characterized the expansion of the Hitachi Group in the postwar period.

In 1970 Hitachi was the only Japanese company to be listed in *Fortune's* Top Ten non-US manufacturing companies. In the space of just twenty years it had been rebuilt into a powerful and vibrant general electric company. It was expanding aggressively into areas that companies like GE and GEC were pulling out of, notably computers. From a primarily domestic focus it was beginning to put more effort into exports; in 1970 a mere 13% of production was exported, but by 1975 this had jumped to 24%, and by 1980 26%. It began exporting technology, too, and by the mid-1980s technology revenue exceeded payments to overseas companies. 'Globalization', however, proceeded more slowly. Growing trade friction and the rise of the yen led first to an international procurement effort, and then to increasing foreign direct investment, but overseas production accounted for only 6.5% of consolidated production in 1990, and 13.4% in 1997. A number of R&D labs were established in North America and Europe from the late 1980s, but they were relatively small in scale.

Table 8.1 gives an indication of the range of products and activities of Hitachi Ltd and its main subsidiaries in the crisis year 1998. In that year there were 976 companies listed in Hitachi's consolidated accounts (684 in Japan and 292 abroad), with 331,494 employees (271,026 and 60,468), and annual sales of US$63.8 billion ($44.0b and $19.8b).

Organization dynamics[13]

Hitachi's rise to prominence is deeply intertwined with the growth of the Japanese economy itself. Hitachi developed as a major infrastructure provider, and diversified into new and growing areas of the economy.

---

[12] R&D expenditure climbed from 3% to 5% of turnover in the 1960s, to 6% in the 1970s, and almost 10% by the end of the 1980s.

[13] The following account is given largely in the past tense, to describe the situation prior to 1998, but of course many of the features described have not been the subject of reform, and are present today.

Table 8.1 *Products/activities of Hitachi, 1998 (consolidated)*

Proportion of sales	Products/activities
Information systems and electronics 31%	mainframe computers, software, computer terminals and peripherals, workstations, PCs, magnetic disks, telephone exchanges, broadcasting equipment, semiconductors, picture tubes, LCDs, semiconductor manufacturing equipment, test and measurement equipment, medical electronics equipment
Power and industrial systems 24%	nuclear power plants, hydroelectric power plants, thermal power plants, control equipment, compressors, rolling mill equipment, chemical plants, elevators, escalators, air conditioning equipment, industrial robots, rolling stock, automotive equipment, construction machinery
Consumer products 9%	room air conditioners, refrigerators, washing machines, microwave ovens, vacuum cleaners, heating appliances, kitchen appliances, lighting fixtures, TVs, VCRs, video cameras, hi-fi audio equipment, audiotapes, videotapes, batteries
Materials 14%	synthetic resin materials and products, PCBs, ceramic materials, special steels, rolls for rolling mills, malleable cast iron products, forged and cast-steel products, pipe fittings, electric wire and cable, copper products, rubber products
Services and other 22%	general trading, transportation, property management, printing, financial services

Source: Hitachi Annual Report, 1998.

Its success, however, lay not simply in its positive response to emerging market opportunities, but to organization structures and dynamics which facilitated both innovation and efficiency. Here we sketch its basic organization structure, management processes, technology and product innovation, rationalization and process innovation, and inter-firm relations.

Factories, divisions and headquarters

Japan's large manufacturing organizations developed differently from their American counterparts in a number of respects, notably greater authority delegated to, and multifunctionality of, the factory. Fruin (1992) attributes the origins of these features to limited resources and a steep learning and innovation curve, and their persistence to the advantages they conferred in product and process innovation. Hitachi's 'factory profit centre' tradition is a prime example, emerging from its prewar heavy electric roots and modified, but never entirely abandoned, in subsequent diversification.[14]

Nevertheless, it began experimenting with divisionalization in 1951–2, when it established an Executive Committee for top-level decision-making, divided its headquarters into operational and corporate management functions, and divided the former into eight divisions. Growth and changing technologies and markets resulted in further modifications and experimentation in the quest for the right balance between centralization and decentralization, synergy and specialization.[15]

In principle, the role of headquarters was limited to strategic planning, raising and managing corporate finance, authorizing expenditure above a certain level, recruitment and personnel management of university graduates, and co-ordination of production. In fact, its activities were extensive, and reflected the importance attached to corporate development and responsibility, as well as to inter-divisional co-ordination.

Management processes

Top down co-ordination and control, and bottom up factory profit centre traditions were accommodated in subtle ways. Division or factory heads – invariably engineers – had an important role, but with strong support from the accounting function.[16] Hitachi is widely known within Japan as 'Hitachi, the technology company', but to some it was also known as 'Hitachi, the accounting company'. Performance targets were based on an internal capital system, established in 1968. This enabled internal performance to be measured and compared with other companies making the same types of products. Long-term planning began in 1959. Recently disparaged as 'management by stapler' – gathering divisional/factory plans and stapling them together – in fact it reflected a delicate balance between central vision and local pragmatism.

---

[14] Not all Hitachi's factories have been profit centres, or multi-functional. A large number of limited product, cost centre 'branch factories' were established in semi-peripheral locations in the 1960s to secure land and labour necessary for the production of standardized goods.

[15] Sugimoto et al., 1990; company mimeo. In the mid-1990s six factories were still formal profit centres, in addition to twenty divisions.

[16] Support functions like accounting and personnel were very specialized in Hitachi, and once assigned to them after initial training (where there may have been some exposure to other functions), employees spent most if not all of their career in that function, though at different sub-specializations and different locations. Engineers, too, were specialized, although they experienced various jobs according to production needs, market and technology shifts. This runs counter to common perceptions of white-collar 'generalists' in Japanese companies.

Technology and product innovation

The processes just mentioned were reflected in Hitachi's R&D organization. Corporate research labs were mandated to follow Odaira's maxim and concentrate on future (10–20 years) technology, divisional research and development labs concentrated on 'tomorrow's technology', and factory development and design centres concentrated on 'today's technology'. In practice, the situation was more fluid. As well as 'future technology' research, corporate labs undertook commissioned 'tomorrow's technology' R&D for divisions and factories. The overall split in 1997 was roughly 40–60.[17]

In addition, there were typically 40–50 'special projects' running at any one time, to which roughly 20% of R&D funds were allocated (Hitachi, 1990). Where competitive pressures required the urgent development of a new product, for instance, the necessary R&D personnel could be gathered from throughout the company. In this way, although Hitachi had a limited number of researchers in any one area compared with specialist manufacturers, it had an institutionalized mechanism to draw on its vast resources at critical times. A second type of 'special project' involved more extensive or long-term research spanning several divisions and research labs, utilizing Hitachi's diversified technological expertise, and ensuring that emerging markets were targeted, even if they straddled or fell between divisional boundaries.

Rationalization and process innovation

Campaigns to improve profitability and efficiency began in earnest following the First World War, when Hitachi's management structure was revamped and process management was implemented, drawing on the ideas of Taylor, Gant, Emerson and others (Sugayama, 1991). In the postwar high growth period they were advanced through a combination of daily management activities, task forces, and small group activities, formalized in 1968 under the banner of 'MI' (management improvement: figure 8.1). MI activities concentrated initially on reducing indirect labour costs, and in the 1970s productivity and regulation improvements, design improvements and sales–division–factory linkage efficiency, and workflow efficiency. Hitachi's reputation for being recession-proof derived from their effectiveness.

---

[17] CRL planning office manager interview, 4 September 1997. At the CRL the split was roughly 50–50. In 1997 about one-quarter of the 13,000 R&D employees were based in corporate labs.

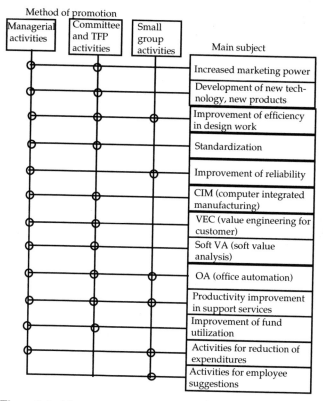

Figure 8.1 Management improvement (MI) activities
Source: Hitachi Ltd (1990), *Introduction to Hitachi and Modern Japan*, p. 33.

Small group (quality control/zero defect circle) activities were launched in 1965. By the mid-1970s they were established in all factories, and subsequently they spread to indirect departments. By 1985 there were 7,600 circles company-wide, with 6–9 employees per circle. The remit of the circles corresponded with MI objectives, but they were also intended to promote employee participation and enthusiasm as well as increase efficiency.

'Soft' efficiency-enhancing campaigns were complemented by 'hard' technological innovation. In 1961 the Hitachi Works took delivery of IBM's first 7070 mainframe computer export to Asia, using it for production control as well as technical calculations. Hitachi started producing its own (HITAC) version in 1964. In 1968, alongside the internal capital system and MI, HIMICS (Hitachi Management Information and

Control System) was launched to promote computer-based efficiency from purchasing to sales.

In production, numerical control (NC) machine tools were introduced in the early 1970s, as were the first robots. These were soon linked into more complex automated systems. FA (factory automation) committees were set up in 1982, and these gave way to CIM (computer integrated manufacturing) committees in 1986, which attempted to integrate FA and OA (office automation: cf. Tokunaga and Sugimoto, 1990). The scope of FA and CIM was extended beyond Hitachi Ltd to include key suppliers.

Needless to say, Hitachi has a long history of commercializing technology developed for in-house innovation, under the concept of 'best maker – best user'.

Inter-firm relations

It is rather artificial talking about the organization dynamics of Hitachi Ltd independent from those of the Hitachi Group. Boundaries were rather fluid; work and people flowed in and out, as did organization concepts and efficiency campaigns. Around 180 companies were incorporated into the budgeting system, some of them directly with the headquarters, and some through operating divisions or factories. Regular function-based meetings were held, and there was extensive joint training.

Relations were based on five principles, formalized in the 1960s:

1. sincerity and trust
2. co-existence and co-prosperity
3. self-management[18]
4. market prices
5. group preference

Just as there has been a factory profit centre tradition within Hitachi Ltd, subsidiaries and affiliates operated comparatively independently. Sixty to seventy per cent of profits were normally left in the subsidiaries, allowing them to develop their own strengths. Consolidated turnover in 1995 and 1996 was twice unconsolidated turnover, and profits were three times as much.

Over 50% of Hitachi's purchases took place within the Hitachi Group, but there were many suppliers with which Hitachi had no capital ties. To varying extents, these also took part in VI (value improvement; launched in 1967) activities, and indeed locally organized social activities.

---

[18] Within set limits; changes to capital required Hitachi Ltd approval, and name changes and making new subsidiaries required notification.

In sum, Hitachi's rapid growth, described in the first section, must be seen not simply as a positive response to market opportunities, but to stringent internal processes which promoted efficiency and competitiveness as the company made its transition to high productivity, high value added and high wage management. The processes also extended beyond corporate boundaries to include group companies, which contributed their own specialist expertise and dynamism.

Employment practices and community

Hitachi's success was based on its people. The company was a pioneer within Japan not just of organizational innovation, but personnel management as well. After the Second World War industrial relations played an important role in shaping the employment relationship and community features.

Early days

From the beginning, Odaira faced a shortage of skilled workers, and in 1911 he set up his own apprentice school, where apprentices studied general and technical subjects off the job, and practical skills on the job. From the apprentice school, a comprehensive education and training system was developed, which stressed the values of 'sincerity, enterprise and harmony' in addition to tangible vocational skills.

Employees were recruited directly by the company, including graduates from top Imperial universities. In the 1920s, along with growing specialization and stratification in the management structure, entry points and promotion became more strictly regulated, and linked to educational qualifications and in-house exam success. This caused considerable dissatisfaction among able blue-collar workers (Sugayama, 1991).

In keeping with the company's mining origins, management was tough but paternalistic (cf. chapter 1). Many workers lived in company housing, with stable basic living conditions. This did not spare the company from the growing labour movement, however; the Yuaikai gained a toehold at the Hitachi Works before a crackdown in 1919, in which some fifty workers – many of them union members – were fired for allegedly not co-operating fully in dealing with the fire and its aftermath. Subsequently an employee association (Onkokai – 'Warm Exchange Association') was formed, and another association at the Kamedo Works, which 'laid the basis for smooth, rapid future growth in employee numbers without labour disputes' as well as 'improving worker welfare and status, and raising production levels' (Hitachi Ltd, 1949: 41).

Industrial relations

These associations were eventually absorbed into the wartime 'industrial service to the nation' council structure (*sampo*), from which emerged Hitachi's first unions, in late 1945 and early 1946. The unions demanded the establishment of collective bargaining, democratization of factory management, livelihood guarantees, shorter working hours, and the abolition of blue-collar–white-collar status and wage differences.[19] Failure to agree on the abolition of status differentials led to the company's first strike, which lasted for three days in December 1946. The outcome was a new wage system, weighted heavily towards living security and seniority.[20] In 1947 the unions (now combined blue-collar and white-collar) joined the Japan Communist Party-oriented Sanbetsu movement. While they demanded that the company introduce one-off payments for weddings, births and funerals (important rites of passage which many members could barely afford), the company reneged on a pay agreement. A strike ensued, ending forty-seven days later after intervention by the Occupation authorities.

The most dramatic confrontation came in 1950, when the company announced that 5,555 employees were to be laid off. The resulting three-month strike ended in defeat for the union, and the purge of fifty 'red' union leaders and workers. The trauma of this event, and the determination to avoid anything like it in future, forms the backdrop for the development of Hitachi's postwar community firm, yet the 'co-operative line' (*kyocho rosen*) of industrial relations which supports it did not emerge overnight.

The company sought to capitalize on its victory and re-establish its 'right to manage' in 1951 by radically overhauling personnel management, introducing appraisal, for instance, and lengthening working hours. (Korean War and hydroelectric orders had begun flowing in, but the company could hardly take on new employees after the mass firing.) As business boomed in the mid-1950s, the introduction of new technology was seen less as a threat to jobs, but as a relief from overwork.[21]

[19] Hitachi Workers Union (Hitachi Branch), 1996, Vols. 1, 2: historical information is from this source unless otherwise noted.
[20] The chief beneficiaries of this new system, in terms of pay increases, were older, blue-collar workers.
[21] For a critical view of industrial relations at Hitachi in this period, see Kawanishi, 1992.

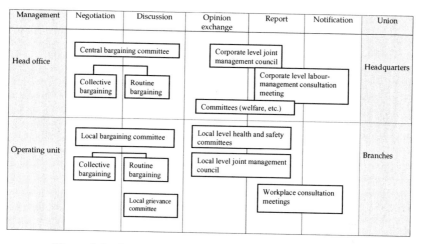

Figure 8.2   Industrial relations: bargaining and consultation bodies
Source: Hitachi Workers' Union (undated), *ing: Hitachi Workers' Union,*
p. 17.

Booming business also meant large numbers of new recruits, who rein-
vigorated union activities. Increasingly, though, the predominant policy
became one of co-operating with management to increase the 'pie', and
bargaining, backed up by short strikes, over its division in the spring
pay round. This trend was promoted internally by the establishment of
joint consultation bodies in the early 1960s, and externally by affiliation
to the Japanese chapter of the International Metalworkers' Federation
(IMF-JC) in 1964.

The 'co-operative line' was further strengthened with the creation of a
unitary body in 1970 – the Hitachi Workers' Union.[22] The defeat of major
enterprise unions in the 1975 wage round led to muted wage demands
and expansion and deepening of consultation. Union emphasis shifted
decisively from persuasion by power (strikes) to the power of persuasion.
Since 1975 there has only been one strike by HWU; over the bonus in
1980.

Although collective agreements set out the items which were subject
to negotiation and agreement, and those which were subject to various
forms of consultation (figure 8.2), formally preserving management's

---

[22] In 1974, too, the loose organization of unions of Hitachi Group companies formed a
tighter-knit Federation of All-Hitachi Workers' Unions, with around seventy member
unions. Group unions aimed to secure wages and conditions as close to HWU members
as possible.

'right to manage' in business areas, in fact consultation became wide-ranging, facilitated by a complex structure of committees on both sides, as well as joint committees. These allowed the union to monitor carefully and debate any proposed changes, for instance, in the *per diem* allowance for overseas travel, or pension administration. In 1996 there were over 200 full-time and 100 part-time union officers *excluding* secretaries.[23]

'Lifetime' employment, training and socialization

After the 1950 mass dismissal, the managers decided it was in their best interests to avoid layoffs wherever possible, thus meeting a basic union demand for job security. This was not set out in the collective agreement or employment regulations, indeed in the former the management retained the right to lay workers off with thirty days' notice and pay. But this did not happen. An implicit contract offered security for loyalty, to both regular white-collar and blue-collar workers. This gave managers flexibility in some areas, restrained their autonomy in others, and exerted a strong but subtle influence on corporate strategy.

Under the implicit contract, recruitment, education and vocational training were taken very seriously, as it was not easy to fire workers once hired. Conversely, however, costs incurred could be recouped, as employees were expected to stay.[24] As an introduction to the company's education system stated: 'To hire a person and not to train him/her is a failure of management.'

Hitachi's apprentice school eventually became an industrial high school. In 1956 there were over 2,000 applicants for 120 entry year places. Forty years later there were still 385 students, spread over three years. By the late 1950s, however, the main blue-collar intake had shifted from middle school to high school leavers. Hitachi established two colleges in 1959 to provide one year training for them, and the colleges also enrolled 360 students between them in 1996. Graduates received a further combination of on and off-job-training, with encouragement to take part in skill certification and skill competitions. Through this, they became core

---

23 Union brochure. A closed shop system operated – with a few exceptions all employees below section manager level belonged. Union dues were set at about the equivalent of four hours' work per month (about 2.5% of basic pay), with most remaining within the branch, and the rest passing to the HWU headquarters, and some to the industrial federation.

24 Labour turnover in the 1990s averaged about 2%, and less than 1% for male university graduates.

members of the workforce and workplace communities. As a 'shop-floor deity'[25] commented:

The most important thing in our workplace is human relations, teamwork. We say that the workplace is the life place; more time is spent here than at home, so it's important they get on. Then you don't get accidents – and accidents here mean death or serious injury – and you get good products.

For the growing numbers of university graduates, initial orientation was followed by two months of 'front line experience', and a two-year training period of OJT punctuated by off-job seminars, plant visits, language training and social events. Initial postings also tended to be near the 'front line', either in factory design sections, accounting sections or sales operations, to socialize new employees into the company's (productionist) culture and nurture an appreciation of front-line work.

Many temporary workers were taken on as work picked up in the 1950s, since the company was unsure how long the growth would last. In 1961 roughly one-third of the Hitachi Works workforce were temporary workers.[26] Thereafter the number declined. Some became regular employees during the growing labour shortage. Changing skill requirements, technological innovation, and surplus *regular* employees in the 1970s reduced their numbers further. Subsequently the number of non-regular workers at Hitachi Ltd itself was very small, but there were sizeable numbers in some subsidiaries, and their subsidiaries.

Wages and promotion

Lifetime employment was reinforced by the pay and promotion system, which rewarded contributions – and loyalty – over time. The company introduced a new system in 1951, modifying the living security emphasis by introducing appraisal. In its attempt to curb seniority-based wages and promotion, it declared that management posts were part of organization design, not part of the incentive system. The following year, however, it introduced a 'special title' system (extra grades) so that morale would not decline in the absence of posts for highly skilled employees. In the 1960s grade ladders were extended, and criteria for promotion made clearer. Seniority was not entirely purged, however, as there were guidelines for early, standard and late promotion, the gap between which widened the higher the grade.

[25] 'Shopfloor deity' is the nickname given to highly skilled craftsmen personally recognized by the president. Fifteen received this recognition in 1996.
[26] Hitachi Works, 1985: 70.

In 1964–5 Hitachi became one of the first companies in Japan to introduce a dual ladder system by adding a professional (or specialist) track beside the management track for researchers and engineers, and later designers, education instructors and sales personnel. And in 1968 the company launched a Personnel Inventory System to better identify and allocate human resources, and to register employee aspirations (written on appraisal forms).

The wage system also underwent major revision in the 1960s, again to purge the hydra-like influence of seniority, this time through job-based wages. The job evaluators set to work in 1963, and eventually came up with some 600 job titles for manual, clerical and supervisory workers. At the same time the piecework system for manual workers was reformed.[27] The result was an extraordinarily complex system, particularly for manual workers, detailed in a very fat handbook produced by the union, but used by company wage specialists as well.

Put simply, the wage packet was part person-related and part job-related. Various mechanisms were designed to prevent disputes over job-based wages from arising, including joint committees, minimum rates (90%) for downtime, and guarantees that wages would not be dropped with new assignments for six months. As more and more workers were moved around, their wages often bore little resemblance to the job they were doing, but the company maintained the system because any reform or simplification 'would like as not have brought us back to the seniority system'.[28]

Mention must also be made of the twice-yearly bonus, which peaked at the equivalent of six months' pay in 1973 and troughed at 4.76 in 1975, but was almost always more than five months' pay in total.

On the one hand, then, the company fought a long battle against seniority in the sense of automatically rewarding age and presence in the company, while on the other it rewarded loyalty and progression through career ladders. A 1996 company mimeo described the key characteristics of the Hitachi wage system as follows:

1. *thoroughgoing ability-related pay* (based on lifetime employment but ability given more emphasis than in referent Japanese companies);
2. *harmonization of person-based and job-based pay*;
3. *stability so that all employees can work with peace of mind* (living security).

Historically these reflect the determination of Hitachi's management to align the wage and promotion system with organization needs on the one hand, and the incorporation of worker needs and concerns on the other. The latter featured prominently in the welfare system.

---

[27] In the late 1990s piecework was still paid in one in five factories.
[28] Personnel director, 1 September 1997.

Welfare

Dore (1973) identified 'welfare corporatism' and 'enterprise as community' as key features of management and employment at Hitachi. 'Welfare' meant much more than sports, culture and recreation, though these activities were important, and were strengthened considerably in 1951 in an attempt to reknit the social fabric of the company, torn during the dispute the previous year.[29]

The cornerstone of Hitachi's formal postwar welfare programme was housing and housing support.[30] As the company took on large numbers of employees in the late 1950s, it built new dormitories to house them in, and as they married in the 1960s, it built new apartments. While employees lived in heavily subsidized dormitories and apartments, with rents about one-fifth of the market rate, they were expected to save up money to buy their own homes, preferably before the age of 40. The company would pay an interest supplement on their savings, and pay part of the interest on their housing loan. This loan would be virtually repaid by the time they retired, the lump sum retirement money would finish it off, and the pension could go towards a retirement free from financial hardship.

The importance of these measures, particularly for the rapidly growing numbers of blue-collar workers, cannot be over-emphasized. Through them the company hoped to lower turnover and enable employees to 'work with peace of mind'. In April 1995, 18,961 employees were housed in company dormitories, and 10,227 in company apartments. Outstanding loans organized under the various housing subsidy schemes amounted to ¥119 billion.[31]

Fitting for lifetime employment, the system aimed at 'lifetime welfare', with support for every stage of the worker's life after joining the company. The main measures are outlined in figure 8.3. In terms of costs, these measures added some 30% to the company's direct wage bill, split roughly equally between statutory, non-statutory and retirement/pension costs.

Community company

Some community features were present in the interwar years. Employment relations were substantially reshaped after the Second Word War,

---

[29] In 1994 a quarter of employees took part in sports club activities, and one in ten in culture club activities, in addition to company-wide festivals and competitions, such as the Spring Celebration, the Summer Festival and the Annual Sports Day.

[30] Housing support comprised over 50% of non-statutory indirect labour costs in 1994, versus less than 10% for sports, culture and recreation support.

[31] Company mimeo. Loan figures are as of March 1996.

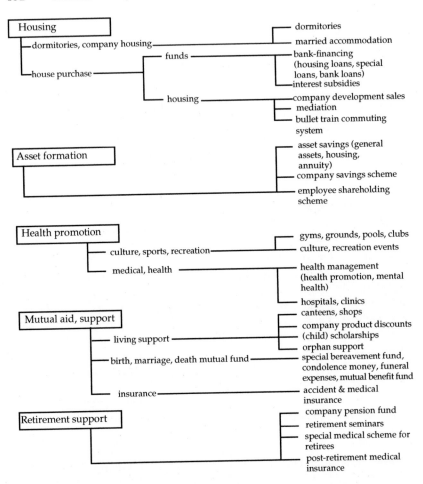

Figure 8.3 Main welfare measures, 1996
Source: Company document (1996).

however, first by the surging labour movement, and then by management's reassertion of its 'right to manage', tempered by the need to
harness employee commitment. A product of these forces was 'homogenization', and the granting of full 'citizenship' to all (male) regular
employees in the 1950s. This meant the extension of staff conditions
to shopfloor workers, as well as gradual compression of wage differences
between them, and between employees and managers. Managers in the
1990s could only look in wonder at the size of houses some prewar

managers lived in, complete with maids' rooms. Socially and economically, managers and workers became much closer.

Citizenship also involved 'holistic engagement'. One aspect was the attempt to engage employees fully in their work, in return for recognition that they had needs outside work which had to be met. Perhaps even more fundamentally, it meant recognition of workers as more than the hands which contribute to production (in contrast to Henry Ford's alleged lament that he had to take workers along with their hands). Socializing outside working hours served to engage parts of the social self which could not be fully expressed through work.

One level, then, was the formal organization structure, with detailed rules and expectations. Another level was a dense network of social relations which was less formal and hierarchical, and which expanded, through social events, career progression and transfers, beyond the individual workplace.

Cleavages between different hierarchical levels were thus minimized, and mechanisms were used to minimize inherent sectionalist tendencies, including the personnel rotations and transfers. The result was the extension of the sense of community beyond the workplace and factory to the company level.

Finance and corporate governance

The final element of the picture, both in accounting for Hitachi's spectacular rise, and the consolidation of its community characteristics, is finance and corporate governance. Stable, supportive finance enabled the company to pursue its growth and technology creating objectives, and at the same time, to deepen its community dimension.

Initially, Kuhara Mining owned most of Hitachi's shares, which it sold to Nissan in 1933. As Hitachi issued new shares after its public listing in 1934 this holding was diluted, and when Nissan registered as a Manchurian company in 1940, it was reduced still further, from 30.9% to 17.6%. The number of shareholders increased from just twenty-nine in 1933 to over 65,000 in late 1940 (Hitachi Ltd, 1960: 9). In seeking to grow as a champion of national technology, Hitachi subsequently attempted not to become too closely identified with any one source of capital. This allegedly enabled the company to withstand pressures for mass dismissals longer than many other companies in the late 1940s, and intensified the bitterness when the mass dismissals were eventually implemented (Hitachi Workers' Union, 1996 vol. 1: 222).

Table 8.2 *Gross value added composition, Hitachi 1957–97 (non-consolidated)*

	Gross value added	Operating profit	Labour share	Depreciation	Other*
1957–61	100	49.6	36.4	12.5	1.4
1962–66	100	41.5	40.2	16.6	1.6
1967–71	100	41.3	48.3	9.2	1.2
1972–76	100	30.4	51.1	11.0	1.5
1977–81	100	24.5	61.8	10.1	3.6
1982–86	100	25.8	55.8	13.9	4.5
1987–91	100	18.3	62.1	16.9	2.6
1992–96	100	10.4	67.2	21.2	1.2
1997–98	100	7.9	70.2	21.5	0.5

Notes: Figures averaged over financial years, ending on 31 March of the year given.
*mainly leasing, taxes
Source: Japan Development Bank Data Base (company code 03074, F6).

In the postwar period, until the early 1980s, about three-quarters of corporate finance was obtained from bank loans.[32] That shareholders did not demand high returns in the face of such leverage was due to stable and reciprocal shareholding. The consequences of 'patient capital' in a relatively benign environment, as well as the consolidation of the company's 'employee favouring' orientation, can be seen through financial data.

Table 8.2 shows trends in the composition of gross value added from 1957–98; notably a steady decline in operating profit, from 49.6% in 1957–61, to a tiny 7.9% in 1997–8, and conversely an increase in labour share, from 36.4% to almost double at 70.2% over the same time period, and an increase in investment (depreciation), from 12.5% to 21.5%.

It is clear that profit maximization was not an overriding management priority. As operating profit declined, so did after tax profit. Until around 1970, the latter averaged 4–4.5% of turnover. It declined to around 3% in the 1970s and 1980s, and dropped well under 2% in the 1990s. Conversely, depreciation remained at 4–5% of turnover for much of the period, but rose to over 5% in the 1990s. Depreciation plus retained earnings was remarkably stable throughout, ranging from 5–7%, suggesting a strategic orientation towards steady growth, and the accumulation of technological and other resources.

[32] Hitachi's insatiable quest for funds also drove the company to issue American Depository Receipts (ADRs) in New York first in 1963, and convertible bonds in London in 1964.

As for the distribution of after tax profits, there was considerable fluctuation in both retained earnings and dividends, but if we calculate dividends as a percentage of paid in capital, we get another remarkably stable figure of 11–16%. The key shareholder policy was to provide stable returns to shareholders, in terms of par value rather than market value. Shareholders were not ignored – in 1997–8 reserves were run down in order to maintain the dividend – but the priority was on stability rather than return maximization.

Table 8.3 lists the top ten shareholders at five-year intervals from 1982–2002. The first four columns tell a consistent story; the final column marks a break with the period until 1997. In the first four columns, shares are widely dispersed. The top ten shareholders collectively own just over a quarter of the company's shares, and no company owns more than 5%. Second, six shareholders figure in each column, and two more figure in three columns. Most of the top ten could be called stable shareholders. Third, directors do not figure, but the Hitachi Group employee shareholding association does – it became the second largest shareholder in March 1997.[33] Fourth, foreign shareholders figure in the first and fourth columns, but not prominently. NATS CUMCO is a nominee for ADRs, while Chase Manhattan and State Street are nominees for institutional investors.

The final column reflects a different financial world; greater participation by shareholders, turbulence and consolidation of the financial sector in Japan after 1998, as well as concentration in the ownership of Hitachi's shares. It accentuates the stability which existed until the mid-1990s.

In sum, financial data suggest a pluralist (stakeholder) orientation, consistent with the classic model described in chapter 2. This enabled the company to pursue growth-oriented strategies, maintain stability, and consolidate its classic model.

Productionist system and the classic model

The main ingredients of Hitachi's dynamic growth have been sketched. Growth was achieved by ambition and design rather than good fortune. We would like to draw particular attention to the postwar innovations which laid the foundations for Hitachi's community firm on the one

---

[33] Employee shareholding was introduced by Hitachi in 1971. It was always referred to as a welfare measure – making it easy for employees to buy shares in the company (through the association they did not have to buy the normal minimum of 1,000 shares), thus providing an additional means of increasing assets – but it undoubtedly served as an additional source of stable shareholding. The upward climb through the ranks appears to have peaked in 1997, and was not part of a union movement to 'socialize capital'.

Table 8.3 *Top ten shareholders of Hitachi Ltd, 1982–2002*

	1982	%	1987	%	1992	%	1997	%	2002	%
1	Japan Life Insurance	3.84	Japan Life Insurance	3.98	Japan Life Insurance	3.88	Japan Life Insurance	3.75	Japan. Trustee Services	5.27
2	Daiichi Life Insurance	2.79	Mitsubishi Trust Bank	3.82	Mitsubishi Trust Bank	2.56	Hitachi Group employees*	3.19	Chase Manhattan	4.50
3	NATS CUMCO	2.75	Daiichi Life Insurance	2.77	Daiichi Life Insurance	2.47	Chase Manhattan	2.75	State Street Bank	4.04
4	Indust. Bank of Japan	2.55	Indust. Bank of Japan	2.56	Hitachi Group employees*	2.44	State Street Bank	2.72	NATS CUMCO	3.82
5	Sanwa Bank	2.46	Sanwa Bank	2.50	Indust. Bank of Japan	2.31	Daiichi Life Insurance	2.53	Japan Life Insurance	3.45
6	Meiji Life Insurance	2.44	Toyo Trust Bank	2.38	Sanwa Bank	2.26	Indust. Bank of Japan	2.23	Mitsubishi Trust Bank	3.40
7	Credit Suisse	2.34	Hitachi Group employees*	2.34	Toyo Trust Bank	2.06	Sanwa Bank	2.21	Mitsui Asset Trust Bank	2.85
8	Daiichi Kangyo Bank	2.24	Meiji Life Insurance	2.26	Sumitomo Trust Bank	2.06	Daiichi Kangyo Bank	1.98	Daiichi Life Insurance	2.79
9	Fuji Bank	2.23	Daiichi Kangyo Bank	2.19	Meiji Life Insurance	2.04	Fuji Bank	1.98	UFJ Trust Bank	2.63
10	Hitachi Group employees*	2.03	Fuji Bank	2.19	Daiichi Kangyo Bank	1.98	Sumitomo Trust Bank	1.88	Hitachi Group employees*	2.46
top ten		25.67		26.99		24.06		25.21		35.21

Note: Figures are for March in the year indicated.
Hitachi Group employees* = shareholder association of Hitachi Group employees

Table 8.4 *Some milestones in the development of the postwar 'classic model' and productionist system, 1951–68*

Area	1951–63 (establishment)	1964–68 (systematization)
Organization	Beginning of 'divisionalization' (1951) Establishment of new operations (consumer elec., semiconductors, Computers: 1952–62) Spinout of major Group companies (H. Cable, H. Metal, H. Chemical, etc.: 1956–66)	Further 'divisionalization' (1964, 1967) Beginning of QC/ZD circles (1965) Company-wide technology upgrading, R&D structures (1967) Management Improvement (MI) campaigns (1968–) Hitachi Information Management and Control System (HIMICS: 1968)
Governance	Executive Committee (1951) Long term planning (1959–) Stable shareholding (1950s)	Internal capital system (1968)
Personnel management, HRM	New personnel management, wage, grade system (1951) Two new colleges for high school graduates (1959) First Comprehensive Housing Measures (pillar of welfare system) Management Training Centre (1961)	New wage system (job and ability-based: 1964) Dual ladder system (1964) Pension scheme (all regular employees: 1964) Personnel Inventory System (PIS: 1968) (Employee shareholding, 1971)
Industrial relations	(Postwar struggle culminating in mass layoff of 5,555 workers and 3-month strike, 1950) Reinvigoration of union activities with new recruits (late 1950s) Joint consultation bodies (early 1960s)	IMF-JC affiliation (1964) (Factory-based unions merge to become Hitachi Workers Union, 1970)

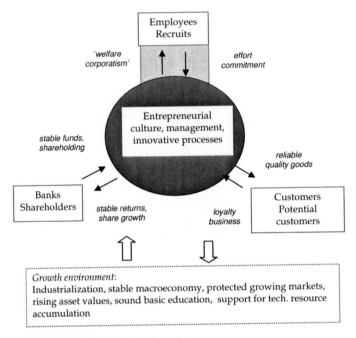

Figure 8.4 Hitachi: a dancing giant

hand, and its production system on the other. Some of the key institutional milestones are listed in table 8.4, which divides the years 1951–68 into two, an establishment period (1951–63), and a systematization period (1964–8). It was remarkable to note in the mid-1990s how many of the building blocks of both the community firm and the production system were slotted into place between 1964 and 1968, thereby creating a strong, mutually reinforcing dynamic. The durability of the community dimension was severely tested during the turbulent 1970s, but not only did it withstand the tests, it allowed the production system to be taken to new heights, through the combination of improvement activities and shopfloor-based technology upgrading.

There are other ingredients, of course. The environment was conducive to strong growth. Domestic markets were still relatively protected, macroeconomic conditions were stable, and the government – MITI in particular – provided support for technology upgrading and accumulation. The education system turned out literate and numerate recruits who knew the meaning of economic hardship and saw work as a vehicle for something better. As we noted in Part 1, the productivity movement emphasized labour–management co-operation (and a sharing of the fruits of productivity improvement between consumers, managers and workers, while labour legislation was built around employment stability and company-based welfare.

Schematically, we have attempted to represent these forces in figure 8.4. The circle delineates corporate management, which was very innovative. Welfare corporatism not only motivated employees, but acted as a magnet for good recruits. For most of the 1960s Hitachi topped the corporate league tables as the preferred destination for engineering graduates. Entry into growing product markets provided them with challenging jobs, and broadened the portfolio of goods Hitachi could offer customers to maintain their loyalty. Patient capital facilitated innovation and attractiveness in labour and product markets. The environment, both directly and through factor and product markets, also facilitated dynamism, while the company could respond swiftly to changes in that environment. By and large, this is the Hitachi depicted in numerous 'excellent company' books which were written about the company in the late 1970s and early 1980s.[34]

---

[34] For example Iwahori, 1978; Okamoto, 1979; Nomura soken, 1981; Nihon noritsu kyokai, 1982.

9 A Victim of its Own Success?

And yet, Hitachi stumbled. Prolonged domestic recession was undoubtedly part of the reason, but Hitachi was supposed to be recession-proof. Instead of nimbly responding, as it had in the past, it appeared lead-footed, and unable to respond decisively to the challenge of Silicon Valley entrepreneurs, domestic specialists and emerging Asian competitors. This chapter explores reasons why it was unable to respond decisively, as well as Hitachi's attempts to cope with the changing environment prior to 1998, paying particular attention to employment and industrial relations considerations. This background is necessary to understand the more far-reaching measures adopted after 1998, which are explored in chapters 10–12.

What went wrong?

Recessionary environment

Various explanations may be offered of Hitachi's stumble. Obvious causes are not hard to find. Semiconductors, which generated almost half of corporate profits in 1995 (and even more in the 1980s), had slumped as the bottom fell out of the DRAM market, and accounted for half the 1998 loss. Consumer electronics were pushed into the red by weak domestic and Asian demand following the Asian Crisis. And electric power and industrial systems, always a steady earner, struggled to break even in a period between major orders. Previously, when one segment was in a slump other segments were able to make up for it – an advantage of being a general electric company. This time, however, key segments were hit simultaneously.

The 'general recession' explanation assigns most of the blame to external conditions, and calls for a measured response. No one was satisfied with this explanation, however.

Large firm malaise

A second set of explanations assigns responsibility to the company, and calls for a major overhaul to bring about rejuvenation. Companies go through various phases of development, from founding through mid-life to maturity, in which ways of doing things are set, and change becomes difficult, even if the environment changes. The result is inertia, and in the absence of major reforms, decline (cf. Schein, 1992).

Until the 1960s, the ethos of Hitachi as a group of unorthodox, itinerant samurai (*nobushi no shudan*) was very much alive, in the bootlegging managers and engineers, for instance, who defied the company directors and developed television in a corner of the Totsuka Works. By the 1970s, however, Hitachi had become a highly structured organization of corporate employees. As such, it sustained formidable competitive strengths, but in the turbulent economic environment of the times, efficiency and caution replaced expansion and exuberance. One corporate planning manager summed up the changing ethos:

I joined the company in 1974. The mood then was all about closing ranks and getting profit. It became safer to concentrate on established business and to cut risk. This happened at various levels.[1]

In the new climate of caution, matters were referred upwards for approval, beyond those which were required by formal rules. *Ringisho* (proposal drafts) began to accumulate more signatures, and more objections. Decision-making slowed. Senior managers spent more of their time resolving internal matters, less time looking outwards. The changing ethos was not just a product of the turbulent times, but the maturation of the company. In Porter's terms, Hitachi was entering the 'wealth-driven' stage of development.[2] In Hitachi's case the compulsion to innovate had hardly diminished, at least in terms of technology and products, but the means of innovation had become institutionalized, and with the establishment of the features depicted in figure 8.1, organizational innovation was less necessary.

The balance between centralization and decentralization, and internal co-ordination became more problematic. Growing *de facto* centralization was counterbalanced by the factory profit centre tradition, but

---

[1] Interview, 24 December 1998.

[2] In this stage: 'Stewards ascend to senior management positions in the place of entrepreneurs and company builders. Belief in competition falls not only in companies but in unions, which both lose the taste for risk-taking. The compulsion to innovate diminishes and the willingness to violate norms and bear disapproval falls' (Porter, 1990: 556).

perversely, some matters like technology (and later IT) specifications, which might have been usefully standardized through central authority, remained locally determined. In production–sales relations, too, there had long been tensions, addressed by periodic attempts to bring them together in new divisional structures, or to separate them.

There were problems in adopting the same structures and processes across all product lines; what made sense for hydroelectric power stations did not necessarily make sense for personal computers. Top managers were selected from the heavy electric factories, in which the roots of the company lay (and in which safety is paramount), and in the computer business, mainframes flourished, while those in personal computers felt like orphans, shunted between divisions in search of a home.

Like other great companies, Hitachi was undoubtedly poisoned in subtle ways by its own success. Success leads to reliance on past proven methods when confronting new challenges, even if these provide a diminishing remedy. Such companies may also become vulnerable to the 'newcomer's/attacker's advantage', even if they are innovative and listening to their customers (Christensen, 1997; Foster, 1986). While Japanese firms were the upstarts in the 1970s and early 1980s, Norton (2001) suggests that they in turn became victims to 'provincial' newcomers in the USA, notably Silicon Valley startups. In Hitachi's case there were other 'upstarts', including specialist manufacturers in Japan, and aggressive tigers in Asia. Whatever the weighting of these reasons, Hitachi was increasingly criticized in the 1990s for failing to exploit fully the technologies it had developed, through lack of speed and excessive caution (e.g. *Nikkei bijinesu*, 1 June 1998). And along with Japan's other general electric companies Toshiba and Mitsubishi Electric, it was criticized for failing to focus (or 'select and concentrate': *Nikkei sangyo shinbun*, 1 January 1998).

Hitachi could still take comfort in being the 'overall competition winner', but it began to claim fewer 'gold medals' in individual events (*sogo yusho, kin medaru nashi*). This became increasingly problematic as individual gold and silver medallists came to claim the bulk of industry profits.

Systemic failure

A third set of explanations sees recession and giant firm blues as part of an even more fundamental problem – one of systemic failure. A moderate version would prescribe reforms complementary to the remedies for large firm malaise; a radical version sees the continued presence of such giants as an obstacle to the transitions Japan must confront.

It is ironic that Hitachi's nascent problems may be traced to the 1970s, a time when it, and other Japanese machine manufacturers, were bursting on to the global stage. The success of such companies in shopfloor-based innovation and improvement, new product development and production co-ordination across corporate boundaries made them the subject of admiration (and fear) and emulation the world over. As Baba has argued, however, this may have locked them into a limited view of competition whose advantages were gradually eroded.[3] Porter et al. (2000) also make this argument, and suggest that Japanese companies failed to develop a strategic approach to business development. Some of Hitachi's (late 1990s) reformers shared this view, arguing that the company concentrated on 'how' and ignored 'what' to make. This is only partly true. Strategies did exist (cf. figure 9.2), but they weren't always implemented effectively.

A related set of issues is the difficulties of many Japanese companies in coming to grips with modular technology and related open product architecture, especially in the information and telecommunications industries, which in the 1990s became increasingly important (Fujimoto, 2001). Cole (2003) sees four related sets of issues which major Japanese manufacturers did not respond effectively to in the 1990s, and which consequently eroded their competitive position: successful emulation of factors making for Japanese success by foreign competitors; the transformation of these industries from domination by large, vertically integrated firms to a pattern of vertical specialization through modularization and open architectures; the growing importance of services, solutions and software; and the growing wave of deregulation. He warns that continued failure to address these issues will result in Japan's large electronics companies losing even more ground, and will continue to stunt the growth of new startups which might address them more effectively.

In a sense it is also ironic that Japanese companies may have pointed the way to modularization, but did not go down that road themselves, and that they achieved spectacular results in quality control in the production process but did not apply them assiduously in indirect areas.[4] And despite the launch of HIMICS (Hitachi Information Management and Control

---

[3] 'The era of manufacturing is coming to an end in which competitiveness is determined by the superiority of shop floor technologies. The principles forming a new type of competitiveness have appeared from outside Japan' (Baba, 1997: 221). An alternative view is that these very competences, as well as the ability to anticipate needs of the market, were eroded over time (e.g. Tsuchiya and Konomi, 1997).

[4] Ironic, indeed, that they were importing Six Sigma concepts in the late 1990s, and 'total supply chain management' as well. History is full of such ironies; many of Japan's competitive strengths came from innovative adaptation of concepts originating in the USA, but only partially applied there.

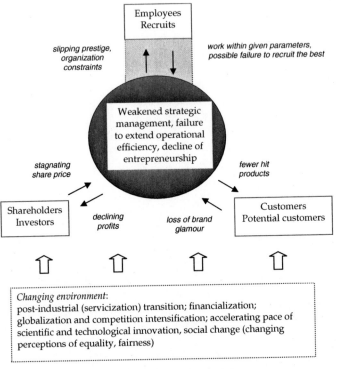

Figure 9.1 Management problems in the 1990s

System – one manager noted with irony the insertion of 'Control') in 1968, and in spite of its ideal of commercializing technology developed in-house, it was not Hitachi – or any other Japanese manufacturer – that set the standards for ERP (enterprise resource planning) in the 1990s, but European companies like SAP and Baan, to which Hitachi then had to orient its own systems.

A third set of systemic failure criticisms relates directly to employment practices and company-as-community. Major Japanese companies lacked reflexivity not simply as a result of their past successes, but their strong cultures of homogenization and normalization, particularly of white-collar workers and their managers (e.g. Chikudate, 1999). Strong communities made it difficult to conceive of different ways of doing things. There is some support for this view from a comparative survey of R, D&E employees in the US, Japan and Korea, which found a positive relationship between openness of HRM systems, and speed of problem solving, an important element of creative working (Appleyard et al., 2002).

As we shall see, Hitachi's senior managers agreed to some extent with many of the systemic failure criticisms, although they did not use the same terminology. They faced severe dilemmas, however, over which systemic features to preserve, which to modify and which to jettison.

A schematic representation of Hitachi's dynamic growth was shown in figure 8.4. We can use the same schematic to depict its growing problems. As figure 9.1 suggests, a rapidly changing environment called for heightened responsiveness at the very time when growing management rigidities were making this difficult. The result was fewer hit products and a loss of brand glamour in product markets, slipping prestige in new graduate markets and a growing sense of concern and frustration by talented employees, and declining profits and a declining share price relative to more nimble competitors.

How would Hitachi's leaders confront its growing problems? The remainder of this chapter explores responses largely prior to the crisis in 1998. Subsequent chapters focus on 1998 and its aftermath.

Employment adjustment

The decision to invest heavily in the emerging areas of computers and semiconductors in the 1960s and 1970s was a strategic one. Profits were siphoned off from consumer products, which in turn had been developed with profits from heavy electric operations. By the 1980s, Hitachi's operations spanned a wide range of industries, and it was becoming increasingly difficult to compete successfully in all of them. Further strategic decisions were made to rationalize or exit operations in low growth, low share markets, and concentrate resources where growth could be expected, as shown in figure 9.2.[5]

Such decisions, and business cycle conditions, had implications for personnel deployment. An advantage of being a general electric company, as far as employment stability was concerned, was the ability to move people – and to some extent work – flexibly, according to need. Such movements increased markedly in the 1970s with harsher business conditions, and institutionalization of employment adjustment steps.[6]

---

[5] This figure clearly resembles Boston Consulting's famous model, which featured the 'cash cow' in the lower right quadrant. It is not clear if Hitachi managers or Sugimoto et al. were applying the model, but certainly some workers we interviewed in consumer electric goods felt they had been used as 'cash cows'.

[6] The steps were: (1) reduction of overtime and curtailing of expenses; followed by (2) non-renewal of fixed-term worker contracts; (3) reduction of new hiring, redeployment through secondments and transfers, retraining, strengthening sales and new business development; (4) overtime freeze, temporary shutdown, application for government employment subsidies and business consolidation; (5) complete hiring freeze and

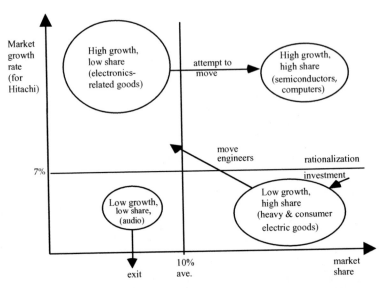

Figure 9.2   Response to 'product polarization' in the 1980s
Source: Sugimoto et al., 1990: 95, 97, compiled from their interviews.

Movement of employees, moreover, crossed company boundaries, as we saw in chapter 6. Table 9.1 shows two sets of employment figures. The first is the number of people on the employment register. The second is the number of people actually working at Hitachi Ltd at the given time. It shows a considerable difference in the mid-1970s, a narrowed difference in the more buoyant 1980s, and an even bigger difference in the 1990s, when several segments were struggling simultaneously, and it was difficult to absorb workers internally. Some of the difference came from employees on sick leave or maternity leave, those doing full-time union duties or health insurance duties, but the vast majority were employees on secondment (10,222 of the 12,360 in 1995, for instance).

Until the late 1980s, this mostly happened within the Hitachi Group, but in the 1990s, secondment spread to non-group companies. Of the 10,222 in 1995, 6,390 were placed with Group companies and 3,832 outside the Group. Increasingly, moreover, such people would not return: 2,823 of those with Group companies and 1,153 of those with outside companies in 1995, or roughly 40% of the total, were eventually transferred, severing their employment with Hitachi Ltd. Transfers were

voluntary redundancies; and then and only then, (6) compulsory redundancies. These are not strictly sequential, as some measures were intensified during subsequent steps, particularly redeployment.

Table 9.1 *Employees of Hitachi Ltd vs employees working in Hitachi Ltd (1975–2000)*

	1975	1980	1985	1990	1995	2000
Employees of Hitachi Ltd	83,797	79,075	85,704	87,415	88,466	66,092
" " working at Hitachi Ltd	75,120	74,373	81,123	81,763	76,106	55,609
Difference	8,677	4,702	4,581	5,652	12,360	10,483

Source: Hitachi Ltd mimeo.

concentrated among senior employees, commonly white-collar workers aged 48–55. Table 9.1 (and 9.2) shows a precipitous drop in employment from 1995, accelerated by spinouts from 1999. The number on secondment dropped too, but as a percentage of total employment, it had risen further by 2000, despite the introduction of consolidated accounting.

Dynamics of the 'quasi internal labour market'

There is insufficient space here to enter the complexities of secondment and transfer. Push and pull factors interacted, sometimes delicately, sometimes less so. The corporate manpower planning section of Hitachi Ltd gradually became involved in intermediation, although there were direct contacts between Group companies as well. Let us give one example of 'push' dynamics.

In autumn 1996, after a temporary – one-day – shutdown, as required by the employment adjustment steps, the union agreed to a restructuring plan for the Hitachi Works which included a 10% reduction of the workforce through secondment and transfer. The 610 selected were in their 50s. Many were blue-collar workers taken on in the boom years of the early 1960s. Four hundred and sixty were to be sent to two 'great grandchild' companies, and the remaining 150 to local subcontractors without a union. Their wages would drop by about 30%.

The union was primarily concerned about two issues: employment security and remuneration.[7] It wanted to be sure that employment would be secure even after the move (i.e. the company would take back any workers who were subsequently made redundant), and that there was no significant financial loss for those involved. Under the agreement those moving permanently would get their retirement sum, and Hitachi Ltd would cover wage differences for up to seven years. Fifty-year-olds would lose out only in their last three years, while those aged 54 and older would

---

[7] Interview, corporate welfare manager, 9 September 1997.

not lose out at all. The savings to Hitachi itself were thus limited, but by paying these costs up front, it could accelerate restructuring.

Spinning companies out: restructuring consumer goods

By the mid-1990s it was clear that pressures for employment adjustment could not be accommodated by secondment and transfers alone. Early retirement appeared on the agenda, though it was a sensitive issue:

Officially, Hitachi has not done early retirement or voluntary redundancies of its own employees, even to this day. In 1993 there was lots of resistance in Japan to early retirement and voluntary redundancies. By 1995, you could often read about it in the newspapers – IBM Japan's 'second career', DEC's early retirement – but these were not traditional, large companies. Our subsidiaries have done it, but large companies that have done it have all been in the red, like Nissan and Oki Electric. Between 1993 and 1995, we debated what to do within Hitachi. If Hitachi does it, the rest of Japan will start doing it. We will forfeit our position. But by late 1995, we couldn't hold off any more.[8]

In fact, Hitachi launched a small-scale, low-key early retirement package for managers (non-union members) aged over 45 in 1993, which gave them two years' pay in addition to their retirement benefits.[9] The uptake was slow at first, but accelerated in 1996. By 1997 about 150 managers had used it. A similar scheme was launched for union members in 1996, which offered a years' paid leave and two years' extra pay on top of the retirement benefits. In the first year there were also about 150 applicants.

Voluntary redundancy was an even more sensitive issue. As the above quote indicates, it did happen in subsidiaries and affiliates. Officially, it did not happen at Hitachi Ltd. Unofficially, it happened in the context of restructuring, which we will now look at.

Hitachi spun out many companies in the postwar years. In the 1950s and 1960s materials operations and support functions were spun out, to improve management efficiency, and for benefits of specialization. In the 1980s many information systems or technology companies were set up or spun out to facilitate the recruitment of engineers. Some 'older worker companies' were also started (cf. Toray in chapter 6). A new wave from the mid-1990s had a stronger emphasis on business restructuring. And it was in this context that the voluntary redundancies occurred.

By the mid-1990s, it was felt that high labour costs were becoming increasingly debilitating in competitive international markets. Labour costs in first tier subsidiaries were some 15% lower, but because of their

---

[8] Interview, personnel manager, 9 September 1996.
[9] The business media soon found out about this scheme: cf. *Nikkei Business*, 18 April 1994.

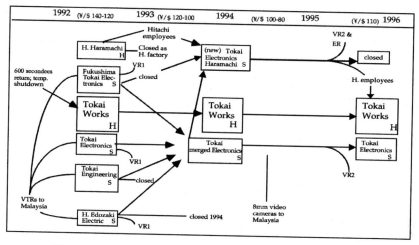

Figure 9.3 Restructuring in and around Tokai Works (consumer electronics), 1992–96

Notes: H – Hitachi. S – subsidiary. VR1 – initial voluntary redundancies, mostly part-timers. VR2 – subsequent voluntary redundancies, regular employees. ER – early retirement.

Source: Interviews, 1996.

alignment with Hitachi, they were often higher than in independent, specialist companies in the same industry. In second and third tier companies, they were some 30% lower. This structure created a centrifugal push from the centre, as workers and work moved outwards (see table 9.2). Increasingly, this took the form of spinouts, often combined with mergers with subsidiaries. The strategic intent was to create stronger subsidiaries, but employment considerations were also influential. Workers in some factories were opposed to being moved to different locations through secondment or transfer. Spinouts, negotiated with the union, provided a way forward. Most workers moved to the new subsidiaries, either on secondment or transfer. Those who did not want to work in the new subsidiaries in effect took voluntary redundancy. The method was developed in consumer electronics, and is illustrated by the Tokai (VCR) Works and its various suppliers (figure 9.3).

In 1992, following the 'bubble' burst and the continued rise of the yen, 600 workers who had been redeployed to factories in Tochigi (air conditioners), Shimizu (industrial air conditioners) and Kanagawa (computers) were forced to return to Tokai, which in line with the employment adjustment understanding, faced a temporary shutdown. Said a manager:

There were reporters everywhere – in front of the Tokai gates, and in front of the headquarters in Tokyo. We were so busy preparing statements. It is my personal feeling that after that, temporary shutdowns spread around Japan.[10]

This measure was only temporary. Workers still got 70% of their wages. And as it was decided that VCR and large video camera production would be moved to Malaysia, something more decisive had to be done, not just at Tokai, but the (Hitachi Ltd) factories and subsidiaries which supplied it. Several of the latter were merged, and with relocations involved, some workers – mainly but not wholly part-timers – took (unofficial) voluntary redundancy. At the Tokai Works itself, some 750 workers were sent to Hitachi's nearby heavy electric factories.

As the yen continued to climb in 1994–5, the decision was made to relocate the production of Tokai's 8mm video camera abroad. Further measures included halving the number of employees at Tokai Electronics and closing of the Haramachi factory, which again involved early retirement and (unofficial) voluntary redundancy. The Tokai Works itself gained a reprieve in the fall of the yen, and the decision to introduce a new product – the MPEG camera.[11]

Restructuring of consumer electronics entered a new phase in 1998–9, when it was decided to place virtually *all* production operations in subsidiaries. The Tochigi Works became Hitachi Tochigi Technology, and the production operations of the Taga Works (one of Dore's two 'Japanese factories', and the centre of Hitachi's consumer electronics manufacturing operations) became Hitachi Taga Electronics. The remaining design, R&D and indirect operations were spun out in 2002 as Hitachi Home and Life Solutions Inc.

Thus, there were three phases of restructuring in consumer electronics, each building on the experiences of the former, increasing in scale, and moving nearer to core operations. In the first stage to 1993, attempts were made to deal with deteriorating results by conventional methods, including redeployment, secondment and permanent transfer. In the second stage, from 1993–7, employment adjustment and restructuring were combined, through spinning out workers with work into new or existing subsidiaries, often with mergers. Spinout restructuring was a response to specific problems at first, but by 1996 had become a central plank in an emerging, generic restructuring strategy. The third phase, from 1998–9,

---

[10] Interview, 20 September 1996.
[11] In its annual report the union noted: 'We have endeavoured to have our views reflected in these (restructuring) measures, premised on stable long-term growth of the company and securing employment, through the central Joint Management Council and the central Labour-Management Consultation Meeting, and have responded in solidarity with the branches affected' (HWU, 1996b: 25).

took this strategy to its logical conclusion by spinning out remaining consumer products operations. The scale of Hitachi's loss in 1998–9 produced a sense of urgency, and accelerated the timetable for spinning out operations. The extent of these measures would have been inconceivable in the mid-1990s, but equally, they did not come out of thin air: the trajectory was already set.

The caution over restructuring reflects in part a hope that the domestic economy would pull out of its slump, and also a concern to maintain employment if at all possible, to minimize the impact upon regular employees and local communities. It reflects a sense of public responsibility on the part of managers. But the media climate changed significantly between 1993 and 1998. In 1993 Hitachi would have been severely criticized for failing its public responsibilities had it failed to maintain employment and created recession in the towns dependent on its factories. By 1998 it was more likely to be criticized for jeopardizing existing and potential employment by failing to take bold restructuring measures. Internally, too, the strength of factory authority made far-reaching measures difficult while profits were being generated, while the plunge after 1998 created a common sense of crisis. These external and internal shifts made it easier to carry out more aggressive measures, but the motivation came from deteriorating performance, and a realization that harder times were yet to come.

On a *Group* basis, restructuring in the mid-1990s did *not* bring about a significant reduction in the number of employees beyond that attained by natural attrition and reduced hiring. Between 1992 and 1997 the number of Hitachi Ltd employees decreased by 14%, but the number in domestic subsidiaries only decreased by 4% (table 9.2), partly as a result of absorbing Hitachi Ltd employees.

This should have resulted in greater price competitiveness, since wages costs were lower in subsidiaries. As noted, however, there were considerable up-front costs in moving workers in this way, as well as intangible costs related to morale. Moreover, wages in many subsidiaries were not as low as in competitor companies, and the proliferation of subsidiaries itself generated co-ordination costs. Such problems had been recognized for some time. An internal survey in the mid-1990s found that purchasing costs within the Group were up to 30% higher than those outside. Efforts were made to push down costs over several years, but with only partial success. The fact that former (senior) colleagues were in the target companies was a complicating factor. Thus Group restructuring was on the agenda, and the imminent introduction of consolidated accounting standards simply underlined its importance in the 1998–9 phase.

Table 9.2 Employees in Hitachi Ltd and subsidiaries, 1988–2002

	1988	1989	1990	1991	1992	1993	1994	1995	1996	1997	2002
Hitachi Ltd	78,352	79,566	81,763	82,221	82,512	80,104	77,185	76,106	72,837	71,160	44,375
Domestic subsidiaries	171,892	181,426	193,149	204,128	208,710	208,343	205,861	203,313	200,942	199,866	211,710
Sub-total	250,244	260,922	274,912	286,349	291,222	288,447	283,046	279,419	273,779	271,026	256,085
Foreign subsidiaries	24,264	29,819	34,845	37,943	40,283	42,190	48,627	52,433	56,473	60,468	83,487
Total	274,508	290,811	309,757	324,292	331,505	330,637	331,673	331,852	330,152	331,494	339,572

Source: Company data.

Internal groups: the first attempt

Spinning out manufacturing operations was not intended solely, or perhaps even primarily, to reduce production costs. Hitachi's problems were seen to lie more in indirect costs, and a lack of market orientation and responsiveness. Greater value chain efficiency was needed, and production needed to become more market-driven. Spinouts were intended to resolve long-standing ambiguities in cost centre–profit centre responsibilities, and to allow greater attention to be focused on these problems.

'Sub-cultures' (Schein, 1992) were an impediment. Comments like the following were not uncommon:

I've heard people in the factories say we're thieves – we have no responsibility for business decisions, and we don't make but we get revenue, and we do this by trickery, like saying to them if they give us something cheaper now, they'll get big orders in a year's time.[12]

Sales–production bickering could no longer be afforded. Hitachi Sales Corporation was merged with the Consumer Products Group in 1994–5. The actual restructuring of sales operations, and particularly distribution, proceeded more slowly, limited by concern for social responsibility. A vice-president summed up the dilemma:

Say a small retail outlet wants something, and they phone the agent. He then phones the distribution centre and they phone sales, who phone the division who contact the factory. This may be extreme, but the process is too long. It needs to be reduced by half and made more speedy. If it is collapsed into two steps there will be job losses, but if nothing is done, we'll all go down. We need to redeploy those affected, so change has to happen at an acceptable pace. The company will be blamed if jobs are lost involuntarily.[13]

Issues of speed and responsiveness went right to the heart of decision-making processes. Too many decisions were being referred to corporate headquarters and its Executive Committee, creating decision-making bottlenecks. And becoming more responsive to markets and customers would require different strategies, structures and processes for different segments. The question was how to decentralize without undermining synergy strengths.

In 1995 a new internal 'group' structure was announced. Divisions were to be placed in four groups – power and industrial systems, electronic components, consumer products and information media, and information (systems) – with automotive products and instruments remaining as separate divisions.[14] Heads were appointed, but there followed an

[12] Interview, 16 October 1998.　[13] Interview, 3 September 1996.
[14] Shortly after, information media was separated from consumer products to create five groups. There was some restructuring of R&D operations as well.

ambivalence as to what authority they possessed. This was particularly marked in HRM and industrial relations matters. If group heads were to have responsibility for business performance, should they not also be given responsibility for these? The overwhelming view in 1996 was 'No':

We need to be able to deal with senior managers at the corporate level, and to carry out personnel rotation from a company-wide perspective. Labour relations won't be divided up because there is one union. The union wouldn't allow us to have different rates or rises in the different groups, although we could do that for (non-union) managers – it's being introduced in their bonuses.[15]

The union was invariably invoked as a reason not to decentralize HRM, but most managers were sceptical as well. The right to fire or lay off people had to reside ultimately at the corporate level, since it would be Hitachi that would be criticized if they were mishandled. Career development would be impeded. And so on. Some successes were achieved, such better use of resources within the groups, but by mid-1997 the general view was that the new system was not functioning well. Instead of tinkering with the system, a decision was made in 1998 to sweep it aside with a reform package more radical than hitherto contemplated.

Restructuring semiconductors

In 1995, semiconductor operations generated half of Hitachi's profits. In 1998, they generated half of its losses. This was not simply a boom and bust phase of the notorious silicon cycle; fundamental changes had occurred in global competition in memory chips – most notably the dramatic reduction in 16 Mb chip size and production costs by Micron Technology of the USA, and the emergence of Taiwanese foundries, both of which increased supply and drove down prices, but more fundamentally, resulted in front runners securing all the profits.[16]

Managers in 1996 noted that their American competitors were busy shedding workers, but their own options were constrained. The 1,000 redeployed workers brought in to help during the boom were returned to their original factories, and negotiations had begun to place semiconductor employees in outside companies. Such measures, however, did not address the fundamental issues. By 1998 media criticism of the company's seemingly lackadaisical stance over its massive semiconductor losses grew sharply. Top management defended its stance in the AGM, but subsequently carried out a reshuffle of personnel, the handling of which drew

[15] Interview, senior director, 3 September 1996.
[16] *Shukan toyo keizai*, 15 November 1997, pp. 156–7.

further criticism.[17] Then a number of subsidiaries were merged, closed or spun into an outer orbit using techniques developed in consumer electronics. In-house operations were reorganized, and foreign operations, some of which were started in the 1980s under political pressure (notably in Europe), were heavily cut back. Still things did not improve.

In February 1999 the management wrote to the union indicating that the very survival of semiconductor operations was in jeopardy unless more far-reaching cost-cutting measures were implemented. It outlined measures it argued were necessary to restore viability, including a 10% reduction in the workforce. A voluntary redundancy scheme was suggested (although the name was studiously avoided) in conjunction with new job mediation. Also proposed were temporary modifications to labour conditions, and a reduction in the bonus.

Although they were relatively modest, and were due to last for only two years, it was the proposals to modify labour conditions which proved most controversial. First, labour conditions had hitherto been considered 'sacred territory', which the company must not breach except in dire circumstances. A breach could open the floodgates. Second, the measures would be applied selectively, to semiconductor workers, violating the principle of equal conditions for all union members. Senior semiconductor shop stewards met and aired their objections in a heated atmosphere, with some calls for a strike. Why should they be victimized, especially after the massive profits they had made in the mid-1990s?

Branch officials responded to the proposed measures with lists of questions, seeking a more detailed justification and a clearer indication of management plans to restore semiconductor viability. The management argued that internal reserves could no longer be relied on to buy time. Either the reserves were required to cover the company's 1998–9 loss, or they were committed or legally required. It noted, too, that the new organization structure being launched in April 1999 required greater independence and accountability in individual division/group operations.

This was the crunch. Semiconductor restructuring had become caught up in wider corporate reforms which we shall look at in the following chapters. The 'victimization' was an announcement that the company meant business over the reforms; it could not backpedal without undermining its broader strategy.

Semiconductor restructuring continued after April 1999 under the new organization structure. In June 1999 it was announced that Hitachi and NEC would pool most of their DRAM operations in a joint venture (now Elpida), catching many inside the company as well as outside by surprise.

[17] *Nikkei sangyo shinbun*, 30 June 1998.

Table 9.3 *Initiatives to restore vitality of Hitachi, 1990–2001*

Reform area	1990–97	1998	1999	2000	2001
Hitachi Group	Secondment, transfer (throughout); restructuring of consumer electronics (spinout restructuring, mid '90s)	H. Group Committee	Consolidated Management Policy Committee; new group pension company	Beginning of mergers, outsourcing service companies	Major personnel reshuffle
Organization	Integration of manufacturing and sales (1994–95); creation of 5 divisional groups (1995); restructuring of corporate level labs (1995)		Reorganization into 11 business groups, 1 spun out, decentralization	Strengthening of new business group structure CVC Centre; business process reforms (BPR) in personnel, finance, purchasing	Delayering
Governance	Most factory profit centres to cost centres (1991–92); upgrading of segment-based investor/analyst meetings	Operating holding company structure; small HQ: 8% ROE targets announced	i.e. Hitachi Plan New governance bodies; advisory committee; IR as separate unit	Assets at present value (including cross-held shares) Stock option scheme (71 top managers)	Quarterly results (internally); pensions on balance Begin strengthening auditor board

				HITACHI VALUE and new pay, grade range system	New specialist system; 'market value' emph.; prepare global grade system; English emph.
Management (non–union) HRM	Small-scale early retirement package (1993) Div. group performance-linked bonuses (1996) MBO (1997)		Executive identification, development programme	Pension reform (*nenko* neutral); cafeteria plan and welfare reforms	Double education expenditure 'Self reliance'; bus. group-specific HRM (Info.);
HRM (union members)	Small-scale early retirement package (1996); increased experienced worker hiring; (c100/yr; 1997); female worker package (1990, 1992)	New pay, promotion, work system; partial extension of MBO	Internal job posting, casual dress code, dropping of formal titles	'Gender free and family friendly' package	H. Financial Community (intranet, pre–401K)

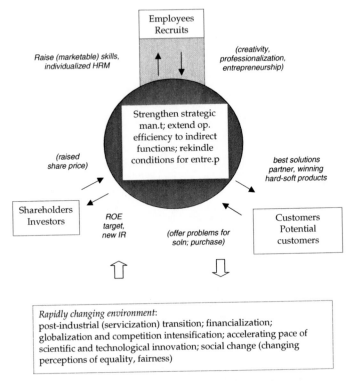

Figure 9.4   (Re)learning to 'dance' in a new environment

The decision was made quickly and 'top down', without any of the lengthy 'bottom up' consultative processes that had hitherto been common. Did this move signal the beginning of a new management style?

In rapid succession, new joint ventures were announced with Taiwan's UMC and STMicroelectronics, and then logic chips were merged with those of Mitsubishi Electric to create Renesas, in the wave of consolidation and transformation of Japan's semiconductor industry at the turn of the century. Less dramatically, other segments were being transformed, too, as chunks of heavy electric operations were merged with those of erstwhile rivals, and in consumer goods and information services, a wide-ranging alliance was struck with Matsushita Electric.

Growing momentum for reform

By 1998 Hitachi was under siege on many fronts. Castigated by analysts and the media, slipping in popularity among recruits, and plunging into the red in a big way for the first time in its history, a mood of pessimism prevailed within the company. The president looked a sorry figure as he faced the nation's press at the Tokyo Stock Exchange to announce the impending loss on 3 September. At the same time, however, he was preparing the ground for his successor to take over the following April, taking on extra restructuring costs to give him a fresh start.[18] Perhaps, too, by intensifying the crisis, lingering internal resistance to change could be overcome, and new energies unleashed.

Reforms planned to mark the company's 90th birthday in 2000 were brought forward. Options previously considered too radical were reconsidered. Under the slogan 'speed and reliability' the company would try to overcome 'large firm malaise', to become more responsive to its environment, even proactive. It would only become more attractive to customers, recruits and employees, and investors by satisfying their demands more promptly, whilst seeking to assure its long-term future.[19]

A schematic representation, similar to one debated in the new top Management Council in late 2000, is given in figure 9.4. Disparate reforms prior to 1998 gradually became linked, as the reform process expanded and was deepened.

By late 2000, then, the reforms were being conceived and carried out more holistically. We have attempted to show this by shading the key areas of reform in table 9.3. In the following chapters we will look at these in more detail.

---

[18] As a Christian, it was perhaps his final cross to bear.
[19] This is a critical but difficult balance to achieve; Ghoshal and Bartlett (1997: 151) call it the 'yin and yang of continuous self-renewal'.

10   Organization Reform

Hitachi's disastrous results in 1998 underscored the fact that major reforms were necessary if the company were to thrive, even survive, into the twenty-first century. At the same time, they unleashed reformist energies which hitherto had been kept in check in favour of a more gradualist approach to change. While sanctioned by the top management, and especially by the incoming president, the details and language of the reforms were to a considerable extent the product of baby boomers who had entered the company around 1970. Loyal to the company, they were also critical. Some had little traditional factory experience and/or had had postings or education in the USA. They used the language of the market, but they also knew that the meanings attached to this language would be modified – sometimes diluted – as the reforms were implemented and diffused throughout the organization.

This chapter outlines the attempts to restructure the organization from 1998, the core of which was decentralization, supplemented by consolidated management. In the process, management structures were questioned at the top governance level, and throughout the organization. Pandora's box was open, at least for debate. The result was, in the words of one manager, a flurry of reform 'balls' thrown from headquarters.

Organization reforms, in turn, had major implications for personnel or human resource management, as well as industrial relations, which we will examine in the following chapters.

Organization reform and the 'i.e. Hitachi Plan'

In 1997 the president started a series of deliberations to produce a new vision for Hitachi on its 90th birthday, in the year 2000. The 1998 disaster, however, resulted in more fundamental reforms being debated, and faster implementation. Options which had been ruled out earlier were now resurrected, and implemented in April 1999.

In mid-1998 Hitachi announced that it would adopt a holding company structure with business operations, in which operating groups would be treated as virtual companies, but would not be legally independent.[1] Non-core operations would be spun out or sold off. Headquarters would be shrunk and concentrate on overall strategy, leaving operations decisions to the new groups. On 15 October, a month after the president's press conference at the Tokyo Stock Exchange, details of the new structure were announced:

1. The present five groups and two divisions are to be reorganized into eleven groups, the number determined as optimum through a study of all relevant factors, including best scale for quick response to changing market conditions and the nature of the company's business. To speed up all aspects of business operation, each business division will be essentially an independent company encompassing affiliated companies with closely related businesses. Group management decisions will be made by a 'group management committee' under the group CEO.
2. A sweeping organizational and functional restructuring and streamlining of the head office will be undertaken and the role of the head office staff will be sharply defined. Specifically, personnel required for management functions and the minimum functions required by the corporation will be defined as 'corporate staff'. The corporate staff will be kept to the minimum number of personnel required. Personnel needed to provide the business divisions with indispensable services of a high-level technical nature will be defined as 'business staff'. The size of the business staff will be adjusted based on the needs of the business divisions.

Hitachi was adopting a more radical option than one rejected four years earlier. The object of the reform was to create a number of smaller 'companies', each of around 6,000 employees with the authority and ability to respond rapidly to changes in markets and technology. If necessary, this response would include customized HRM and pay and conditions, which was hitherto inconceivable. Groups failing strategic or performance requirements would follow industrial air conditioners, the first of the eleven groups to be formally spun out.

The announcement was greeted with scepticism. Some (mainly internal) sceptics wondered if this were simply the old centralization–decentralization see-saw, especially as it was claimed that the reforms would not be allowed to undermine corporate development and synergies. Some (mainly external) sceptics argued that organization reform without

[1] Holding companies had been banned by the Occupation authorities following the Second World War as part of the initial drive to break down the *zaibatsu* and extend economic democracy. The ban was lifted in 1997 in response to lobbying by business organizations, arguing that holding companies would facilitate restructuring and substitute for declining cross-shareholding. Toshiba announced it would adopt a pure holding company structure, but Hitachi believed this was premature until further legislative changes were in place.

a select and concentrate (focus) strategy was futile.[2] They were not convinced that the top management had even an implicit strategic vision. Just what did 'information infrastructure' – the avowed new business core – mean? Indeed, in a number of interviews the incumbent president had rejected an 'American approach' to restructuring by getting rid of unprofitable operations and concentrating on profitable ones. Hitachi had played a role in building the national and corporate infrastructures, and could not simply move to where the pickings were best.[3] The new reforms were to be carried out under the slogan 'speed and reliability (trust)', but implicit in the latter was the promise that Hitachi would not abandon major customers of its infrastructure business.

Unperturbed, the company pressed on with developing performance indicators for the new groups. These would be crucial in signalling the expected relationship with headquarters. The outcome was evaluation 'basically on, within a given period, profitability measures such as ROA (return on assets), growth, improvement and accomplishment of accounting objectives, and in addition customer satisfaction, proactive investment, preparations for the future through R&D, contribution to society, etc.'[4] In addition, the ceiling for investments not requiring headquarters approval was raised by a factor of ten to ¥1 billion.

Governance structure

A new corporate level decision-making structure was created. Hitherto the key forum for debate and executive decision-making had been the Executive Committee (*jomukai*, with twenty-two members at the Senior Executive Managing Director level and above). Creeping centralization had made this a bottleneck for decision-making, and various attempts had been made to clear the backlog by creating other committees, with little lasting success:

There was the Executive Committee, the Vice Presidents Committee, and there have been lots of other committees in the past, started and stopped, in order to speed things up. But they didn't really work. The Executive Committee was meant to debate strategy, but it couldn't really, because members represented divisional interests, and so the Vice Presidents Committee was set up, and so on.[5]

---

[2] Cf. a report by H. Wakabayashi (an authority on Hitachi among Japan's financial community) of Dresdner Kleinwort Benson, 14 July 1998; also *Nikkei sangyo shinbun*, 30 October 1998.

[3] Eg. *Nikkei Business*, 2 November 1998, pp. 70–3; also 1 June 1998, p. 25.

[4] www.hitachi.co.jp/topics/99.4/01a-6.hmtl (accessed 9 July 1999). ROE (return on equity) was subsequently added. The corporate R&D labs were simultaneously reorganized as a business division equivalent, with their own evaluation criteria.

[5] Interview, corporate planning manager, 5 January 2000.

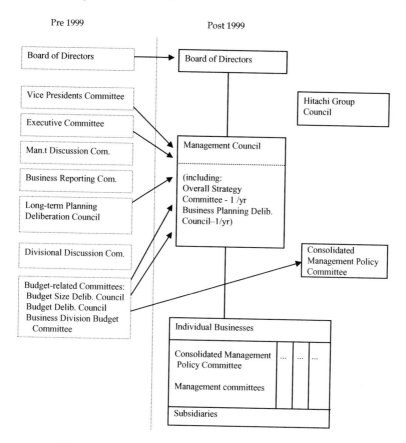

Figure 10.1   Decision-making bodies, pre-1999 and post-1999
Source: Company document.

Under the new structure, these committees were rationalized (figure 10.1). The key forum for debate became the new Management Council (MC, *keiei kaigi*), with eleven members – the president (chair of the council), the chairman, vice-chairman, five vice-presidents, and three corporate senior executive managing directors (from finance, personnel and the secretariat). The number of Board members was also halved, from over thirty to fourteen (the MC members plus the CEOs of key groups – semiconductors, information and electric power – chaired by the chairman). The MC was to be the main forum for debate and *de facto* decision-making about Hitachi Ltd and direct subsidiaries, but the Board was not simply to be a legal rubber stamp – it was also to take into account broader Hitachi Group issues from the perspective of consolidated management. These, however, would mainly be debated elsewhere, as we shall see.

In 1999, therefore, the role of the Board was modified slightly, but not radically. Hitachi did not introduce outside directors, as a number of other companies (like Sony) were beginning to do. To bring in outside views, it instituted an Advisory Board, with five external members, to meet with the president and vice-chairman twice a year.[6] Despite growing debate in Japan about creating stronger, more independent auditing bodies, too, initially at least this was not seen as a reform priority.[7]

A key objective was to speed up decision-making. There were tangible results at the corporate level. Within weeks the MC was said to be dealing with 10–12% of the business of the former Executive Committee.[8] Decisions were being devolved to the groups, individual responsibilities were clarified, and directors were required to make decisions on the spot, with little time to arm themselves with the customary wadges of documents and staff advice. The new president was critical in forcing through these changes. He downplayed traditional 'root binding' and internal consensus mechanisms, and as we noted, in June he announced that he had agreed with the president of NEC to merge most of their DRAM operations, to the surprise of most within the company.

Creating the same momentum within the new groups was more problematic. On the one hand, headquarters was reluctant to take the lead and enforce changes, since it would undermine the objective of devolving authority. On the other hand, there was some confusion within the groups as to just what they should now be doing. The problem was manifest in the process of choosing the new CEOs: 'It was like trying to find ten company presidents, who could manage risk, all at once', mused a senior personnel manager.

'i.e. Hitachi Plan'

The focus sceptics got their answer with the 'i.e. Hitachi Plan' ('i.e.' referring to information and electronics), unveiled in November 1999. To effect a shift 'from a manufacturer to a solutions-providing company', ¥300 billion would be invested in acquisitions, equity participation and

---

[6] The initial members were the chairman of Japan Life Insurance, Hitachi's largest shareholder, the chairman of Morgan Stanley Japan, an Emeritus Professor of Keio University (an authority on women's studies), a prominent lawyer, and a former US Assistant Secretary of Commerce.

[7] Four of the six corporate auditors in 1999 were former senior directors, a fifth was an ex-director who had become the president of a subsidiary and the other was a former diplomat.

[8] It exceeded the target 80% reduction: *Hitachi shaho*, March 1999, p. 5.

alliances (at least 80% in sectors related to information systems; sixty projects were reported to be under consideration), ¥200 billion in existing IT business, and ¥50 billion in a new Internet-based solutions business. Conversely, (unnamed) products would be selected for pruning, with manufacture ceasing 'within one year'. The goal was to achieve 70% of sales in information-related sectors by 2003, including 25% in services.

The medium-term plan focused on business expansion rather than employee reduction. It was set out in unprecedented detail and market approval was signalled by a rise in the share price of 3%. Managers claimed it represented a break from 'stapler planning' (*hotchikisu chokei* – assembling plans from the divisions and stapling them together; a caricature of former long-term planning). The mood inside the company, at least in and around headquarters, began to change. Perhaps change was possible. With the benefit of hindsight, of course, the plan was doomed by the bursting of the IT bubble just months later.

Hitachi Group reforms

At the same time that the new organization structure was created, new bodies were launched for generating Hitachi Group strategy, and improving Group co-ordination, efficiency and responsiveness.[9]

As described in chapter 8, beyond highly dependent subsidiaries, Group companies were traditionally quite independent. Little active effort had been made to co-ordinate Group company strategies. Several factors converged to change this tradition. First, it had become imperative to address high purchasing costs within the Group. Second, reforms within Hitachi Ltd sometimes had adverse consequences for Group companies, which in the long run could come back to haunt the core company. As the company embarked on restructuring, more attention had to be paid to these. Third, the introduction of new consolidated reporting requirements in 1999 would raise the visibility and hence importance of Group results. And fourth, in a positive sense, it was recognized that there were many resources within the Group which could be leveraged more effectively to generate new business.

A new Hitachi Group Council, described in Hitachi Ltd's Annual Report (2000) as 'a virtual board of directors for the whole group', was established to discuss and propose strategy.[10] At the same time, a

---

[9] 'Group' is written with a capital 'G' here to avoid confusion with the internal groups ('virtual companies').

[10] The 'wise men' at the inaugural meeting were the chairman and president of Hitachi Ltd, and the chairmen or presidents of Hitachi Metal, Hitachi Cable, Hitachi Credit, Hitachi Software Engineering, Nissei Sangyo (trading company) and Hitachi Chemical.

Group Strategy Office was established 'to formulate and oversee concrete strategies based on decisions made by the Committee'. A new post of vice-chairman was created to concentrate on Group development.[11] Said the designee at his first press conference: 'The company will move aggressively in merging affiliates and acquiring companies outside the group to create a company that can win in the world market.'[12]

The flurry of resulting initiatives cannot be reviewed in any depth here. The new net company was created, armed with Hitachi's B2B infrastructure platform TWX-21. A corporate venture capital office with a ¥10 billion fund was set up to invest in new technology business (in-house and external, but especially in the USA, or Silicon Valley). An array of domestic and international alliances, mergers and spinouts was announced.[13] Bits of Hitachi Ltd's operations were separated off and merged with Group companies.[14] The consolidated management strategy identified different kinds of Group companies – large 'independents', subsidiaries of the Hitachi Ltd virtual company groups, and service operations – and proposed a different strategy for each.

Service operations included financial services. In 1998 financial service companies were given the goal of generating 30% of consolidated profits on a stable basis. In October 2000 the biggest companies, Hitachi Credit and Hitachi Lease, were merged to create Hitachi Capital, Japan's largest leasing company, with growing business in retail, credit cards, securitization and business outsourcing. Clearly inspiration was derived from GE Capital, which expanded aggressively in Japan in the late 1990s, and whose share of GE turnover and profits reached 48% and 27% respectively by 1998.[15] The president of Hitachi Capital denied that GE Capital was his model, however, and declared that as part of the Hitachi Group his job was to support manufacture, and that the company's growth would be organic.[16]

---

[11] The chairman was still officially responsible for overall Group matters. The media speculated that the new post was the product of succession politics.

[12] H. Kuwahara, cited in *Nikkei Weekly*, 28 December 1998.

[13] Alliances included, for instance, a joint venture with GE and Toshiba in nuclear fuels, with Matsushita (National/Panasonic) in a broad range of consumer electronics, with Fujitsu in plasma display panels, and UMC in wafer fabrication.

[14] Examples include the merger of Nissei Sangyo with Hitachi Ltd's instruments and semiconductor equipment operations to create Hitachi High Technologies, of Hitachi Techno Engineering with industrial machinery systems operations to create Hitachi Industries Co Ltd, and in telecommunications the merger of Kokusai Electric, Hitachi Denshi and Yagi Antenna to create Hitachi Kokusai Electric Inc.

[15] Sasaki, 1999. Plender dubbed GE Capital as 'an ever-larger cuckoo in the GE group's nest' (FT.com, 31 July 2000).

[16] M. Hanabusa, interviewed in *Nikkei Business*, 5 June 2000, pp. 72–5. GE Capital accounted for two-thirds of GE's 100 or so acquisitions (worth a cumulative $51 billion) between 1997 and 2000.

In late 1999 Hitachi Investment Management was established to manage Group pension fund assets. A joint venture was announced with Tohmatsu, a major accounting firm, to develop, market and support software for calculating retirement lump sum and pension packages. Hitachi was not abandoning manufacture by any stretch of the imagination, but it was also seeking rapid development in services, both to improve internal efficiency, and as a source of new business. From a technology development perspective, it was also investing significantly in cashless finance and e-commerce, participating for instance in the (ill-fated) Mondex consortium.

Job design and business processes

The new organization structure envisaged a reduction in corporate headquarters staff, from 1,200 to 400. Some of the balance would become 'business staff', providing specialized services to the new groups.[17] But just what jobs were to be done by corporate staff and business staff, and staff within the new groups? How would they be linked? Should they basically be doing their old jobs, only better, or something else? Could some jobs be automated? Or outsourced?

The opening salvo of a business process reform campaign was the establishment in early 2000 of a new outsourcing company – Triple Win – to handle payroll administration and routinized accounting and finance work, first for Hitachi Ltd, and subsequently for Group companies. A project team headed by a vice-president subsequently started work to: propose and implement ways to professionalize, systematize and make more efficient management and service activities; drastically improve business processes through IT; and construct a new database architecture for knowledge management.[18] Targeting purchasing, accounting and HRM, it envisaged more extensive changes over the next two years than those hitherto achieved under MI (management improvement) activities.

The HRM team, including external consultants ('to get an outside perspective'), began by debating the types of human resources and hence HRM the company would need (based on figure 11.3), HRM in referent companies such as GE, HP and Sony, and current work organization. A survey showed that 50% of the time of managers and white-collar staff was being spent on processing work which was 'unlikely to produce value added'. They concluded that too much work was being done

---

[17] In 2000 the notion of 'corporate staff' and 'business staff' was applied to the group headquarters as well.

[18] *Hitachi shaho*, October 2000, p. 2.

through habit, there were too many duplicated procedures and overlapping responsibilities, too much reliance on paper and poor management of knowledge. A major shakeup was needed to achieve 'global level process excellence'.

The next few months were spent gathering knowledge of some 300 HRM and general affairs processes and their local variations, systematizing the information, and preparing a shared service call centre. Loosely modelled after that of Fujitsu, the call centre was opened in late 2001. As part of a simultaneous move towards 'self responsibility', employees would input web-based requests for information and services at their work or home terminals. Indirect employees would no longer receive printed pay slips. They would not be able to order new name cards locally. They would input their working hours which, after approval by their superior, would be sucked up into the Triple Win pay calculation computers. Requests for travel costs would be similarly handled. Long a bone of contention and symbol of bureaucracy (and power of the accounting function), these requests would no longer have to wind their way through personnel and accounting departments collecting signatures.

As a result of these measures, it was envisaged that the ratio of HRM staff to employees would be reduced by two-thirds, to one in a hundred. Some of those displaced at the local level were absorbed by the call centre, others were redeployed to functions like sales. Those left had to redefine their 'mission', in the words of one senior manager 'from translation (explaining systems to employees) and transaction (pay calculations, etc.) to transition (responding to external change) and transformation'. On the one hand HR and general affairs managers were glad that deep-rooted inefficiencies were being addressed ('there were five factories in our area, and we couldn't even get standard pay calculation forms'), but on the other they were concerned that if their numbers were pruned too heavily they would end up without the capacity to know the employees well and facilitate smooth workplace relations ('you'd end up like in the West, with just management–subordinate relations, and no third leg').[19]

The quest for speed, efficiency and devolved decision-making produced simultaneous efforts to flatten management and reporting hierarchies. Again, these efforts were not new, but were more concerted than in the past. In February 2001 the company announced that all posts carrying the title 'deputy' or 'vice' (*fuku shokui*) would be abolished, reducing

[19] Interview, HR and general affairs managers, 2 August 2001. The particular manager quoted was an industrial relations specialist. By implication he did not expect that grievance procedures could or should be subject to reform.

a potential ten layers to five, but with simultaneous devolution of authority, effectively reducing them even more. About 250, mostly middle-aged, managers would be affected. Some were assigned to new project teams to devise new business or efficiency plans, others were assigned officer titles, like chief marketing officer (CMO) and chief strategy officer (CSO). Commented one general manager: 'I think they're good – they're mission oriented titles. We've never really liked the deputy titles.'[20]

In sum, as flattening hierarchies and devolution raised basic questions about what managers should be doing, the organization reforms raised questions about what support staff should be doing. For some time white-collar employees had wrestled with the notion of being a 'professional', as expressed on a billboard in front of the Ebina (PC) Works: 'I am a professional, you are a professional. More speedily, more radically . . . Create 21 campaign, 21 March 1996–20 March 2001.' 'Professional', however, had been more of a slogan than a concrete concept. Now the notion of support staff was being infused with concepts of innovator and value creator, doing work which could not be purchased in the marketplace. At least that was the intent, but Hitachi is a big organization, and for some employees in far-flung parts these ideals were tempered by the daily realities of work loads and deadlines. For some, the welter of reform 'balls' being thrown from the centre threatened not liberation, but yet more work, or the prospect of being hived off into a new company.

Maximizing shareholder value?

As we have presented them so far, the organization reforms were motivated mainly by the need to restore competitiveness and to improve responsiveness to rapidly changing market conditions. In the conceptual scheme of figure 9.1, the main thrust came from product markets rather than capital or labour markets. Decision-making bodies were reformed, but outside directors were not introduced, and the auditing function was not radically strengthened.

It would be wrong, however, to say that pressures from financial markets, particularly shareholders, analysts and the finance media were inconsequential. The 'i.e. Hitachi Plan' stated:

The management of the Hitachi Group is committed to reciprocating the trust placed in it by its shareholders by improving asset efficiency and increasing the market capitalization of Hitachi Ltd. With the aim of achieving an ROE of 8%, the Hitachi Group will be managed on a consolidated basis . . . (Section 4)

[20] Interview, 12 July 2001.

At the press conference to launch the plan the new president declared: 'Our priority is to imagine ourselves in the shoes of shareholders. We must change our mindset.'[21] Did they?

Hitachi began individual meetings with major investors in the USA and Europe in 1973–4, as well as segment-based meetings with analysts and (buy side) investors. It began such meetings in Japan from around 1980, but they were rather perfunctory, as (from Hitachi's viewpoint) 'the institutional investor representatives weren't very professional'.[22]

Such meetings took on a new meaning in the post-bubble early 1990s, when stable and reciprocal shareholding began to come under strain, and business leaders and the media began to debate just who would hold the shares of Japanese companies. Maintaining share prices would require making the company more attractive to investors, and providing them with better information. By 1996, when IR (investor relations) began to emerge from the shadows of PR (public relations) in the secretariat office, segment-based quarterly meetings – for computers, semiconductors, consumer products, and power and industrial systems respectively – had been regularized, and their quality was recognized by an award from the Japan Investor Relations Association.[23]

According to the IR manager just cited, the participants were becoming much more sophisticated, so much so that Hitachi's top executives began to see these meetings as mutually beneficial, in contrast to the AGM, at which malcontents would try to air their grievances.[24] In the mid-1990s, too, it became easier for disgruntled minority shareholders to sue corporate representatives at very little cost, and this indeed happened at Hitachi over a public tender scandal.

Nonetheless, it would be safe to say that IR remained the job of a small group of specialists; most of Hitachi's managers or even directors still did not spend a great deal of time, if any, thinking about it. Even in 1997, our questions on financial deregulation were more likely to be met with relief that the pension fund could be managed more efficiently, reducing the corporate top-up burden,[25] than disquiet that the collective effect of

---

[21] Cited in the *Financial Times*, 11 November 1999.

[22] Interview, IR manager, 24 December 1998.

[23] By 1999 IR had become a separate unit, headed by a department-level manager, an almost full-time deputy manager and four staff, with additional staff in San Francisco, Singapore and London. Responsibility for credit rating agency relations was also shifted to the unit.

[24] These included people charging unfair dismissal, nuclear protesters, etc. Such a tendency in AGMs is not unique to Japan; see Charkham (1995: 28) on Germany.

[25] In 1996 Hitachi had had to pay ¥30 billion into its employee pension fund to make up for a shortfall over the previous two years. Deregulation and a buoyant US stock market helped raise the return from 3% to 5% in 1997, just short of the 5.5% which the fund required.

efficient pension fund management might be to increase pressures for higher shareholder returns.

This is despite the fact that the proportion of Hitachi's shares owned by foreign shareholders had increased to 27% by 1997 (and almost 32% by the end of 1999, where it hovered for the next few years). IR staff acknowledged that such shareholders sometimes demanded greater efforts to raise profits during investor meetings, but they were not activists. They were more interested, they suggested, in capital gains – Hitachi's shares tended to fluctuate with the Nikkei average – and currency gains. If investors wanted spectacular returns, they would invest in high risk–high return ventures. One manager pointed out that in the year of Hitachi's massive loss, when no dividend was paid in the second half of the year, the company's share price actually rose by almost 40%![26]

Things started to change in 1999. IR awareness began to spread beyond the confines of the IR unit. Commented one manager:

In the past it was like they (shareholders) were air or water, or public infrastructure – you don't notice them, but you're in trouble if they're not there. I guess this was because of reciprocal shareholding. This is breaking down, and it has introduced a certain tension into the relationship. A new relationship may emerge from this, but at the moment it's rather tense as we recognize them for the first time.[27]

One factor promoting awareness was the 8% ROE (return on equity) target, to be attained within five years. This target was set with 'global standards' in mind – if other leading companies were achieving double digit ROEs, Hitachi had to get at least 8%. It was also felt, however, that 8% was needed to ensure future development of the company, from a *management* perspective. There were no immediate plans to raise the dividend of ¥11, or 22% of the par value of the shares. Even top union officials believed that 8% ROE was in principle a good target to be aiming for:

Emphasizing shareholders is the trend these days. That's fine, as long as the attitude towards employees and customers isn't adversely effected. Support of and respect for customers and employees is needed, or the company will disappear as trust collapses . . . I met with the President and Chairman today, and they haven't changed . . . The union will benefit if we can get 8%.[28]

Second, 'imagining ourselves in the shoes of shareholders' and adopting 'global standards' required greater efforts to improve the quality and clarity of information. Senior accounting managers decided that Hitachi

---

[26] Interview, 24 December 1998.   [27] Interview, 5 January 2000.
[28] Interview, 6 January 2000. The reasons for the last sentence will become clear in chapter 12.

would be one of the first major Japanese companies to list shareholdings at market rather than purchase value, and they embarked on a campaign to establish quarterly accounting, internally from 2001, and publicly from 2002, as well as to publish non-consolidated and consolidated results simultaneously. The release of consolidated performance information was reorganized around seven segments. Again however, from a management perspective the establishment of quarterly accounting was a step in the quest to establish a 'real time' management capability, which those in the rapid product cycle and market change segments had long complained was impeded by procedures originating in the heavy electric segment.

Stock options

In 1996 the general opinion within Hitachi was that stock options might work for image-conscious companies like Sony, or for fast-growth startups, but not for Hitachi. In 1997, a vice-president suggested they were 'a possibility', but there were tax and other obstacles, so they could not be introduced right away.[29] The 1999 'i.e. Hitachi Plan' announced that 'the introduction of a stock option system is being studied as part of the increased management emphasis on the shareholders' perspective'. In April 2000 a scheme was introduced which featured options for the fourteen directors and fifty-seven corporate officers, together with a new Hitachi Executives' Shareholding Association, and a new measure for the existing Hitachi Employees' Shareholding Association. Together they were 'intended to contribute to the maximization of corporate value by heightening the motivation of directors and employees'.[30]

The seventy-one stock option recipients would receive shares ranging from 20,000 for the chairman, vice-chairman and president, to 5,000 for corporate officers and corporate fellows. In total, this would mean a maximum of 527,000 shares, a small drop in the existing bucket of 3.4 billion shares. As one of the architects of the system commented:

To be honest, I feel a certain contradiction. I personally think that selflessness (*mu-shi*) is an important part of the management mind, like the founder of IBJ (Industrial Bank of Japan) once said, but this is a mechanism to link management thinking to the share price and company assets.[31]

It was unlikely that the scheme would make up for the directors' remuneration cuts during the restructuring, but it was another signal

---

[29] Interview, 5 September 1997.   [30] Press release, 28 April 2000.
[31] Interview, 6 January 2000.

to investors that managers were being encouraged to be more mindful of their interests. The Hitachi Executives' Shareholding Association was intended to do the same thing for Group executives (of around 150 domestic companies) 'by making it easier for them to purchase the Company's stocks', though no details were offered at the time.

The third feature of the scheme was a new measure for the Hitachi Employees' Shareholding Association, which was started in 1971 as a measure to help employees in asset building, while at the same time increasing the stable shareholder base of the company.[32] Hitherto, employees of Hitachi Ltd and non-listed Group companies could purchase shares, and the company would add 5% to their investment as an 'encouragement allowance'. In 1998 there were almost 30,000 members with 68 million shares, enough to place the Association in the top five shareholders. The new scheme would provide an *additional* allowance of 1–10%, depending on the company's performance. According to the press release: 'The new measure is aimed both at encouraging members to build their assets and at raising their awareness and motivation regarding consolidated business performance.' Again, it was primarily a signalling measure, and the financial significance was limited.

We should also note that in April 2001 a campaign was launched (assisted by Fidelity), with meetings, an intranet site and call centre to educate employees about personal asset management, called Hitachi Financial Community. Subsequently, when enabling legislation came into effect in October 2001, Hitachi was a front-runner in introducing a 401K-type pension. The company gave employees the option of taking half of the old lump sum retirement money and putting it into their wages, or converting it into a 401K-type pension, with a choice of seven fund management companies. While linked more to efforts to promote 'self-reliance' (which we shall look at below) in the press release, indirectly these developments can be seen as supporting attempts to promote greater employee awareness of shareholders.

New governance system

The reforms embarked on by Hitachi in 1998–9 are ongoing. A new phase was entered in 2003 with the launch of a new medium term plan – 'i.e. Hitachi Plan II' – and, as we have noted several times, a new governance system for Hitachi Ltd and its eighteen listed subsidiaries. The former featured a plan to exit businesses accounting for 20% of its current turnover

---

[32] Normally they would have to buy shares in bundles of 1,000, but through the Association, employees could buy smaller lots.

by 2005–6, using an economic value added indicator to inform exit decisions (see chapter 13). The latter featured the new 'American-style' committee system, with external directors, and nomination, compensation and audit committees. At first glance these developments suggest a conversion to shareholder capitalism, finally, whereas the earlier reforms merely created a half-way house. A closer look suggests continuity with the earlier reform trajectory, emphasizing restoration of corporate vitality and an acceptable return on capital.

The new Board of June 2003 had thirteen members. Six were serving directors, and two were auditors and former directors. One was the chairman of Hitachi Capital (underlining the importance of consolidated management, the growing importance of financial services, as well as the personal skills of the appointee). The remaining four were outsiders – a former ranking Labour Ministry official, and president of the Japan Association for the Advancement of Working Women;[33] the chairman of Asahi Glass; the chairman of Nippon Steel; and a senior partner of the law firm Nishimura and Partners.

None could be considered a direct representative of shareholder interests. The selection reflected a perceived need for external management perspectives, and the need to keep abreast of rapid changes in the legal environment while giving due consideration to employee relations, particularly better utilization of the skills of women. This was particularly evident in the composition of the audit committee.[34]

Several of the 1999 bodies were abolished or streamlined, including the Advisory Board and the Hitachi Group Committee, to promote faster decision-making, and more substantive external input. (External directors now had legal responsibilities, former advisers did not.) The news release gave four reasons for the adoption of the new system: improved speed; greater transparency; strengthened consolidated management; and strengthened global management.[35]

It is significant that all of Japan's general electric companies adopted the committee system. Whether they would have done so had their performance been better, like Toyota or Canon (two vocal advocates of the classic model and critics of the American-style system) is a moot point.

---

[33] Sato Ginko, who was closely involved in the drafting of the Equal Employment Opportunity Law in the mid-1980s.

[34] The audit committee consisted of the two current (former senior director) auditors, the chairman of Nippon Steel Corporation (well versed in corporate restructuring), the former Labour Ministry official and the legal expert.

[35] Regarding global management, it noted 'While preserving the strengths of its existing corporate governance structure, Hitachi will adopt a corporate governance format that is easily understood by institutional investors based in the US and Europe, its customers and other parties, to foster greater trust in its governance, and thus speed up the pace of global business development' (news release, 31 January 2003).

The sheer complexity of their operations, too, may have encouraged them to adopt a system which appears more open. But it is difficult to argue that the new system signifies – or will bring about – a conversion to shareholder capitalism.

Labour markets and HRM

And what of pressures from labour markets, the third set of relations in figures 9.1 and 9.4? Here we shall consider this question briefly, as well as the implications for employment relations of the organization reforms, while deferring our discussion of actual changes in employment relations and HRM to chapter 11.

Throughout the 1970s and into the 1980s, Recruit surveys placed Hitachi at or near the top of preferred destinations for Japanese science and engineering graduates. Its popularity began to dip in the bubble years of the late 1980s, not dramatically, but apparently enough to alarm top managers, who attributed the dip to too few hit products and ageing facilities, especially dormitories. They embarked on a campaign to upgrade facilities, and to rectify their 'second runner' (follower) image.[36] Hitachi climbed back up the table, but in 1996 it dropped to eighth place, then to seventeenth, twenty-fifth, and by 1999 in the depth of its crisis, it plunged to an unprecedented fortieth. It fared even worse in the arts and humanities graduate table. It is little wonder the top management felt they had to restore the attractiveness of the company.[37]

This feeling was compounded by a growing fear of losing able employees. The overall separation figures gave little cause for alarm – for male graduates they were still under 1%, and long-term the increase had not been dramatic.[38] However, managers were reporting that in jobs in which an external labour market was growing – notably for systems, software and IT engineers, and indirect staff with international skills – they were now losing good people. An increase in non-Japanese businesses offering challenging work and more pay meant that leaving was no longer tantamount to downgrading career prospects, and persistent calls from headhunters meant that such employees were likely to know what their options were.

It was not enough to upgrade welfare facilities to keep such people. They needed to be given choices, challenging jobs, and chances to increase their employability. Managers acknowledged that efforts to

---

[36] Kono, 2000: 14–16. Hitachi did have hit products, but its 'second runner' image stuck.
[37] In 2000 it climbed back up to eleventh, and in 2001 to eighth. It dropped back to thirteenth following its second disastrous result, in 2002.
[38] Eighteen per cent of the 1985 male cohort had left by 2000, up from 15% for the cohort five years earlier. For women the comparable figures were 62%, up from 50%.

provide these might actually increase the separation rates, but failure to do so would also lead to an increase, as well as an increase in demotivated workers. While not advertised prominently, therefore, restoring the attractiveness of the company as a challenging place to work, and gaining appeal as a place to develop skills and employability (which might potentially be used outside the company at a later date), were actually important considerations in the reforms.

Conversely, the organization reforms had implications for employment practices and HRM. One was the devolution of authority for employment and human resource management. As we saw, the initial attempt to create internal groups in 1995 avoided this issue, for good reason. It was a critical industrial relations issue, and the company would have to move very carefully. No change, however, could send the message that devolution was, again, partial. Irrespective of signals, the purpose of the organization reforms was to re-establish competitiveness in different markets. Failure to do so would cost jobs and/or result in units being spun out, so it was in the interests of both management and the union to come up with appropriate solutions. The reformist view, that HRM needs of the various groups were very different, and were an integral part of developing group strategies, is shown in figure 11.3.

Devolution would not just introduce diversity between groups, but some CEOs would want to introduce more diverse employment contracts for their own employees. There were other pressures, too. What would happen to employees who now found themselves stuck in a 'virtual company' group they did not want to be in through a quirk of posting? This was not simply a question of how movement between groups would be handled, but as part of a simultaneous move to emphasize performance in pay and promotion, it was only fair that employees should be in a workplace they felt they could perform in. As a result, an internal job posting system was introduced in 1999. The reforms also envisaged a greater proactive movement of personnel between Group companies. Both measures were extended under the 2003 'i.e. Hitachi Plan II'.

As pieces of the company were increasingly spun out, or sold off altogether, it was becoming increasingly unlikely that employees who began their working lives in the company would continue to work there until retirement. In which case, was it more responsible to carry on under the assumption that they would, or to recast the company's responsibility to employees in terms of facilitating their career development through raising their 'employability'? And who was the best judge of how to raise employability, anyway? 'Standing on your own feet' (jiritsu) and choice were new concepts introduced into the reforms, as we shall see.

These concepts were congruent with the principles of devolution, which emphasized clarifying loci of responsibility as well as placing responsibility in operating units. They were also congruent with some aspects of the business process reforms, which required employees to input data into IT systems themselves, or seek information themselves. And they matched the emphasis in the new remuneration system on performance and contribution. In other words, pressures from labour markets, as well as from product and finance markets, and management attempts to restore entrepreneurial vigour, were leading to conceptually coherent changes in the employment relationship which were in principle as fundamental as those of the 1960s, and certainly more significant than anything since.

Concluding comments: market forces and the spirit of the reforms

If there is something in common between the pressures from product, finance and labour markets, it is that they were compelling the company to address them in the short term, rather than promise that they would be satisfied in the long term. Customers wanted new products right away; in some markets product cycles had been reduced to a matter of months. Shareholders wanted evidence of management action now. And employees with marketable skills wanted challenging job assignments and recognition of their performance now, faster than in the past. Propelling these pressures was greater choice. These pressures do not necessarily bring about short term*ism*, but they demand responses in the short term.

Second, they were compelling the company to become more open and outward looking. In some cases this meant the penetration of market principles. A number of functions became profit centres – manufacturing technology, for instance, which led a 'Hi Speed 21' digital engineering campaign, as well as intellectual property, and some general affairs functions (these were typically functions of the old headquarters but not the new) – and others were outsourced. The centrifugal push of work and employees from the core company outward was also propelled in part at least by market referencing. But it is difficult to argue that market forces were the main ideological driver of the reforms. Paradoxically, perhaps, it was felt that monitoring costs, which were rising under the reforms, could begin to outweigh savings if they were given too free a rein.

At an ideological level, therefore, classic model principles were modified, but not abandoned.

11   Recasting the Employment Relationship

In chapter 5 we saw that executives' views of corporate governance and employment reforms were only loosely coupled, at least in the late 1990s. So it was at Hitachi. Employment and human resource management (HRM) reforms actually began in April 1998, before the organization reforms outlined in the last chapter. It was only later that they became interlinked, and at the same time more ambitious.

Classic model employment practices had remained relatively unchanged at Hitachi for three decades because, personnel managers argued, they worked. By the mid-1990s, however, there were growing misgivings. The practices had been designed primarily around blue-collar workers, who in the 1960s constituted over half of the workforce. By the mid-1990s the proportion had declined to less than 30%. Most employees were now white-collar workers. The proportion of university graduates had risen from 10% to over 30%, and 1,750 had Ph.Ds.[1] Increasingly, the future of the company depended on the creative output of such employees.

The practices were also designed around a youthful workforce, with an average age of 28 in the mid-1960s. By the mid-1990s this had risen to 39, and average tenure from seven years to eighteen years. This created pressures on labour costs, as well as on management tracks.

Stimulating white-collar creativity and performance, rethinking posts and promotion criteria, and controlling labour costs, therefore, were critical objects of reform. Then came moves to link management behaviour with the organization reforms described in chapter 10. The growing momentum for reform soon developed into a broad-based attempt to recast the employment relationship, de-emphasizing loyalty and stressing self-responsibility, and sometimes employability. Ultimately all employees were covered by a new HRM package introduced in 2004. The

---

[1] The majority of Ph.D.s were gained while working as part of the career development of R&D employees.

abolition of automatic annual wage increases (*teiki shokyu*) was seemingly for employment practices what the committee system was for corporate governance – a negation of the classic model. But was it?

The 1998 HRM reforms: fostering and rewarding creativity

Background to reform

Hitachi's classic model employment practices were largely built around blue-collar workers, but the company also introduced a number of innovations in the management of white-collar workers in the 1960s. It was one of the first Japanese companies to introduce a dual ladder system, in 1964–5. In 1966, too, sections in indirect departments were abolished, to reduce sectionalism and to encourage flexibility. In theory, this flattened the organization and reduced the number of formal management posts, but in practice section managers were replaced by deputy department managers. These posts were finally abolished in 2001. And in 1968 a nascent form of management-by-objectives (MBO) was introduced, although it was never really developed.

The 1998 reforms, then, had echoes as far back as the 1960s. As growth became more modest in the 1970s and 1980s, and the 1960s recruits were promoted, the number of 'professionals' (or 'specialists' – this term is closer to the Japanese *senmon shoku*) increased, and their functions became less clear.[2] By the mid-1990s these employees were coming into their 50s, and attempts were made to curb their growing wage bill.[3] Many were transferred to subsidiaries.

If the baby boomer bulge were the only problem, the company might have been prepared to wait it out. An even more threatening bulge making its way through the company, however, was the 'Heisei bubblers'. Based on optimistic economic forecasts and gloomy demographic projections, Hitachi had joined other major Japanese companies in a scramble for recruits during the 'Heisei bubble' years of the late 1980s, doubling its normal graduate intake. In the scramble, recruitment standards (as measured, for instance, by general aptitude tests) fell. By the mid-1990s

---

[2] In 1971 only 4% of employees were either managers or specialists. By the mid-1990s the proportion had risen to 15%, mostly through an increase in the latter.

[3] From 1993 those aged 52 or older who got poor evaluations faced wage increase curbs and potential cuts in their bonus. The age is significant; it was calculated that living costs began to diminish after 52.

these recruits were surging towards the management and specialist tracks, which were already under strain.[4]

> Everyone rises to T6 (the intermediate grade). There are about 5,000 people there at the moment, and they are union members. As it is, most will join the management ranks (as managers or specialists). There will be too many bosses, and wage push. Posts are normally pyramid shaped, but this is like an inverse pyramid. An organization can't survive with an inverse pyramid.[5]

Further, there was the time-based management problem, symbolized by the 'sleeping bag affair'. Managers in 1997 told of an employee who had slept in a sleeping bag at the office while working at a design company in Silicon Valley, but was prevented from doing this back in Japan by working hour restrictions. In part this was seen as a difficulty of having a single union for both blue-collar and white-collar workers, and standardized conditions in collective agreements to cover them, with legal restrictions as well, but it was said to adversely affect the way creative workers approached their work. They weren't clock watchers, but ticking clocks prevented them from focusing fully on their work.

And, of course, there was the *nenko*-based management problem, the ancient thorn-cum-pillar of personnel management.

A major review of the pay and promotion system started in 1995, with a view to increasing emphasis on performance. The qualitative question for the committee was how to create a new, results-focused approach to working. The quantitative question was total labour costs. As a proportion of value added (but not necessarily turnover) these had risen markedly (cf. table 8.2), and threatened to rise even more. Some middle managers in particular felt strongly that this was a management problem, and it was unreasonable to make employees pay for the consequences:

> I think it's wrong for the management just to demand wage restraint without improving management itself – that's an abrogation of responsibility. If we dropped wages by 50% would we be able to get more orders? I don't think that's the real problem.[6]

Of these two concerns – white-collar productivity and total wage costs – by mid-1997 the former had emerged as the central thrust of the reforms planned for 1998. Said the personnel director:

[4] Promotion through the lower 'planning' grades was automatic. High fliers were promoted from these to the first of two intermediate grades at age 29, and into the ranks of specialists of managers at 34. Half the cohort could achieve this promotion by 38, and 90% would achieve it during the course of their career.

[5] Interview, personnel manager, 5 September 1997. This was a problem for the union, too, as the employees would cease to be union members when they left the intermediate grades.

[6] Interview, 19 September 1996.

Table 11.1 *Summary of 1998 employment reforms*

System	Key area of reform
Employment system	Consider more diverse forms of employment for increasing fluidity
Qualification system	Reform planning (comprehensive) grades, emphasizing ability and performance (grades, etc. based on written descriptions)
Wage system	Reduce seniority element, reconsider wage curve, structure, allowances, greater emphasis on ability, performance
Work	Introduce new working system
Retirement lump sum, pension	Stabilize finances in medium to long term; measures to ensure post-retirement livelihood security in view of potential lowering of public pension rate, etc.
Welfare, health and safety	Reconsider club and recreation activities based on changing aspirations, health needs; strengthen mental health care
Health insurance	Stabilize finances in medium to long term
Mutual aid ass.n	Reconsider fee, prioritize provision

Source: Company mimeo, also *Rosei jiho*, 11 September 1998, p. 47 (*shading in original*).

The president says we shouldn't think of cutting costs. If we stimulate white-collar workers, costs will decrease as well. Of course we should cut unnecessary costs. There's scope for this in the pension and health insurance, and I will ask the union to show restraint on these.[7]

The HRM reforms introduced in April 1998 aimed to change the way employees in the planning grades – those destined to become managers or specialists – approached their work, to make them more reflexive, innovative and oriented towards results. The reforms were the first stage of an evolving and expanding agenda, but as they were introduced before the organization reforms were even drawn up, and before facilitating legal reforms, the actual path was not clear at the time. A summary of the reforms is given in table 11.1.

Qualification system

The first feature was a new qualification system. This did not replace 'ability' as the key consideration for advancement, but sought to make the criteria more transparent and objective, and to de-emphasize seniority. Under the old system the criteria were particularly fuzzy in the intermediate grades, which the Heisei bubblers were about to surge into. Now all planning, management and specialist grades were placed in a single hierarchy, and pre-management grades would have both a general description

[7] Interview, 5 September 1997.

of the qualities needed to achieve that grade, and fifteen job type-based descriptions, which did not exist before. Promotion through the lower grades would no longer be automatic. Assessment would not be relative – there would not be a fixed number of promotions in a given year. It would be possible to skip grades, and, after a lead-in period, demotions would also be possible.

Wage system

The second feature was a new wage system, again for planning grades. The base component, which made up 40% of the wage, was retained, but now called the 'base ability wage', with more emphasis on ability and less on seniority. Fixed and variable supplements were merged into a new 'job ability wage', constituting most of the balance, based on the grades and five steps within the grades. Personnel managers were determined to keep seniority not just out of the grades, but the steps as well. Only minor changes were made to the supervisory, manual and clerical grades at this time.

Work system

The third feature was a new system to promote working flexibility in terms of time and place, to encourage individual responsibility and creativity. Flex-time for indirect workers, with four hours of 'core time' was introduced in 1988. It was widely used, although sometimes, managers lamented, as an excuse for coming in late. In 1990, too, the company had bought out thirty hours of overtime (reduced to twenty hours in 1997). The new scheme systematized these developments, and linked them to the new pay system.

As managers and specialists were already fully salaried the new system did not directly affect them, except that they were now eligible to work from a satellite office or home. The main group targeted again, as table 11.2 shows, was those in the intermediate planning grades (now C6 and lower C5). Under the new system they, too, were eligible to work from home or from a satellite office, but in addition they could work to a new flex-time regime with no core time, and they would not be paid for overtime. In return, they would receive an allowance equivalent to thirty hours of overtime per month, and a results-based supplement to the biannual bonus. To avoid breaking the Labour Standards Law, the system had to be voluntary, those consistently putting in more than thirty hours of overtime would have to come off it, and night and holiday working would require further supplements.

Table 11.2 *New work system*

Qualification	Time management system	Remuneration	Satellite office, home working?
Upper C5+	n.a.	(salaried)	yes
C6, lower C5	new work system	new work allowance; results-based bonus	yes
-C7 and supervisory	flex-time	allowance in lieu of overtime	no
Others	flex-time (indirect)	allowance in lieu of overtime	no

Source: *Rosei jiho*, 11 September 1998, p. 54.

Intellectual property

Finally, although not directly related to these reforms, Hitachi was also beginning to raise the payback it gave to individual researchers as a result of technology licence income. Such moves by leading Japanese companies in 1998–9 reflected a growing pro-patent mood in Japan, a recognition of the growing contribution of licence fees to corporate income, a growing emphasis on patent quality rather than quantity, and a desire to keep leading researchers and their technology know-how. Relative to other companies, Hitachi had always rewarded its patenting researchers well, but it doubled the limit paid from ¥5–6 million per year to over ¥10 million.[8]

There was caution over raising the limit much higher, however, because of difficulties in measuring individuals' contributions to patents, and fears of collegial dissatisfaction. These fears, indeed, marked the caution with which the new remuneration system was drawn up and implemented. Problems in performance-based pay in other companies – notably Fujitsu – showed that these fears were well founded.

Stand on your own feet

Self-selected welfare

By themselves, the 1998 HRM reforms do not support the claim for a recasting of the employment relationship. The company now had new tools for creating incentives, but just how they were to be used is another

---

[8] *Nikkei shinbun*, 28 July 1997; 12 May 1998. The top amount it actually paid a researcher in 1998 was ¥8 million: *Nikkei sangyo shinbun*, 11 May 1999.

matter. Indeed, despite the fanfare with which they were introduced, the effects would no doubt have been modest without complementary organization and management reforms which allowed employees to work more creatively.

Reforms in welfare were measured, but were nonetheless symbolically important. As indirect labour costs amounted to 30% of direct labour costs, they naturally came under scrutiny in the 'total labour costs' debate. Both statutory and non-statutory costs were expected to rise in the coming years, and if the latter were considered 'fringe' benefits, they might well come in for heavy pruning. HRM managers, however, believed that heavy cuts in non-statutory costs would be difficult to achieve without raising wages. Instead, measures were put in place to control costs more effectively, and greater choice introduced for the sake of fairness. However, this was soon linked to the emerging emphasis on self-reliance.

The cornerstone of Hitachi's welfare policies was house ownership. Housing support measures accounted for more than half of non-statutory indirect labour costs in the mid-1990s. Rents for company dormitories and housing were raised in steps from 1997 by an average of 20–30%, and again from 2000 by roughly the same amount. This was from a very low base, however, and even with the rise, the rents would still be below the rate for (subsidized) public housing.[9] In addition, employees were expected to move out of company housing and dormitories earlier, and sliding rent scales were introduced to discourage prolonged occupancy. The company wanted to reduce the number of employees living in company housing and scrap old facilities, and at the same time extend housing support for those eligible to be living in company housing but not doing so, thereby catering for diversifying tastes and ending the disadvantage for those making their own arrangements.

In stages, too, the company withdrew from direct involvement in housing finance. Employees were encouraged to make their own arrangements with Hitachi Capital (or other sources), and to switch to floating rates. The company would now pay only half the interest above 3%. The in-house savings scheme into which the company paid a 3% interest supplement was scrapped in 1997. The company continued to pay an interest supplement for savings, but with an upper limit.

After housing support, the biggest non-statutory cost for the company was meal subsidies. These were phased out from 2000–3, and most of the ¥3.5 billion annual savings were ploughed back into a new 'cafeteria'

---

[9] Rent for a standard company '3DK' (three rooms, plus dining room, kitchen and bathroom) apartment in the capital region in 2003 was ¥32,300.

scheme, under which all employees were awarded points each year for purposes of their choice; housing, health, childcare, support for elderly parents, study, purchase of company goods, leisure and so on.[10]

The cafeteria plan had several benefits from the company's point of view. Quantification of benefits/costs in this way would not only make them easier to control, but would make them more visible to employees, who would then be less inclined to take them for granted. It would be relatively easy to add new services and remove less popular ones. And critically, not only would there be a greater sense of equity, as more employees would benefit, but they would be able to use the money for things they really wanted. This reinforced the message the company was now propagating elsewhere – employees should take charge of their own lives, and not rely on the company to arrange it for them.

Long-service awards were also incorporated into the scheme. The company proposed abolishing them, saying that choice and initiative should extend to employment, and job changers should not be disadvantaged. The union objected, and under the compromise employees aged between 35 and 45 who had been with the company for at least *one* year were eligible for a one-off award of 500 cafeteria points.

In, sports, recreation and cultural activities, the number of company-wide events was reduced. Support was focused on local activities which encouraged family participation.[11] Employees were expected to contribute more to circle activities. While there was an element of cost saving in these measures, again the main objective was to address diversifying employee interests, and dissatisfaction over some activities being sponsored by the company and others not, as well as to foster self-choice and self-responsibility.

Finally, with the same reasoning as abolishing long-service awards, in September 2000 the company introduced changes which made pension increases with years of service linear rather than S-shaped. From 2001, employees were given the new options of converting half of the retirement lump sum into a 401K-style pension, or having it incorporated into wages. Career changers joining the company should no longer be disadvantaged, the company argued, and conversely if employees thought they could better develop their careers elsewhere, they should not be prevented from doing so. The company should not try to handcuff employees, but keep them because they wanted to be there.

---

[10] The scheme was launched in 2000, when employees received 400 points, worth ¥100 each. Operation of the scheme was largely outsourced: *Fukuri kosei*, 18 July 2000, pp. 5–8.

[11] 'Pun pon' – a cross between table tennis and handball – would be retained as a company sport, however, as it was unique to the company.

By introducing these measures, the company risked sending a signal that it no longer valued loyalty. It was a calculated risk. The message was that it was not loyalty *per se* that the company valued; the company wanted people who thought about what the company should be doing, questioned it, and took initiative rather than simply taking orders. Loyalty should be a by-product of finding the company an enriching place to work in. The 'standing on your own feet' message was also a calculated risk. In the minds of many employees, such terms were of the same ilk as banners used for voluntary redundancy schemes, which the company might well be softening them up for.

Along with performance-based management of the 1998 reforms, however, these were messages that growing portions of the workforce, especially younger employees and those with externally marketable skills, were already receptive to. These were the very people whose loyalty the company was especially keen to maintain, and who managers hoped would become agents of transformation.

Although not specifically couched in this language, the company was trying to move away from the idea that it was an all-embracing 'community of fate' (*unmei kyodotai*). Over time the original purpose of the employment relationship had been obscured. It was time to bring this into focus. The message was repeated in education.

Education, training and employability

The HRM reforms were followed by the first major overhaul of education and training for over thirty years.[12] The three main features were a doubling of expenditure, revision and expansion of the contents, and a shift to self-responsibility.

Hitachi was well known for its comprehensive education and training system. In chapter 8 we quoted a company brochure which stated: 'To hire a person and not to train him/her is a failure in management.' In their survey of HRM systems in global referent companies, however, managers were alarmed to find that Hitachi's education and training expenditure relative to turnover was less than a fifth of the published figures of companies like GE, Siemens, ABB and Motorola.[13] They also felt that Hitachi's education and training system had become too insular, and failed to keep abreast of best practice, especially as a tool for business transformation.

---

[12] *Nikkei shinbun*, 8 January 2001; *Nikkei sangyo shinbun* 15 January 2001.
[13] Officially Hitachi spent ¥17 billion on education in 1999, or 0.46% of its turnover, but the figures do not include on-job training, QC circle activities or rotation training.

Content-wise, it was operations focused, and weak on strategy. Without an overhaul, they concluded, it would contribute little to the realization of the 'i.e. Hitachi Plan', and Hitachi would get left further behind in the global competition stakes.[14]

For starters, they would raise expenditure to 1% of turnover by 2002, doubling the annual number of education hours per employee from twenty to forty. The Hitachi Institute of Management Development (HIMD), now a subsidiary aiming to become a corporate university, revised its curriculum and brought in more outside lecturers. It also created an advisory board, with four internal members, three professors from Japanese universities, one from IMD and one from Michigan University. It signed a partnership agreement with the University of Maryland University College (UMUC) to provide online MBA and other graduate programmes. And more managers, especially the select L1–4 (see section 3), were sent on executive programmes at leading foreign business schools.

To participate in such programmes, to function internationally and to advance a global strategy, improved competence in English was required. In 2001 TOEIC scores became a criterion for promotion. New recruits were advised to clear 500 points (out of 990; in 2001 the average was 586), general managers needed 650 points, and to be eligible for executive selection, it was announced, 800 points would be required, a higher hurdle than any other major Japanese company.[15] The message was: 'back to school'.

Back to school meant learning to improve business performance. Since at least 1997 HRM managers had debated the balance between education to produce a 'rounded' manager, which included elements of tea ceremony, zen, haiku and music appreciation, and education to produce a 'professional' manager, which focused more on strategy, core competences and leadership. With 'fire at the gates', said one manager, the emphasis swung towards the latter.

For pre-management employees, course grids were drawn up, with levels (years in the company) on one axis, and types of training – technical/functional and various management skills – on the other, showing courses and hours or points needed for advancement. Employees were told to develop their own plans rather than waiting until they were told to go on courses. Said an HRM manager:

---

[14] Interview, training managers, 26 February 2001.
[15] Specialists in areas clearly not requiring English might be exempted and the requirements would be phased in; *Nikkei BPExpert*, 7 February 2001; *Nikkei shinbun*, 16 January 2001.

We want employees to be more entrepreneurial, to find out for themselves what direction the company should go in, and not to be ordered. But the company wants to support them in this. We have to provide a menu, but this is not enough, either. They can find good courses elsewhere, and we will make it easier for them to take these.[16]

It was better for employees to take ownership of their career development and to raise their employability, the rationale went, given the possibility of future change and reorganization. This would be good for the company, as employees would become less passive, more reflexive and innovative. Here we can discern an emerging strategic attempt to change the nature of the employment relationship, especially when considered together with the HRM, welfare and organization reforms.

HRM reform, rounds 2 and 3

Managers and HITACHI VALUE

The 1998 HRM reforms targeted pre-management employees, especially those in intermediate planning grades. Manager HRM was largely unaffected, except for the introduction of management by objectives (MBO) in 1997, which was subsequently extended to the intermediate grades. The future of the company depended more than ever on its managers and specialists, however, and in 2000 they became the subject of HRM reform, in a way that introduced a clear difference from the pre-management grades.

In February the company unveiled a chart called HITACHI VALUE (table 11.3), the background of which is as follows. When the founder died in 1951 his closest managers had debated the essence of his management philosophy, and decided on 'pioneering spirit, sincerity and harmony'. Every new recruit was told about these, but there was a sense that, over time, their real meaning was being lost, or that they needed rethinking. And with the plan to make the new groups virtual companies, something was needed to maintain a common identity. A list of ten core qualities, and behaviour exhibiting these qualities, was drawn up and presented to the new president. He is said to have gone down the list and stopped at 'harmony', insisting that this should be changed to 'respect for individuality'. In the days of the founder, he reasoned, issues were debated fully, but then they had to come to a resolution, hence 'harmony'. Over time this had come to mean obedience without debate.

---

[16] Interview, 19 February 2001. Corporate managers prepared sample grids, but details would differ by internal group.

Table 11.3 *HITACHI VALUE*

Categories		Qualities
Behaviour based on business vision	1	Customer satisfaction
	2	Trust
	3	Speed
Creation and accomplishment of change	4	Challenge and reform initiative
	5	Clarification and application of organization vision and business strategy
	6	Accomplishment of goals
Professional expertise	7	Knowledge, skills, abilities
Organization management	8	Leadership
	9	Respect for individuality
Human resource management	10	Human resource development

Source: Company mimeo.

To revive the original culture, the individual needed more respect. And so the list of table 11.3 was decided.

HITACHI VALUE clearly drew inspiration from the USA, but it was more than a normative statement about corporate culture.[17] It was introduced to better align management behaviour with corporate objectives, specifically realization of the 'i.e. Hitachi Plan'. In fact, it was to become a central feature of manager HRM.

Managers and specialists would rate themselves on each value on a scale of 1–4, their managers would give their ranking, and based on this, they would be evaluated as super, high, A, B or C.[18] With further reference to their MBO evaluation, they would be given an overall evaluation (J1 outstanding; J2 excellent; J3 good; and J4 unsatisfactory), which would largely determine their pay and promotion, as well as assignments and training. One J1 evaluation would be sufficient for promotion (and in principle necessary as well), speeding up promotion of high performers from three years to one. Under the 'range' system simultaneously introduced, average performers would eventually hit a ceiling in their grade, thus putting a cap on seniority increases.[19] Two J4s would result

---

[17] Like 'GE Values', HITACHI VALUE was printed on cards distributed to managers. The English expression was used, but in the singular form to further suggest value *to* the company.

[18] Discrepancies in the respective evaluations would be dealt with in feedback sessions.

[19] The ceiling would be hit after about ten consecutive J3 evaluations in the bottom management grade, and earlier in higher grades. A special adjustment allowance ensured that those above the ceiling would not be adversely affected until (at least) 2003. Skipping of grades became possible.

in demotion. Path dependency built into the old system would be weakened, and present contributions – 'present value' – emphasized.

A separate initiative introduced selective training and postings. In chapter 10 we noted the difficulties of finding CEOs for the new internal groups. The difficulties reinforced the message personnel managers had brought back from visits to referent foreign and Japanese companies; executive selection should start earlier, and those identified should be given special training and postings assignments to prepare them for leadership roles. Selective training and postings had hitherto been resisted for fear of demotivating those not selected. Although not publicly identified, four tiers of high fliers were selected (L1–L4), the top two under the direct authority of the president and the third and fourth under the authority of the group CEOs. Adjustments to the pool would be made on an annual basis, depending on appraisal results. Special training of the top tier began immediately in 1999 when groups were called to the HIMD for three days of debates and exercises, giving the new president a chance to observe and interact with the new executive pool. The top two tiers were given very different assignments from in the past, to broaden their experience, and to help break down boundaries and sectional walls. From these tiers an even more select group of eleven were designated 'corporate senior staff' in 2001 and charged either with setting up new businesses, or making existing ones radically more efficient. Thus, selected individuals were to spearhead the organization reforms and create new businesses (cf. Mizuno, 2004).

Round 3: the end of seniority?

The third round of HRM reform came in 2004, when a new HRM system was applied to *all* non-management employees, incorporating elements from both the 1998 reforms for the (former) planning grades, and the manager HRM reforms. Newspaper headlines announced that Hitachi was comprehensively abandoning *nenko* wages and ending automatic annual wage increases (*teiki shokyu*):

Among the companies that have already implemented company-wide performance-oriented wage systems, Canon Inc. and Honda Motor Co. still maintain de-facto periodic wage hikes for workers up to a certain age or position. Hitachi is taking the idea one step further by scrapping periodic wage hikes for all workers who have finished their initial training.[20]

---

[20] *Nikkei Weekly*, 24 November 2003. Cf. also *Asahi shinbun*, 5 November 2003.

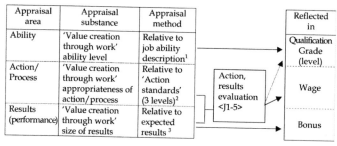

Figure 11.1 Appraisal framework, 2004
Notes:
[1] Descriptions for grades and job types form the basis of appraisal.
[2] 'Action standards' are adapted from HITACHI VALUE, with weightings by employee type.
[3] Based on MBO for planning/comprehensive grades; work performance over the period for others.
Source: Company mimeo.

The aim of the new system was to clarify, evaluate and reward 'value creation through work'.[21] First, the 1998 qualification system, with its combination of general skill level and job-type skill level definitions was retained, and generalized to the clerical and technical grades. Second, 'action standards' were set out, adapted from the HITACHI VALUE chart. And third, performance appraisal was generalized. This was based on MBO for the former planning and related grades, and work done over the appraised period for others. The system is shown in figure 11.1.

Another element taken from the management HRM reforms was the range concept, eliminating the pay overlap between the top of one grade and the bottom of the next, which previously allowed older 'plodders' in one grade to earn more than younger high fliers in the next. This is shown in figure 11.2. Within the grades, moreover, pay would be decided purely by appraisal. Those with a J1–3 appraisal would move up the range, those with J4 would not, and those with successive J5 appraisals would get a pay cut. (This would be exceptional, however, and recovery routes were considered vital. A *sine qua non* was effective feedback sessions.)

The news release declared: 'The system for determining qualifications, wages, etc. based on appraisal results will be thoroughgoing, and other

---

[21] 'For the survival and development of Hitachi, we need to continuously create "value" that customers and markets recognize. "Value creation through work" is the contribution to Hitachi's value creation that each employee contributes through their work' (company mimeo).

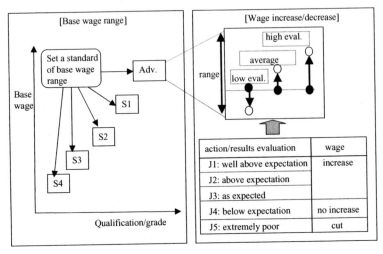

Figure 11.2 Grade, range and wage system, 2004
Source: Company mimeo.

uniform considerations like age, service and education will essentially be excluded.' The ambiguity of 'essentially' is telling; the proof of the pudding will be in the eating. As we noted in chapter 2, the very way jobs are assigned tends to create a link between *nen* and *ko*, and declaring a singular interest in *ko* does not in itself sever that connection. That said, the intention is clear, and the range system simultaneously extends the earnings differential of workers of a given age and seniority, attenuating the egalitarian aspect of *nenko*.

On the other hand, we should also note the intention to simplify, standardize and clarify the link between work, pay and promotion. All employees were being urged to contribute to HITACHI VALUE creation through their work, and their contributions would be recognized through similar principles. The wage packet itself was greatly simplified – at least for blue-collar workers – and largely standardized, with a common base component (grade × appraisal result), and various supplements (for foremen, etc.) and adjustment allowances (for new recruits with no previous appraisals).[22]

This standardizing objective is significant, and was probably intended to counterbalance centrifugal forces through growing diversity, or to set the parameters within which diversity could operate.

---

[22] The family allowance was retained, unlike Sony, which abolished it around the same time.

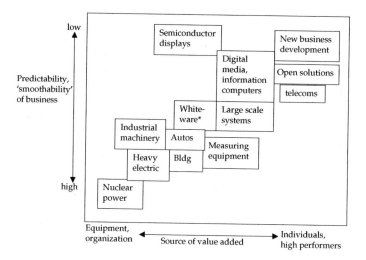

Figure 11.3 Business diversity and HRM
Note: *White-ware – refrigerators, washing machines, air conditioners, etc.
Source: Adapted from internal document; Sekijima, 2001.

From homogeneity to diversity

Diversity became an increasingly important concept from 1998, in two different senses; diversity of HRM by (internal) group, and diversity of the workforce and their contracts.

Diversity through group-based HRM

Decentralization of decision-making authority, or devolution, and the creation of internal groups, were supposed to include HRM systems. The HRM needs of telecoms and solutions business were seen to be different from those of the heavy electric operations, as suggested by figure 11.3. The classic model was formed when business was primarily in the bottom left and central portions of this figure, but the 'i.e. Hitachi Plan' envisaged the company extending more towards the top right, necessitating new systems.

Indeed IT divisions in the top right had already begun to innovate.[23] These divisions had grown rapidly from the 1970s, and recruiting was unable to keep up with growth. Numerous subsidiaries were created in

---

[23] Ideas from IT, in fact, influenced the central reforms.

various parts of Japan to enlarge the intake of systems engineers, software engineers and hardware designers. Large numbers of engineers from dispatching agencies were hired (creating workforce diversity). In some businesses, regular employees constituted a minority in the workforce. In addition, qualifications offered by Microsoft, Oracle and others became widely recognized in the 1990s, and were a factor in determining wages, and also unit prices. The 'market value' of a business could be increased with employee qualifications in a direct way.

In this context, in 1996 the (old) Information Systems Group and key subsidiaries launched their own examination system, with ten job types and three levels. Internal qualifications could be related to external ones. They would help in determining pay and costings in the rising number of collaborative projects with other companies.

In 2001 the new IT groups launched their own full-blown HRM system for pre-management employees, again with ten job types,[24] a hierarchy of ability specifications, and associated education and training grids. Financial incentives were given to gain qualifications, and pay and promotion were based on qualifications, performance and other criteria.

It was originally envisaged that each of the groups would develop its own HRM system. Corporate reforms were drawn up in the form of frameworks so as not to undermine this understanding. Subsequently, however, there was a rethink on devolution (see chapter 12), and three main types were developed – for heavy electric operations, IT, and the ubiquitous platform group. This resulted in a large number of job-type ability descriptions, but the 2004 reforms were intended to provide a common framework and hence identity.

Workforce diversity

The second type of diversity is workforce diversity, both in workforce composition and types of employment contract. This type of diversity is still in its early stages, but there has been growing recognition of its importance, as we shall see.

Some of the measures we looked at earlier in the chapter decreased the costs of mid-career movement, both into the company, and potentially out of it. Logically speaking, too, the increased emphasis on self-responsibility and individual choice should find expression in employment diversity. The 1998 reforms, as table 11.1 shows, made this an

---

[24] The ten types were: client relationship partner, solution partner, sales specialist, business promoter, business producer, project manager, system integrator, software professional, business planner and IT professional – all English terms.

explicit goal. Traditionally, of course, many workers in Japanese companies have not been 'standard' lifetime employees, and there has always been a diversity of contract types. In contrast to this diversity, though, in which the (large) company creates discrete categories, each with standardized conditions on a take-it-or-leave-it basis, the diversity we are talking about here introduces individual choice and blurs past boundaries.

Like other major Japanese technology companies, Hitachi began to experiment with hiring researchers on fixed-term contracts in the mid-1990s. The aim was to attract high-powered researchers, including foreigners, some of whom it was hoped would subsequently convert to long-term contracts. The use of such contracts, however, was purpose-specific, and limited.

Typically over 90% of Hitachi's employees had been recruited directly from school or university. A small number were hired mid-career to meet specific needs, but in the mid-1990s these had been reduced to a mere trickle – 10, 9, 6 and 5 from 1993 to 1996 respectively. The figures for 1997 to 2000, however, jumped to 122, 125, 69 (following the major loss) and 145 (almost 15% of all hires). Of the 1997 intake, 70% were posted to information systems. Forty were from financial institutions which had either gone bankrupt or were heavily restructuring (such as Nissan Life Insurance, Yamaichi Securities, Hokkaido Takushoku Bank).[25] The skills of these people would help propel Hitachi's push into financial services and solutions.

The introduction of new contracts and the increase of mid-term hires may be termed 'flexibility at the fringes'. The personnel director at the time summed up the situation neatly: 'There will be no basic change to the premise of long-term employment, but some will not be employed long-term.'[26]

Diversity was also entering the core, however, through more flexible forms of employment for existing employees. Notable here were 'gender free and family friendly' (FF) measures. Hitachi started to recruit female university graduates for its management track in the 1970s, but to a very limited extent. In the absence of supporting policies, few moved into management positions, or even stayed long-term. Recruiting was increased in the late 1980s, in the wake of the Equal Employment Opportunity Law, the recruiting boom, and a desire to present a progressive image. In 1990, in addition to maternity leave, it became possible to take childcare leave until 1 April following the child's first birthday, and short (six) hours were possible for a further two years. Re-employment was offered to those quitting for childbirth or raising children, within three years. In

<hr />

[25] *Nikkei kin'yu shinbun*, 23 April 1998.   [26] Interview, 1 September 1997.

1992 similar short hours and re-employment schemes were introduced for those taking care of elderly parents or relatives.

These measures were extended in 2000 – childcare leave for a month so that infants starting nursery in April could be settled, and the short hour option until the start of school, or until the need to take care of the elderly relative disappeared. The re-employment scheme was similarly extended. It became possible for some to work from home for the same period as well. A 'work and childrearing' site was set up on the intranet to provide information and support, and in 2003 a nursery was started by the union with company support.

The FF measures were reinforced by the new work system, and the cafeteria system. They contributed to the growing acceptance of diversity. Of course this was more noticeable in some parts of the company than others, and top HRM managers felt they still had a long way to go. Commented one manager:

Only 10% of comprehensive (pre-management/specialist) track workers in R&D and engineering are women, but in non-technical areas it is 40%, whereas six or seven years ago it was only 10%. This is having a big impact. It is introducing a different culture. I think there is growing awareness that the company can't change if we're *kintaro ame* (candy which looks the same wherever you slice it). Diversity can be a tool to bring about change.[27]

Increasing diversity and flexibility extended to retirement. From 2001, after lengthy negotiations with the union, a re-employment system for those reaching the retirement age was introduced. Four hundred employees reached the retirement age in the next six months. Of these roughly half wanted to be re-employed, and jobs were found for 80–90% of them, in subsidiaries in the majority of cases. Wages were negotiated individually, as were the hours of work.

In principle, FF policies create new opportunities for long-term employment for female employees, and re-employment of retirees also extends the length of employment. It would be wrong to assume, therefore, that diversity, flexibility and individuation will undermine long-term employment, as we argued in chapter 3. They do, however, introduce qualitative changes to the employment relationship. It is no longer a matter of accepting *the* system on offer; there is growing scope for choice and reciprocal agreement.

---

[27] Interview, 27 March 2003. The external director appointment of Sato Ginko (see chapter 10) is suggestive of a willingness to move more concertedly in this direction.

In 1996 there were only twenty female section managers or higher. In 2003 there were 130 (1.8% of the total). The number was rising rapidly, as the 40%+ remaining from the hiring surge in 1989–91 began to enter management ranks.

Concluding comments

The 1998 reforms began the first major overhaul of HRM for thirty years. They initially targeted white-collar 'knowledge workers' and their creative output and performance. They were soon complemented by the 1999 organization reforms, and this led to a more ambitious, though subtle, attempt to modify the employment relationship. The implicit contract had succeeded only too well in reducing the tension in the relationship, and top managers felt some needed to be reintroduced. They wanted employees (and managers) to be more subjective, and take more initiative in confronting the challenges the company now faced.

Relatedly, managers felt they had gone too far in the past with uniformity, and this had become dysfunctional. This was to be countered with choice, and enhancement of diversity. Shaking up psychological comfort and increasing diversity, however, created new risks, which HITACHI VALUE and its derivatives were supposed to counter. New centrifugal forces were to be balanced with a clear understanding of value creation missions, to ensure the continued survival and development of the company. This was subtly different from the centripetal forces that had operated under the classic model.

Massive organizations do not change overnight, however. Initiating reforms is not the same as embedding them. They are frequently modified and reinterpreted as they are implemented. In the next chapter we will look at the *process* of reform, and the industrial relations of reform, before attempting an evaluation.

12 The Impact on Industrial Relations

Our discussion of organization and governance reforms (chapter 10) and HRM reforms (chapter 11) would be incomplete without considering the collective, industrial relations dimension. What were the implications of the reforms for industrial relations? Conversely, how did industrial relations considerations influence the design and implementation of the reforms?

As we shall see, the union had its own reasons to seek change, in part to preserve employment, but also to meet the changing aspirations of its members. Failure to participate in reform, too, would diminish its influence. On the other hand, participation could also diminish its influence, through a fracturing or even break-up of the union, and individualized HRM. How did the union face this dilemma? And, independently of such challenges, how did it deal with challenges from within, such as growing member apathy, and the ascendance of 'knowledge workers'? These are questions we will consider in this chapter.

First we will look at industrial relations developments in the 1990s prior to 1998, and then at the industrial relations dimension of the HRM and organization reforms. Most corporate restructuring programmes have both 'high road' (value creating) and 'low road' (cost cutting) elements. We will see that industrial relations considerations and processes helped to tip the balance towards the former. Additionally, in order to avoid the danger of becoming a victim of change, accomplice of 'low road' policies or simply a bearer of bad news, the union also undertook reforms, and changed its modus operandi which was predicated on (pre-reform) corporate and industrial relations stability.

These arguments are challenged by the fallout from Hitachi's second big loss, of ¥480 billion in 2001–2, when the company sought an unprecedented 5% wage cut, and introduced its first early retirement scheme for union members for over fifty years. After considering this debacle, we offer an assessment of changing industrial relations from a stakeholder perspective.

We draw on a number of company and union surveys throughout this chapter. Such surveys are vital for the conduct of industrial relations where the power of persuasion is preferred to the persuasion of power. They form the basis for identifying employee/member dissatisfactions, demands, approval, etc. and for justifying positions taken. Both company and union are very sensitive about their use for purposes other than originally intended, however, and for reasons of confidentiality they are not individually attributed and direct figures are not taken from them.

Industrial relations to 1998

Co-operative industrial relations at Hitachi were established in the aftermath of a monumental dispute in 1950, as described in chapter 8. In fact, 'co-operative industrial relations' does not fully express the overlapping interests that evolved between the union and the management. What this means in brief is, first, that the union was bound to give ultimate priority to the continued prosperity of the company, as jobs and livelihoods depended on this. On the other hand, managers internalized the importance of protecting jobs and livelihoods.

Second, conventional bargaining constituted a relatively minor – if important – part of the collective employee–employer relationship. Consultation mechanisms were extensive and crucial. Failure to consult sufficiently would constitute a severe breech of trust. Formally, management guarded its 'right to manage', and the collective contract laid out clearly which issues were subject to negotiation, which were subject to discussion-debate (but not necessarily agreement), to opinion exchange, reporting, and notification only. Matters such as labour efficiency and welfare measures came under opinion exchange, while management plans, including manning, came under reporting. In principle, there was no union 'participation in management'. However, as a senior union executive put it: 'Things are not cut and dry like that. That's not how industrial relations work. We have the right to know early on, and we let them know what we're going to be bringing up.'[1]

As a result of overlapping interests and extensive consultation, the union did not face an outright assault on its existence through derecognition, bullying or bypassing, as happened to many unions in the USA and UK in the 1990s. On the contrary, implications for industrial relations *and the union* were considered very carefully before reforms were introduced.

[1] Interview, 5 September 1996.

On the other hand, this maturation of industrial relations brought problems of its own. Adversarial wage bargaining is visible; overlapping interests and extensive consultation reduce differences to nuances. When high nominal wages reduce the scope for bargaining to a matter of a few hundred yen, moreover, questions are raised about the meaning of the annual wage 'struggle'. Technically, this may be compensated for by a broader approach to living standards, but the broader approach creates complexity. The web of committees set up to deal with this increasingly comes to appear like a bureaucracy. Bureaucracies tend not to excite passion.

Compounding the potential for apathy were changes on the part of members themselves. Hitachi's union was formed in the crucible of postwar desperation; fifty years later that desperation only existed in collective memory. By the mid-1990s more than 90% of male members over 40 owned their own house or expected to shortly. Despite discontent about wage levels, in many ways Hitachi's union members could be considered part of Japan's 'labour aristocracy'. In such a situation, the 'who needs unions?' attitude is as likely to come from within as from top management.

Membership composition had changed over time as well. While it is not correct to say that 'knowledge workers' have no interest in union activities – militancy at the Central Research Laboratory (CRL) union (now branch) persisted into the 1960s – they are usually seen as more individualistic and less inclined to take part in solidaristic activities than production workers, more interested in having their creative output recognized than looking to collective bargaining to improve their lot. Eventually, most become non-union members.

Union membership was a part of the community consciousness of shopfloor workers in heartland factories in a way that it was not in white-collar workplaces. At the CRL, in fact, few of the top branch officials were full-time, by choice. They were younger than their counterparts at the factories, and had less experience in union activities and committees. They tended to get 'thrown in at the deep end' and serve for just two years before stepping down:

The term here is one year, as at corporate HQ, rather than two years, and we tend to serve two terms. Even after two years, and not full time, it is difficult to get re-integrated into the research group.[2]

The union response to these developments, as at other major Japanese companies, was 'UI' (union identity) activities. The first things to change were the symbols of struggle. In 1991 the colour of the union's flag was

2 Interview, vice-president, CRL Branch, 18 September 1996.

changed from red to blue. The 180-strong delegation to the 'spring struggle' wage bargaining was reduced to a team. Demonstrations preceding the annual mass meeting were abandoned. The monthly magazine was made glossier, and its name changed from Labour Critique to HUNT (Hitachi Union New Trend).

Although the union provided various services to its members – access to loans, insurance schemes, a co-operative shop, etc. – and had developed activities for various types of member – young, older, women – these could only supplement its core activities. Surveys showed that members most wanted it to work for better wages and conditions. If this meant 'participation in management', then fine, as long as the union retained an independent voice and strongly argued its case.[3] A key question for the union, therefore, was how to maintain its relevance, and levels of participation, in its core areas. This involved new efforts, first to keep members informed about what was happening in central negotiations and consultations, and second to gather the views of members through stewards and representatives.[4]

All these efforts yielded some results. Surveys suggested that member views of union activities improved, and more felt their views were being reflected in these activities. It would be safe to say, however, that like company management the initiatives took place within established frameworks, and the frameworks themselves were not the object of reform.

HRM reform

The high road to reform

Faced with deteriorating performance and growing pressures for more far-reaching reforms than those previously contemplated, top managers in 1996 considered a number of options. Some focused on cost cutting, and others on regeneration. There was growing concern that they would adopt a 'low road' approach to restructuring and employment. This concern was articulated by a number of middle managers, who thought that top managers were becoming 'drier', and were starting to look at 'US-style' restructuring with a certain fascination. Said one labour relations manager of the Hitachi Works:

---

[3] A very small minority – 7–8% – believed the union's stance should basically be one of resistance or confrontation, and a similar minority believed in unitary interests.

[4] In 1999 all the wage, bonus, retirement money and contract bargaining activities were concentrated in the 'spring offensive', and to fill the autumn activity gap a 'NEEDS Month' (Network, Everybody, Everything, Discussion, Strengthen) was inaugurated, focusing on UI issues.

There is a view which is spreading among top management in this country that unions are no longer needed. What I think about this is that the centripetal forces put in place for blue-collar workers – *nenko joretsu*, housing, sports, hospitals, fire brigade, even helping at their parents' funeral – this is how our companies have been built up. But with 'mega competition' the top managements think they can't be kept. All right, I say, what do you have in mind to replace all this? . . . If you start cutting things here and there, there's no telling where it will end . . . Well, I might be able to swallow some diminution of labour conditions, but I would fight tooth and nail (together) with the union to prevent layoffs.[5]

Shortly after these comments, labour costs were debated in the corporate level joint management council. One (management) participant related the debate:

At the joint council yesterday the (company) president took the line of costs, and the (union) chairman pushed on value added and management responsibility. These are the causes of the problem, he argued, not just wages. Things were very tense. I haven't often seen them like this.[6]

The debates continued afterwards, and the eventual outcome was the 1998 HRM reforms, discussed in chapter 11, in which the 'high road' view had clearly gained the ascendancy. Either the middle management and union view had won out, or the senior management was not really as 'dry' as it had been portrayed.

The background to the high road package reveals a lot about overlapping interests and the nature of industrial relations. Cluster analysis of a 1995 company survey identified five groups of employees: self-actualizers interested in developing themselves through work; company loyalists who devoted themselves to the company; me-firsters who put their own gain first; company dependants who relied on the company and its stability; and the apathy-smitten. Numerous surveys, both within Hitachi and in other companies, had plotted the decline of company loyalists over the years, and identified a growing proportion of would-be self-actualizers, whose drive could be harnessed by appropriate personnel policies (cf. Whittaker, 1990b). Of particular concern in this survey, however, was the size of the last two categories – company dependants and the apathy-smitten – for whom there was little obvious drive to harness.

Union surveys had also picked up this apathy, which applied to union activities as well (often, though not always, on the part of the same people). They also registered a decreasing interest in promotion offset by an increasing concern for doing fulfilling work, weakening support for *nenko* and growing support for performance-based HRM (within limits).

[5] Interview, 9 September 1996.   [6] Interview, 19 September 1996.

These feelings were particularly strong amongst creative workers in R&D, technology centres, divisional headquarters, etc.

The company and the union shared a common interest in minimizing generalized apathy towards work, company and union, and encouraging fuller engagement. They agreed that systemic changes were needed, and set up a corporate level joint Committee for Considering the Remuneration System, with ten specialist sub-committees to consider implications for specific issues in the collective contract. In principle, the union did not oppose the creation of a new system which would increase the spread of pay and promotion on an age basis. It was concerned, however, with how much the spread should be widened, who would be classed a 'discretionary worker', and especially how performance was to be conceived and measured. The chairman of the CRL branch commented:

We've been studying discretionary working for 4–5 years now. For researchers, we think it is good. We did a questionnaire this May and eighty per cent of our members had heard of it, but most said they don't know if they'd like to use it, because they don't know what will be included and what won't. They've been studying it seriously at the HQ since last year, but there is a difference in what they are saying and what we have studied . . . The company wants to apply it more widely, but if they do, it might dilute the benefits in freedom we would gain. And as for the evaluation, we have visited research labs of other companies that have introduced it experimentally, but the company says that they will be thinking about it from now. It's all very well and good to talk about performance, but it has to be transparent – whose performance, over what period, how much.[7]

Evaluating the performance of R&D employees is extremely difficult – the results of research might not become apparent for many years, while promising directions might turn out to be dead ends, and there may be many reasons for the failure to reach targets. Excessive emphasis on targets may have pernicious side-effects, such as opportunism and a breakdown in co-operative effort. With problems emerging in performance-based systems over the next few years, the union's caution was well placed. In fact, according to the R&D group's senior HRM manager, the company heeded these concerns:

You have to look at how the targets are achieved – the process. The CRL branch raised this issue, and asked for it to be included from the beginning, so an analysis could be made if the target were not reached. We took it on board, and it spread around the company . . . Results are produced by teams.[8]

The union thus participated in the design of the reforms, and as a result their implementation did not pose the threat to traditional industrial relations that 'individualized' performance-based wages and HRM often did

[7] Interview, 4 September 1997.   [8] Interview, 12 July 2001.

Table 12.1 *Company and union objectives for C21 Committee*

What the company is aiming for	What we (HWU) are aiming for
21st century vision Hitachi is aiming for: Solving Hitachi's management problems: (1) Overcoming the unprecedented crisis situation, based on reliability and speed – improving performance, strengthening competitiveness, energizing human resources; (2) Deepening the new business structure (as *de facto* independent companies), spinouts, consolidated management; (3) Improving profitability – 8%+ ROE by f.2002.	21st century society we are aiming for: (1) From stable employment and living, the realization of well-being; (2) Human society emphasizing psychological well-being rather than just material wealth; (3) Living style enabling self-actualization, responding to greater fluidity and diversity of employment types; (4) Creation of new working styles, with matching fair, just, open and attractive remuneration; (5) Society with participation by men and women together; (6) Extending employment (beyond retirement) in response to the low birthrate.

Source: Rodo Hitachi, No. 780 (26 November 1999), p. 1.

in the UK and USA. While this potential also existed at Hitachi, the union's interest in successful HRM reform overlapped with its interest in developing UI activities, while the company had an interest in building on this willingness to co-operate rather than undermining it.

Coping with the accelerating pace of reform

From 1999, however, the accelerating pace of reform began to impose a new, indirect threat to the union by overloading the industrial relations machinery. The union could have become pinned down with immediate or symbolic issues, and failed to address more strategic challenges. For the company, too, there was a danger that the reforms would get bogged down over minutiae, with a consequent loss of momentum.

Recognizing this danger, and to avoid a piecemeal and purely reactive response to reform, the union began work on a 'Comprehensive Labour Policy and Welfare Vision'. In addition a 'Joint Labour–Management Committee to Consider Hitachi in the 21st Century' (C21 Committee) was set up. The respective motives/objectives for participating in the Committee are given (by the union) in table 12.1. The Committee divided industrial relations issues into four categories. Category A items were linked to the spring bargaining round of 2000 and were to be settled within 1999. Category B items were to be taken up and implemented in the next financial year. Categories C and D were longer-term issues; they would be debated in parallel, but without the same time restrictions.[9]

In the initial rounds of debate on category A issues, agreement was reached to extend the coverage of discretionary 'E-work' downwards by one grade, to introduce a new incentive scheme for employees in sales, to introduce re-employment after age 60, to introduce a qualification system for all non-management workers, to expand MBO and to reform welfare measures to give more individual choice (the 'cafeteria plan').[10] Thus the company had made some progress towards its aim of 'energizing human resources', while the union had made some progress towards its objectives, particularly 4 (new working styles) and 6 (extending employment) in table 12.1.

Category B issues included reform of the spring bargaining round, the retirement lump sum (including the introduction of a 401K-type option), and a review of various allowances. C items included devolution of industrial relations, group-based HRM, and reforming categories of employee (merging clerical and manual grades, which happened in 2004), while D items included a range of corporate culture-related items, morale surveys and reform evaluation, removing barriers for female employees (one immediate product of which was the family friendly package of 2000), internal job posting, (internal) corporate venturing, mental health, and social and environmental responsibility.

The thrust and direction of the HRM reforms, like the organization reforms, were set by the company. But as the HRM reforms were, broadly speaking, supported by the union, co-operation on the part of both sides was clearly the preferred option. The C21 Committee constituted a mechanism through which the industrial relations implications of reform could be resolved without getting bogged down in logjams. The union was able to ensure that it was not overrun by the pace of reform, and that both the big issues and the details could be debated. It sought to partner change, rather than being forced into a purely defensive position. The potential reward for the company was morale maintenance. As a result, co-operative industrial relations became an agent of change rather than a victim.

---

[9] Not surprisingly, there were differences of opinion as to which category certain items belonged to, and these were resolved by give and take. The list was revised in September 2000, and new items like business process reform, mobile working, education and self-responsibility were added.

[10] *Rodo Hitachi*, Nos. 780 (26 November 1999) and 785 (31 January 2000).

The organization challenge

A similar analysis may be offered of the organization reforms. A low road approach to organization reform would be characterized by a defensive emphasis on spinouts and fixed cost reduction, while a high road approach would seek to position the company for new growth. The spinout restructuring of consumer electronics in the mid-1990s was necessarily defensive; the question was whether this would set the pattern for the subsequent company-wide reforms as well. The measures announced in 1998 were ambiguous in this regard, and the new president in 1999 had overseen the restructuring in consumer electronics. As the reforms unfolded, however, they began to take a high road emphasis, which was particularly marked in the quest for synergies in the Group restructuring. Again, industrial relations played a part.

The union set out its position to the company's crisis in September 1998 with a list of ten proposals:

1 The company should make clear its strategy to restore the company to health rather than simply pursuing policies of shrinkage, organization reform and reducing fixed costs.
2 If it does so, it will gain the willing co-operation of employees, rather than simply impacting negatively on morale.
3 This positive co-operation is absolutely necessary for any rehabilitation strategy, and policies should be implemented to improve morale.
4 The company is its people, and its future depends on them. This should be reaffirmed.
5 All information should be widely shared in the pursuit of solutions, and a management think tank should be set up.
6 Unnecessary work should be thoroughly purged. For instance, the budget process takes six months of the year and takes up many people's time. There is room for major improvements.
7 People, money and goods should be invested strategically, based on a clear vision, which should include subsidiaries.
8 There are 330,000 employees in the Hitachi Group; this market should be used more fully.
9 Sales and customer relations should be strengthened, with improved incentives and support for developing new customers and markets.
10 Spinoff companies should be given the resources to create their own value added and independent management, while being integrated into the Hitachi Group.

The union proposals had a number of points in common with those of financial analysts, but emphasized the role employees/members would play in bringing about renewal, and the importance of maintaining (or boosting) morale. It did not simply advocate employment maintenance, in fact in point 7 it argued against continued cross-subsidization of loss-making operations, which logically would result in fewer jobs. The same applies to point 6. Its position was that without a return to entrepreneurial dynamism, the future for its members was bleak. Tacitly, it was giving the go-ahead to major organization reforms, even though there would be bitter pills to swallow.

Virtual companies

The first of these came almost immediately. During the autumn bonus negotiations the company proposed emergency measures until March 2000 which included a cut in the bonus, extension of scheduled working hours from 7:45 minutes back to 8 hours, and lowering the overtime rate by 5%. It also proposed that, for the first time for union members, the bonus would differ by (internal) group. The union for its part demanded 2.6 months' pay for the winter bonus, claiming that it had co-operated with the company, and the losses were the responsibility of management. Its first fallback position was 2.4 months, the same as the previous year, and then 2.2 months, which would mean a single digit reduction. The final figure was 2.15 months, which was a blow to the union. The company argued that this was exceptional, and necessary to send a message to shareholders, who would not be getting a dividend. The differential bonus was applied to managers and intermediate grade employees only on the grounds that they had some responsibility for performance, and not to younger employees. The HRM director said of the negotiations:

The union had to give a lot in these negotiations, and I'm grateful to them. 20% of members got a business-linked bonus. It was difficult for the union to accept this when the bonus itself was reduced.[11]

This was just a precursor of what was to come, as we shall see. Although the HRM director had achieved differentiation in the bonus, he did not intend to try to push it through into wages. He did, however, see further decentralization in matters like working hours. To prepare for this, the union agreed in the first instance to set up joint councils at the group level with authority to debate, but not to formally negotiate. Said a senior union leader:

[11] 5 November 1998. The union felt obliged to express 'deep gratitude' to its members in the Annual Report for their understanding and co-operation over the emergency measures, particularly to members in semiconductor divisions, already subjected to other emergency measures. The approval rating of the union's performance dropped the next year.

What we are saying is we need time to prepare. We are just recovering from our loss, the members are nervous, and they think devolution will lead to lots of concessions. Do it when things are better.[12]

(At that point a company manager who had entered the room quipped: 'Perhaps things will get better quicker if there is devolution faster.')

Just as the company had a struggle to find CEOs for the new groups, to put in place new decision-making bodies and to rethink its task allocations, the union faced the same issues. Its branch structure would need to be reorganized. New group level committees and industrial relations bodies would have to be put in place, in addition to the joint councils. The union called for a step-by step devolution as these were carried out.

In mid-2001 a compromise was reached in which the work system, travel expenses and welfare could be decided (negotiated) at the group council level, but the qualification system, wages, evaluation and bonus needed 'four party' agreement (of management and union at both the group and corporate levels). In 2002 bonus differences based on group performance would be extended to all employees, but within a 10% band.

The company was clearly treading carefully. In fact it appeared to be re-evaluating its devolution strategy. The president indicated he was not heading towards a pure holding company structure, and an industrial relations manager suggested that three models (rather than one for every group) were appropriate for HRM needs of the different groups.[13] This was very good news for the union, which agreed with the objectives of the reforms, and that speedy industrial relations machinery was necessary to complement speedy management decision-making, but found its very survival threatened.

Group reforms

Initially the virtual companies were seen as a precursor to some if not all being spun out as independent companies. If some of the groups were retained within the company fold, in all likelihood there would only be 20,000–30,000 members left. If a pure holding company structure were adopted, there would be a tenth of this figure! Already membership was plummeting; between 1998 and 2001 the union lost 20% of its members, and a commensurate share of income.

As for those spun out:

---

[12] Interview, 6 January 2000.   [13] *Nikkei shinbun*, 16 September 2001.

When they are individual companies, and business conditions are bad, it will be difficult for the unions to resist cuts in wages and conditions. That is the problem of small units . . . Mr Shoyama (president) and Mr Muneoka (HRM director) are fine people, but the heads of these new businesses might not have the same qualities.[14]

According to the 'one company, one union, one collective contract' logic, employees in the companies spun out would be organized in new unions. The situation was complicated, however, by the fact that units were simultaneously being spun out and merged with other companies – some with no union – both within the Hitachi Group and outside it. After negotiations, agreement was reached to create new unions at these companies, even when the companies the units were being merged with had no existing union. Further, in April 2002 a new union council encompassing the HWU and these new unions was created. For the union, this offered the prospect that the haemorrhage of membership would be stemmed, wages and conditions across companies could be maintained, and industrial relations issues accompanying the new strategic thrust could be addressed.[15]

The company stood to benefit from simplified restructuring procedures, particularly the ability to move employees between companies more easily. (Employees would no longer have to formally retire before moving as they had in the past.) A corollary, however, was that cost-cutting and wage reductions were no longer a primary motive for such restructuring. The new companies would compete on the basis of value and service rather than low costs. This shift was a recognition of negative morale effects of transferring people from Hitachi Ltd to other Group companies in the past, as well as a means of reducing up-front restructuring costs. The morale problems were aggravated by the widely held view that Hitachi was the pre-eminent company, superior to other Group companies. High road restructuring, however, required that there be a greater sense of parity between the different companies. This was explicitly advocated by Hitachi's president, although in reality it applied to a select inner group of companies rather than the whole Group.[16]

---

[14] Interview, HWU president, 6 January 2000.

[15] Ambiguities related to the new structure remained. Formally, the council would be the organization affiliated with the industrial federation, but under the name Hitachi Workers' Union.

[16] Similarly, two-way movement of personnel (the 'maturation' of quasi internal labour markets referred to in chapter 6) was limited to a small group of companies. Hitachi Ltd personnel might move to others and return, but most subsidiaries were reluctant to lose key personnel to Hitachi Ltd.

The implementation of Group reforms initially posed a great threat to the union. This threat receded with the adoption of a high road approach to restructuring, which enabled the maintenance of, and was enabled by, co-operative industrial relations.

Business process reforms

Finally in this section we consider business process reforms. In its response to the company's crisis the union called for the purging of 'unnecessary work' (item 6 above), notably in the budget-making and monitoring process which spilled out of the accounting function and ate up the time of engineers, line managers and workers throughout the year. Its origin was in the heavy electric factories, and to many it epitomized the cautious, safety-first approach of those factories which dominated corporate management thinking. Despite a long-standing undertone of dissent, and many years of MI (management improvement) activities on the one hand, and union campaigns to reduce working hours on the other, its influence was pervasive through to the end of the 1990s. There were long-standing complaints as well about other procedures such as travel expense reimbursement, which needed multiple signatures for authorization.

The union's surveys also showed strong dissatisfaction over workloads and manning levels; for R, D&E members these were easily the biggest sources of work-related complaints, ahead of wage and bonus levels. Similar frustrations were expressed in our workplace group interviews. In fact, a number of interviewees expressed concern about improvement or reform initiatives, including those designed to promote creative work, because they would add to their workloads. The status quo was maintained by busy-ness. Said one engineer:

> If you thought time was being wasted, you would have to produce data and a counterproposal, and a convincing argument that if you did this, you would save this amount of time . . . Even if we produced a report on how improvements could be made, the report would end up in the department and go no further. And even if the department changed, the chances are others wouldn't, and things would revert to the former state.[17]

The situation may perversely have been exacerbated by management's 'right to manage' work organization, historically more zealously guarded than other areas. As a result, it may have become an industrial relations 'blind spot', limiting the types of issues members brought to meetings, and reinforcing the view that the union failed to grapple with pressing issues. On the other hand, management campaigns – MI and QC

---

[17] Group interview, 21 February 2001.

activities – had made little headway in improving indirect work organization. The result was the kind of resignation this person expresses, the very opposite of what the company was aiming for. While the company wanted to move away from 'management based on time' and encourage a new approach to work, ironically the pressures of time constraints and manning levels obstructed this.[18]

For both the union and the company, therefore, overcoming long-standing inertia and reforming business processes were timely. The union became involved in discussions on how to simplify budget-making and monitoring, travel reimbursement and other cumbersome procedures. In some cases this involved unpicking procedural stitches which had been sewn with industrial relations machinery in years gone by, as in reporting late arrival at work. The management was interested not just in saving money, but in promoting self-responsibility, as we have noted. On the union side there was support for this thinking, and as some managers remarked, a similar change of focus away from procedural minutiae to larger issues.

These developments raise the possibility that, rather than being a victim of reform, the union can become involved in areas from which it was hitherto excluded. Although it is necessary to distinguish between business process reforms and the reform of work organization itself, it is logical that when or if the scope is extended to work organization, union involvement will be similarly extended.[19] If so, a historical scar of postwar conflict could be healed, and the union could become a fuller partner of reform.

The spring wage round of 2002

The 2002 Japanese spring wage round was thrown into confusion at the *twelfth* hour when, hours after Hitachi announced a settlement of 2% and a (total) bonus of four months' pay, it was announced that the company would immediately enter into negotiations with the union over a 5% wage cut. On the face of it, the incident casts doubt on the stability of industrial relations at Hitachi, and the arguments developed in this chapter. On the contrary, it suggests a counter-argument, of progressive encroachment into the 'inviolable' areas of wages and conditions, starting in 1998 (bonuses varying by group performance, and emergency measures for employees in the semiconductor group) and expanding with each downturn.

---

[18] Thus, many of the key impediments to creative work, identified in chapter 4, applied to Hitachi.

[19] Ishida (2003) has argued, similarly, that union involvement might be extended to work organization through attempts to link wages to organization objectives.

Closer inspection reveals a complex picture. The backdrop to the wage round was continued domestic recession (and deflation), compounded by the global IT slump, plummeting DRAM prices, and post 11 September economic uncertainty. Hitachi had projected a loss for the financial year of ¥480 billion (c.$3.7 billion), briefly the second biggest annual loss in Japanese corporate history, after Nissan in 1998, and much heavier than its crisis inducing loss in 1998–9.[20] In this light, the 2% increase and four months' bonus were remarkably generous, foolhardy even. The top directors themselves had just taken pay cuts of 10–20% – the higher the rank, the larger the cut – and managers were to get a cut of 5% (with no raise, either).

The 5% cut after a 2% increase would have the effect of a 3% wage cut. Why was it handled in this way? Why didn't the negotiations just focus on the wage cut? The main reason is that both parties intended to separate the wage cut from the spring wage round. In the spring round they were part of a wider context of co-ordinated bargaining, which had come under strain by the late 1990s with minuscule settlements. Putting the cut into this setting would have dealt a heavy blow not just to the 2002 wage round, but to co-ordinated spring wage bargaining itself. The union was especially anxious to avoid this outcome, as it had fought against what it saw as moves within the industry federation to weaken the spring round (for instance through alternate-year bargaining).

The wage cut, therefore, was to be separated from the spring round, as part of a subsequent package of emergency measures which were scheduled to last for one year. Details of the emergency package were leaked in the press on the settlement date, however. The company was forced to declare its package, and the union was forced into negotiating a delay of the cut until June.[21]

The measures also included an early retirement scheme, the first officially applied to union members since 1950, as part of an attempt to reduce employment within the Group by 8%. The scheme was heavily oversubscribed, with 9,000 applicants compared with a target of 4,000.[22]

---

[20] Of this loss, over half – ¥280 billion – was restructuring costs, half for special retirement allowances and half for restructuring and consolidation. The bulk of the operating loss came from semiconductors. NTT announced a heavier loss shortly afterwards.

[21] The cut was ended two months early, on 31 March 2003. The level negotiated a year earlier was restored, and the union agreed to consider the grade system, and an end to the seniority annual wage increase (introduced, as we saw, in 2004).

[22] Some employees and managers were critical of the way the scheme was handled; many good managers were lost. There has been growing concern in Japan about 'leakage' of tacit knowledge of engineers and managers to Asian competitors paying high salaries to such people in recent years, too, especially in semiconductors.

Both measures made new inroads into hitherto inviolable wages and conditions areas. For the company, no doubt, the situation was sufficiently grave to make such an incursion, albeit a temporary one. And externally, it would send a message to the media and investors that it was prepared to take action, and internally to rekindle a sense of crisis. The union was receptive:

If any other company made a loss of ¥480 billion they'd go under. There'd be no bonus, full stop. If we have another loss like this, we'll be in deep trouble. The employees need to understand the seriousness of the situation. We can't pretend nothing has happened . . . If we make a recovery next year, we'll get it back . . . But unlike 1998, there is no guarantee things will get better next year.[23]

It would be wrong to say that the measures represented a basic shift towards 'low road' restructuring, but in the short term at least, efforts to improve bottom line results had to include such cost cutting. The question arises, however, as to whether, once violated, the way might be opened for more extensive inroads into wages and conditions in the future. This, of course, remains a possibility if losses continue, but the preference on the part of the company – evident in the 'i.e. Hitachi Plan II' for instance (see chapter 13) – clearly remains value creation through untapped synergy, and energizing employees.

Just days after the incident the new union council was announced. The council was compatible with a joint vision of high road restructuring, not cost-cutting spinouts. If anything, therefore, the wage rise–cut incident demonstrated not so much the unpredictability or volatility of industrial relations at Hitachi, but its underlying stability.

The stakeholder, or *a* stakeholder?

The late 1990s are widely seen as a period of growing union impotence in Japan, both at the enterprise level, and at the national policy level. If union influence is taken as the ability to forestall restructuring, or to extract higher wages – or even to prevent cuts – Japan's unions have been impotent. As we saw in Part 1, moreover, management reforms threaten to weaken union influence in subtle ways, also.

In the case of Hitachi, however, union engagement in the reforms was able to bring about a greater emphasis on 'high road' measures, and a continuation of overlapping interests forged under the 'co-operative line' during the golden growth years, specifically:

[23] Interview with HWU president, 20 March 2002. A purchasing manager also expressed the view that the emergency package would send a signal through the supply chain on the need for change.

1. *Long-term employment*: The union saw stability of employment (and living security) as fundamental, and employee engagement with the company as based on this. The company saw long-term employment as fundamental to its HRM.

2. Both sides, however, believed that long-term employment for core members should be supplemented by new options, with greater *fluidity*. The company believed this was necessary to give it flexibility, and to allow it to adapt to rapidly changing markets and global competition. The union saw it as desirable to increase the options for workers with increasingly diverse life aims and situations. Both parties agreed that various reforms were necessary, including legal changes and pension reform to enable greater portability of pensions.

3. In addition, greater *flexibility* in working practices. For the company, the extra costs of flexibility were expected to be outweighed by improved morale and creativity, and a better balance between work and family and other interests outside the workplace. Providing this flexibility was becoming an indicator of employer 'progressiveness'. For the union, too, the same merits outweighed the potential demerit of reduced cohesiveness.

4. Along with greater fluidity and flexibility, greater focus on *creative work* by company professionals. More challenging jobs were in everyone's interests. This was linked, in HRM, to greater emphasis on *individual contributions*, in turn supported by a changing sense of fairness (those who contribute more should be rewarded more, within limits). It was also linked to organization reforms, including business process reforms.

5. Organization reform meant increasing personnel *movement across corporate boundaries*. The company was forced to address resulting morale problems, and the union, membership decline. Morale problems could only be reduced through addressing the implicit pyramid of corporate prestige and a high road emphasis. These in turn made it easier for the union to create a new, flexible structure, which would help to maintain not just union influence but morale as well.

Of course there were stresses and strains associated with the reforms – the wave of applicants for the early retirement scheme points to the stresses on individuals, and in some cases disillusionment – and many managers believed that the union would inevitably become weaker over time. And even if there are continued overlapping interests, the question remains as to whether these might be upset by the emerging claims of other stakeholders, notably shareholders, or changes in the environment.

We saw in chapter 10 that top union officials were not opposed to ROE targets 'as long as the attitude towards employees and customers isn't adversely affected'. They believed members would benefit through investment in growth areas and renewed dynamism. They were less happy with the changing media climate associated with shareholder emphasis. The business media increasingly wanted to see bold restructuring measures, irrespective of the resulting influence on the workforce. Union leaders were particularly chafed by similar calls for bold union reforms, and the feting of those who responded.[24] We have noted the 'special responsibilities' felt by the company prior to 1998 (and to some extent after that). The union also felt it had 'special responsibilities' to uphold for labour. The media was increasingly apt to interpret this as foot-dragging.

Continuity in industrial relations cannot be taken for granted. Challenges abound, and leadership is needed to address those challenges. This will determine, for instance, whether union influence over business process and work organization reform is actually achieved, and whether the inter-firm council develops or atrophies. It is premature, however, to write the obituary of the union. Earlier we quoted managers who felt that in the past shareholders had been like air or water – something you take for granted as being there, and only come to notice it when its supply is threatened. If the company was waking up to the presence of shareholders, the same might be said of some of the employees about their union. Said the union president:

It's interesting, you know, that it is very difficult to organize employees of software companies where they haven't been organized before. But if you spin out a software company – and some will no doubt be spun out – the first thing that happens is the members come and say you'll make a union for us, won't you, even if they haven't been interested in the union before. It's something they take for granted, like air or water, until something like this happens.[25]

---

[24] It was opposed to moves within the industry federation to move to biennial spring bargaining, determine bonus by formula, end co-ordinated bargaining, formalize rules for layoffs, etc. Cf. *Nikkei sangyo shinbun*, 26 January 2001; *Nikkei shinbun*, 30 January 2002.
[25] Interview, 19 February 2001.

13 Evaluation

Hitachi's reforms can be evaluated in a number of ways, including the following. First, in terms of their own objectives, have they brought about the kinds of changes envisaged when they were launched? Second, how do they compare with the reforms of other companies which have similarly attempted to bring about corporate renewal? And third, what do the outcomes mean for the classic model of the community company?

This chapter evaluates the reforms on these three counts. We start with a brief summary of the reforms and an interpretation of deeper cultural changes. We then look at the extent to which the reforms have diffused and taken root, based on interviews of managers at various levels, group interviews in diverse workplaces, and survey findings. In addition to the qualitative aspects of reform, we consider briefly the quantitative, bottom line results.

Next we take a comparative view. Although various companies might be selected for comparison, both within Japan and abroad, we have chosen GE, the premier US general electric company whose transformation under Jack Welch was widely admired, and in many ways symbolized the transformation of corporate America in the 1980s and 1990s. As we shall see, there are both similarities as well as contrasts between the two. The contrasts reveal important aspects of continuity in the community firm.

Finally, we assess the reforms in terms of implications for Hitachi's community firm, through changes in employment practices, corporate governance and managers' priorities, as well as membership, boundaries and internal cohesion. Is the classic model intact, being modified, or abandoned? Can we discern a new model in the making?

Hitachi's reforms: a brief summary

For many years Hitachi was a paragon of entrepreneurial vigour. It grew rapidly through organic growth and acquisition in prewar Japan, and successfully relaunched itself after the Second World War, expanding from its heavy electric base into consumer electric goods, then subsequently computers, semiconductors and IT products and systems. Many books were written trying to explain its innovativeness and the secrets of its spectacular growth.

From the mid-1980s, however, Hitachi's star began to shine less brightly. Corporate culture became more conservative, and it became slower to respond to changes in the business environment, and to seize emerging opportunities. The fact that it was still 'overall winner' despite gaining few gold medals (*sogo yusho, kin medaru nashi*; in the domestic electric/electronic industry turnover competition) offered only temporary solace, as gold and silver medal winners began to reap all the profits. Attempts to rekindle dynamic growth produced little lasting success. Within the company some began to favour US-style restructuring, while others began to resign themselves to shrinkage and ceding volatile IT markets to those with a bent for self-flagellation.

While the conceptual tools were still rather blunt, new plans for reform were drawn up in the late 1990s. They were intended to mark the company's 90th birthday in 2000, but as a result of the company's first loss in fifty years in 1998, their implementation was brought forward. A sense of crisis helped to overcome resistance to change, and to generate consensus for deepening the reforms. In principle, no areas of business or management were off limits.

When implemented, reforms in one area began to generate new ideas for reform in others. Eventually they began to acquire a coherent, transformational quality, thus marking the most significant programme of change since the reforms of the 1950s and 1960s.

We grouped the reforms into two main categories, organization and human resource management (HRM), and the former into organization, Group and business process. The main thrust of the organization reforms was to speed up decision-making and increase responsiveness to diverse market needs. The new 'virtual companies' were intended to create small company responsiveness within the framework of a large company – 'downsizing' in a sense, without layoffs. The streamlined headquarters was to concentrate on strategy and co-ordination, and soon produced the 'i.e. Hitachi Plan' which outlined how Hitachi was to be transformed 'from a manufacturer to a solutions-providing company' over the next few years.

The Group reforms were to address the high cost structure, improve efficiency through consolidated management, and create new businesses through synergistic combination. The creation of companies such as Hitachi Capital, as well as new outsourcing companies, signified the growing importance of services within the Group. Business process reforms in purchasing, HRM and accounting combined IT investment with process and job design reform to reduce bureaucracy, increase speed and free up employees for value creating work. Measures were adopted to flatten management hierarchies.

The HRM reforms actually started in 1998, before the organization reforms, with new qualification, pay and work systems for pre-management white-collar workers, aimed at stimulating and rewarding creative performance. These were followed by a new approach to the management of managers which attempted to align their work with the strategic objectives and the reform agenda through HITACHI VALUE. Early executive selection and selective education were also introduced, albeit cautiously.

In the area of welfare, the 'cafeteria plan' signalled a new emphasis on choice and self-responsibility, which was taken further with the 'free agent' system launched in 2003. The new emphases were evident in employee education, while pension reform in effect de-emphasized loyalty, and options for the retirement lump sum were introduced. A new package of 'family friendly' measures increased the scope for diverse work and career patterns. Mid-career hiring was stepped up. The virtual companies were expected to tailor HRM to their own needs, while strategic postings beyond corporate boundaries began to emerge within the Group. HRM reforms were systematized and generalized in 2004, when *nenko* (or at least the *nen* part of *nenko*) was finally shackled. Through such measures the company was trying to redefine the employment relationship.

In the past, industrial relations considerations had subtly circumscribed reform agendas. In the crisis atmosphere from late 1998, such circumscription was overridden. The union faced plunging membership and splintering through the organization reforms, and potential loss of its collective role through 'individualized' HRM. In fact, however, there were new innovations in industrial relations which minimized the damage and established industrial relations as a more positive force for change. The result was an increasing emphasis on high road restructuring – value creation rather than cost cutting – after initial trial and error.

At a deeper cultural level changes were also underway. Social relations in the classic model were organized around the manufacture of products, with a strong emphasis on shopfloor processes and efficiency, and a productionist culture. (In Hitachi's case it was a very particular culture, derived from the company's roots in heavy industry.) Those not engaged in these activities were literally 'support staff'. Even sales was a kind of support function; 'real' value creation took place on the shopfloor. Those working in offices were reminded of this in various ways, from their 'factory experience' when entering the company, to resistance to improving their office work environments. Even R&D employees felt the questioning gaze of those involved directly in production, including line managers.[1]

The productionist concept of 'support staff' was not fundamentally challenged until the mid-1990s when, as we saw in chapter 10, slogans began to refer to white-collar employees as 'professionals'. The debate about just what this meant intensified with the organization and business process reforms. Questions were asked about what needed to be done within the company, and what could be bought from outside. What value could such 'professionals' add that could not be bought? In the process of this questioning, the old identity of 'support staff' began to give way to a new identity of 'professional' or 'value creator', which is diffused in the 2004 HRM reforms.

This transformation is still in its early days. In a giant organization like Hitachi, many employees are in fact specialists, even within functions. The idea of a professional as someone who creatively combines specialist knowledge with other (specialist or broader, generic) knowledge has not been applied concertedly. But the direction of change, and the broader cultural transformation towards 'total value creation', encompassing indirect, white-collar employees, is evident. So, too, is the parallel transformation of reining in technology/product push dynamics and strengthening customer focus through teams of planners, R&D employees and sales staff (Mizuno, 2004).

There were parallel developments at the business level. The 'i.e. Hitachi Plan' declared that Hitachi was being transformed 'from a manufacturing company to a solutions-providing company' or a 'best solutions partner': 'Hitachi will undergo a qualitative and structural change to being a trusted solutions enterprise that utilizes its manufacturer's values such as high quality and productivity as it helps customers through the provision of services and systems.' Financial services were strengthened. Noteworthy, too, was the attempt to recombine activities within and across Group companies, from a 'solutions' perspective. These combined hardware and services in areas such as e-government, education, business management, distribution and financial services. A Group-wide 'one stop security solution' initiative, ranging from cyber security to physical security such as in distribution, attempted to turn Hitachi's traditional emphasis on safety and security into new business, and a

---

[1] This was captured in a cartoon-style history of Hitachi's R&D (Kato, 1996: 80), which shows two production workers walking past two researchers, who were sitting outside trying to solve a problem of an election microscope in 1941. 'Look at them,' says one to the other, 'They get paid for lazing about.' Shortly afterwards the research lab was moved from the Hitachi Works to an idyllic location in west Tokyo, which created a much better environment for research, but did not change such attitudes.

Group-wide Medical Strategy Council was launched to promote biomedical business.

Supertanker to speedboat?

Hitachi's problem, as expressed in the Asahi newspaper's commentary on its loss in 1998, was that it had become an unmanoeuvrable supertanker. Serious reforms were needed if it was to become manouevrable again. It is one thing to introduce measures to improve speed and manouevrability, but a different matter to achieve it, for the measures might be blocked by the very resistance to change they are designed to overcome. Our first type of evaluation is whether the reforms diffused and took root, or whether they were blocked or watered down in the process. Some preliminary observations are necessary.

First, the reform architects were quite aware of the difficulties of turning a supertanker, and internal scepticism about whether it could be achieved. They had been with the company for almost thirty years, and had seen reforms come and go. That much of their inspiration was initially drawn from the USA was hardly accidental. First, postings to the USA and in some cases participation in business school executive programmes had provided them with ideas for reform. Second, however, they believed that without presenting the reforms as being radically different, they would get bogged down and dissipated. To some extent their adoption of 'market' vocabulary was based on conviction that this was the only way to achieve change, but to some extent it was tactical. The tactical calculation, at least, was correct. In the process of reform, however, some of the architects themselves modified their positions, aspiring to a 'third way' of reform which maintained strengths of the classic model while drawing selectively on US restructuring concepts.

Second, reforms are not simply impeded by resistance in a quantitative sense. As they diffuse, concepts are translated, and in the process their meaning is subtly – sometimes creatively – changed. The notion of 'market value', for instance, was initially invoked in the context of market reforms. It soon took on a number of meanings, however. In the context of the new HRM system, it came to mean emphasis on current contributions rather than reliance on seniority or past contributions. In the context of redesigning jobs and business processes, it inspired the question 'what can we contribute, as organization professionals, that cannot be purchased in the market place' (through outsourcing)? Similarly, the concept of 'self-responsibility' was originally conceived as 'take responsibility for your own future because the company might not be able to', but was subtly translated by some managers as 'take responsibility as a citizen' (a good citizen → loyal employee → does not passively accept the status quo, but if necessary acts to change it).

That such translations occur is not surprising, as people and groups seek to interpret language in terms meaningful to them. Nor is it surprising that interpretations in areas subject to cost-cutting restructuring or spinout were more pessimistic than those in areas set to gain more resources. Thus perceptions differed as to what the reforms were trying to achieve, but dominant meanings were the result of translation and negotiation, and not simply imposition.

With these preliminary observations in mind, did the reforms diffuse and take root – were the balls thrown by the centre, as some line managers expressed it, caught by those in far-flung reaches? Surveys and group interviews of employees in various parts of the company offer some clues. Apprehension appears to have been outweighed by relief that at last serious efforts were being made to address the company's problems, and the debilitating sense that nothing could be done. The reforms seem to have tapped a reservoir of goodwill; a much greater proportion of union members in 1999 indicated that they were prepared to do their best for the company than in 1994, sharply reversing a decline in such sentiment over the past fifteen years.[2] There was, however, still a sense of scepticism as to whether many of the HRM reform measures, at least, could be effectively implemented.

A massive (40,000 responses) survey by the company in 2001 also picked up this sense of goodwill, and the strong sense of responsibility employees felt towards their jobs. What was shocking for the company, however, was the predominant view of the company culture as conservative. While the management (organization) vision was quite widely diffused (though not the Group vision), many employees felt that the HRM reforms had not gone far enough, and that there were still not enough openness and feedback. Views of specific measures, like family-friendly measures, were favourable, but employees felt they had been insufficiently embedded in their workplaces.[3]

This survey was intended to be administered annually, as part of the reform process itself. It was intended to provide a feedback loop to gather views from throughout the organization (there were open questions as well

[2] The reversal was especially pronounced for female employees. The reservoir of goodwill was deepest on the shopfloor, while engineers were more reserved – their view of a 'good company' was more conditionally tied to the nature of their work, and reforms in this area were only just beginning.

[3] The number of employees taking childcare leave quadrupled between 1990 and 1998, from 67 to 239. This was clearly linked to the increase in female career track employees, but proportionately, there was also greater uptake.

as tick box ones) for corporate strategy planners. Group CEOs were to be provided with an analysis of the results for their group, and expected to act on it. And, the questionnaire and general communication of the results were intended to contribute towards a culture of openness and transparency, which were seen as an important element of the new corporate culture, and which employees felt were still insufficient. Similar themes emerged from the 2002 survey, and resulted in a 360° appraisal system (by superiors, colleagues and subordinates) of managers. This was intended to inject a new impetus into the diffusion of the reforms, which had only been partial.[4]

Restoring speedy, responsive management on the one hand, and eliciting creative employee performance on the other were major objectives of the reforms, but ultimately, of course, these are the means through which corporate objectives are reached, rather than the ends. A second type of evaluation is whether the reforms enabled corporate objectives to be reached, specifically those set out in the i.e. Hitachi Plans I and II. In fact, the distinction between means and ends is not always clear-cut, and the medium-term plans might themselves be seen as a means of promoting reform as well as the end.[5]

Top managers did not assign overriding priority to reaching the numerical targets of the original plan, which would have required veering towards low road restructuring as the IT slump and global economic slowdown began to weigh heavily on corporate results. Far from registering higher profits, Hitachi slumped to a record loss in the financial year 2001, and barely managed to pull itself out of the hole with a small profit in the following two years.[6] The 7.5% ROE target remained distant.[7] Many within the company thought that the numerical goals had been over-optimistic, and the plan itself should have been overhauled earlier, in the light of unfolding events.

The president did announce a shift in the i.e. Hitachi Plan II in February 2004, indicating that the 20% divestment target would be

---

[4] Said one of the survey's administrators: 'Whether we can get rid of the culture of superficiality and conservatism will depend on how managers behave. 360° appraisals will let them know' (interview, 27 March 2003).

[5] As a means, failure to attain the numerical targets of the plan is not necessarily damning, while single-minded pursuit of the targets as an end could be counterproductive if it created undesirable side-effects which impede performance in the long-run.

[6] The 2002 ¥27.8 billion profit was made possible by labour cost (including pay) cuts of ¥170 billion, as well as a ¥290 billion reduction in fixed costs: *Nikkei Weekly*, 5 May 2003.

[7] Management obtained permission at the 2002 AGM for a share buy-back of up to 300 million or roughly 9% of its common shares, presumably to boost ROE. In the dismal business climate, and after a $2 billion hard disk drive deal with IBM, only some 30 million were actually purchased in May 2003. In late 2003, however, the company was its own tenth biggest shareholder.

revised downwards to 10% (two-thirds of which was already accounted for by spinning out logic chip operations into Renesas), and that candidate operations would be strengthened instead: 'Divestiture itself is not the goal. Unless individual operations are strengthened, they can't be sold, either.'[8]

In terms of the reforms' own objectives, then, it is safe to say that they were only partially successful by 2004. Quantitatively, however, we believe a longer time frame is necessary.

Comparison with GE

We next turn to a comparison in our attempt to evaluate Hitachi's reforms. Dore's (1973) study compared Hitachi with English Electric around the time it was absorbed into GEC,[9] as eventually was most of the British electric-electronics sector under Arnold Weinstock. The factories Dore studied became part of GEC-Alsthom in 1989, which was spun out as Alstom in 1998, as Lord Simpson dismantled Weinstock's conglomerate. Production had long since ceased at the Bradford works; a small repair shop remained, but a large superstore on the site epitomized Britain's deindustrialization.

Simpson sought to focus the GEC group on Marconi's operations and to bring about a 'fundamental culture change': 'The new GEC will be a risk-taking, technology-driven group with its eyes on growth, its main focus on telecommunications and £2.7 billion in cash to fund its ambitions.' By 2001 GEC-Marconi had began to implode. From its record valuation in September 2000, the share price had plunged 99% by March 2002. Many of its assets had been sold, and the remainder were judged by many to be less than its net debts.[10] Whatever lessons this drama might provide, there is not much left of this once-leading British company to compare Hitachi with, and we will not pursue the comparison here.[11]

Another possibility is IBM, and Lou Gerstner's reforms in the 1990s following the collapse of the company's performance. Under Gerstner,

---

[8] *Nikkei shinbun*, 5 February 2004. The dilemma for the company was that it is much easier to sell healthy operations, which the company would sooner keep, than unhealthy ones. This was seen as foot-dragging, if not a U-turn on reform.

[9] General Electric Company, founded in the 1880s, not to be confused with the American GE.

[10] *Financial Times*, 3 July 1998; 20 January 1999; 23–24 April 2002. Alstom, too, had to be rescued with a € 4.7 billion package backed by the French government in 2003.

[11] One possible lesson is that those who live by the stock market will perish by it. (This view has become less heretical in recent years; cf. Jensen and Fuller, 2002, 'Just Say No to Wall Street'.)

the 'elephant' began to dance again, to a new tune. There are important similarities, especially in attempts to change deeply institutionalized culture sanctified by past success.

The most natural comparison, however, is with the USA general electric giant GE, whose transformation under Jack Welch was the subject of countless articles and books, both in the USA and Japan. Welch took what was already a well-managed company and turned it into a stellar performer in the 1980s and 1990s. At the time he retired in 2001, GE was the world's most valuable company in terms of stock market value. According to Ghoshal and Bartlett (1997), GE achieved what many tried but few succeeded in its reforms; it dramatically improved the performance of its individual business units, and also succeeded in integrating them synergistically. As a result GE became the 'best practice of the individualized corporation'.

Welch's reforms and those of Hitachi share a lot in common. Both sought to redefine business focus on the one hand while drawing on cross-business synergies on the other, to move from a traditional manufacturing focus to encompass services without abandoning manufacturing strengths. Both sought to overcome creeping organizational sclerosis, to revive small company entrepreneurship and responsiveness in a large company setting, and to speed up decision-making – learning to dance, or supertanker to speedboat in Welch's language. Both sought to create organizations conducive to creativity and high performance, and to reward such contributions. Management was reconceived, and linked to transformation objectives through explicit 'Values'. And both sought to redefine the employment relationship – 'lifetime employment' was replaced by 'lifetime employability'.

The similarities should not be surprising. First, there were similarities in the nature of the problems both giant groups and many others like them faced. Second, GE had long been a periodic source of management inspiration for Hitachi – some features of its accounting system attest to this. With the US resurgence in the 1990s, and the success of Welch's GE reforms (some of them, conversely, inspired by Japan), it is only natural that Hitachi should look to a business with many similarities for new ideas.

Strategy

But there are striking differences as well, at a fundamental level, and Hitachi's managers were reluctant to draw on the model Welch presented. These differences highlight important features of Hitachi's reforms.

Like Hitachi's top managers, Welch was an engineer. He clearly had a keen interest in technology and manufacturing, and his aversion to the 'culture of finance' is palpable in his account of GE's acquisition of the Wall Street investment banking firm Kidder, Peabody: 'It's a place where the lifeboats carrying millionaires were always going to make it to the shore while the Titanic sank' (Welch, 2001: 222). But he also clearly relished the cut and thrust of making business deals, including an enormous array of acquisitions, many in financial services. He brought an engineer's mind to these deals; the ultimate test for these was 'in the numbers'. This thinking, too, was behind his 'No. 1 and No. 2' strategy.

Hitachi's top managers shared the passion for technology and manufacturing; non-engineer directors told of their difficulties in following technology debates in management council meetings. But the logic of their M&A (itself at a much diminished level compared to GE) and alliance activities reveals a different approach, less focused on 'the numbers' and more guided by a strategic view of the technology itself. They might abandon individual products incorporating a technology if the numbers did not add up, but they would be loath to abandon a technology itself which they viewed as strategically important. As a result, Hitachi remained in fiercely contested areas which GE had long since abandoned.

Although the i.e. Hitachi Plan envisaged the company/Group moving into services and becoming a solutions provider, this was done very differently from GE. Hitachi Capital and other financial service companies were given a mission to increase substantially their contribution to Group profits, but it is hard to imagine them becoming as prominent as GE Capital. (Becoming a 'best solutions partner' in finance was more likely to involve developing technology for cashless commerce, embodied in products such as smart cards, or infrastructure systems.) GE Capital powered GE's globalization, and for many (young) non-Americans GE Capital and GE are virtually synonymous.[12] Hitachi's nascent globalization strategy (under the i.e. Hitachi Plan II) of a limited number of 'global products incorporating advanced technology' was quite different.[13]

Relatedly, it is hard to imagine the following response from a president of Hitachi to intense competitive challenges, say from Silicon Valley ICT champions:

[12] By the late 1990s over 40% of GE's turnover was generated outside the USA. This expansion was powered most visibly by GE Capital, which made over 300 acquisitions outside the US during the decade; Sasaki, 1999.

[13] 'Global products' included hard disk drives, technologies included Ipv6, embodied for instance in the Mu chip, and solutions included multi-faceted security.

I was looking for a business that would give us a place to hide. In the early 1980s three businesses seemed to ring the bell: food, pharmaceuticals, and television broadcasting. Everyone needed to eat, and the United States had a strong agricultural position in the world. We evaluated several food companies, including General Foods, but couldn't make the numbers work. At the time their price-earnings ratios were much higher than GE's. As for pharmaceuticals, the numbers weren't even close. The government's foreign ownership restrictions made TV attractive. Like the food industry it had strong cash flow that could strengthen and expand our businesses . . . We bought RCA primarily to get NBC. (Welch, 2001: 140)

Hitachi's lengthy list of M&A, spinoffs and alliances in 2002–4 reveals a contrasting, strategic technology rationale. The numbers appeared all wrong for its $2.5 billion acquisition of (the bulk of) IBM's hard disk drive business in 2003, for instance. If analysts were right, HDDs would be a loss-making operation, not just for the next few years, but perhaps forever, as commoditization and cut-throat competition intensified. Hitachi's top management, by contrast, saw HDDs as a key element in storage solutions, which was a strategic business domain for integrating a range of technologies, including their new perpendicular recording technology. Time will tell if they were right. The point here is that 'integrated diversity' meant different things for GE and Hitachi.

Implementation

Second, these differences were also evident in the implementation of restructuring reforms. In the 1980s GE made disposals worth $10 billion, and acquisitions worth $17 billion (Ghoshal, 2001: 130). As with businesses, so with people. In his first four 'Neutron' years, Welch slashed GE's workforce by a quarter, or more than 100,000 employees. It was crucial for Welch to hire the best, and he often went outside GE to do so. He made no bones, however, about getting rid of those who did not perform in the way expected of them, or who were in businesses no longer deemed necessary.

Hitachi, by contrast, attempted 'downsizing' without large-scale layoffs – creating smaller 'virtual companies', some of which were spun out. The number of Hitachi Ltd employees was *also* reduced by a quarter between 1998 and 2002, but Group-wide, there was little reduction (cf. table 9.2), and compulsory redundancies were avoided. Although the new employment relationship stressed 'employability', the basic premise of long-term employment for the majority of employees remained.

In part these differences might be attributed to the respective environments in which the two companies operated. The M&A market has been much less active in Japan, and in particular, the labour market for mid-career employees was much less active. The consequences of being laid off for a Hitachi worker were thus amplified. However, the contrasts also reflected underlying philosophical differences in approaches to business and employment. One of these is what has been termed a 'logic of commitment', as opposed to a 'logic of exit'. The former is not just a reluctance on the part of Japanese managers to shed businesses once started and workers once employed, but the use of 'barriers to exit' (Kagono and Kobayashi, 1994) as a means of eliciting relationship-specific investments and co-operative effort. Such barriers are no longer locked, but they still exist.

The logic has important implications for leadership. Hitachi's top managers were not free to buy and sell businesses (or employees) as Jack Welch did. They could not claim: 'We didn't fire the people. We fired the positions and the people had to go' (Welch, 2001: 128). If Hitachi's leaders wanted to dispose of a business together with employees, it was incumbent on them to do it in a way in which the business was seen to have a viable future. If positions and people had to go, it had to be seen to be necessary for the greater good (of the community firm membership), and as fair as possible for those adversely affected.[14]

Conversely, even supposing Hitachi's leaders had become interested in buying a major food business, and the numbers added up, it is doubtful that they could have done so. They could conceivably – just – have acquired a major media network, but only on the grounds that it would help to develop existing business or technology, or that it was beneficial for community members. Price–earnings ratios were much less likely to be understood and actively supported by middle managers and employees than concentrating resources in strategic technologies and their applications in growth areas, preferably those seen as contributing to the greater social good. Thus the president announced to new recruits in 2002 that Hitachi would be concentrating future resources in:

'Solutions for comfortable living' – applying IT to the creation of 'ubiquitous knowledge society'; 'clean environment solutions' – creating a safe basis for living through energy and environment technology; 'well-being/health solutions' – creating well-being/healthy living through industrializing advanced medical and biotechnology; and 'knowledge management solutions' – contributing to corporate innovation with Hitachi's rich experience and technology.[15]

[14] As Kagono and Kobayashi (1994: 94–5) put it: 'The option of leaving the sinking ship is not freely available, either to the crew or the captain. The sense of sharing in a common destiny also is a source of the captain's authority and the legitimacy of his orders.'
[15] Press release, 1 April 2002.

Remaking cultural 'software'

Third and relatedly, while there were similarities in attempts to rebuild the cultural 'software' of the companies, there are clear differences as well. Similarities included attempts to get rid of bureaucracy which slowed decision-making and impeded creativity, to devolve authority to those nearer production and customers, to shape behaviour through explicit 'Values' (printed on cards), and to offer greater rewards to high performers.

The means used by GE to achieve these are well known: Boundary-less, Work-Out, Stretch, Six Sigma, GE Values. Culture was important for Welch; it was not enough for managers to reach numerical targets if the culture of empowerment and learning was sacrificed in the process. In this culture, people came first, but in a particular way. Welch's autobiography is about people with names and characters, which Welch responded to strongly. Self-confidence, simplicity, speed and passion were cardinal virtues. Those combining cultural virtues and performance were rewarded with new challenges and stock options.

Those who did not, however, could pack their bags. Getting rid of the 'Cs' – the bottom 10% in Welch's 'vitality curve' – was a vital part of building up high performing businesses. The title for the 'vitality curve' was 'Differentiation'. Differentiation was necessary to 'get out of the pile'. It was also a necessary tool for managers; those unable to differentiate their subordinates according to the vitality curve would soon find themselves not just back in the pile, but on the 'C' list. As got big rewards, Bs got modest rewards, Cs got nothing.

Hitachi's new HRM system introduced the possibility of demotion, but without a numerical target for the underperformer category; the assumption was that its use would be exceptional, and much concern was expressed about providing 'rehabilitation routes'. Conversely, individuals were expected to strive harder, both for their own sake as well as the company, but A performers were not lionized, and their rewards were comparatively modest. While inevitably some kind of differentiation is needed in promotion, it was not given the same emphasis as the heart of the HRM system, and the use of new sticks and carrots was restrained. 360° appraisal, for instance, was not linked to pay, at least initially. Stock options, too, were introduced very cautiously. Indeed they were introduced to promote awareness of shareholder interests, not as a mechanism to motivate individual performance.

Welch's autobiography is about (high performing) individuals. Few would be able to name more than two or three of Hitachi's leaders, if any. Shoyama is probably more widely known than his predecessors, as he gives more press conferences, attends more analysts' meetings, and is accessible on-line in the company. He emphasizes the need for clear responsibilities in his management style, but the creed of the individual is muted. (And so are individual rewards. Shoyama earns less than twenty times the salary of a new recruit. Welch's remuneration package was said to be 1,400 times the average factory worker in 1997! (Lowe, 2001: 185).)[16]

Hitachi's leaders were keen to improve performance while minimizing divisiveness. Undoubtedly they were aware of the contradiction described so well by Cappelli et al. (1997), of creating insecurity and stress through restructuring on the one hand, and requiring creativity and higher commitment on the other. They tried not to undermine the latter through pushing the former too aggressively.[17] Particularly in a situation where external labour markets were only partially developed, a lack of caution could easily undermine higher commitment.

Commitment to employees still started at the point of employment, not emergence from the 'pile'. It was not just a matter of fairness to the Cs, but if the Cs were seen to be treated unfairly, the extra effort needed of the Bs, and even the As, might be lost. In other words, community values were still strong. In GE's more individualistic approach, managers were charged with educating and empowering others and behaving in a boundaryless manner, but the norms were justified by reference to results, rather than an underlying shared sense of fairness.[18]

Half baked?

These three areas of difference – strategy, implementation and cultural 'software' – are systematically linked, in both cases. They exhibit what

---

[16] Welch's reputation was subsequently tarnished by the enormity of his retirement package, but while he was CEO, few shareholders complained.

[17] Cappelli et al. (1997: 57–8) cite a 1993 *New York Times* article in which employees in a GE jet engine plant are described as 'working scared' but also 'working smarter, harder, more flexibly and more co-operatively'. Konzelmann and Forrant (2000), also describe the stress of workers in GE's Lynn factory, as well as those of suppliers under pressure to relocate production to Mexico under GE's Globalization and Supplier Migration initiative.

[18] Richard Ellsworth says this about GE's culture under Welch: 'Welch has created a cadre of professionals and given them a focus on serving their self interest. He has told them that GE will make them better professionals, more marketable professionals, and has subjected them to intense pressures to perform. But he has not given them a sense of loyalty to the organization, to some higher goal of the organization. He is still hammering away at being number one, competing and winning, but what he may not realize is that the message to managers is "look out for yourself, win at any cost, do whatever you have to do"' (cited in Lowe, 2001: 168).

Dore (2000) describes as 'institutional interlock' and 'motivational congruence'. On current evidence, Hitachi is destined not to become GE.

Is this good or bad? Is this interpretation just an academic way of dressing up the fact that Hitachi's managers failed to go beyond what Welch denounced as 'superficial congeniality', or as failing the 'reality test' (the reality of competitive global – US – capitalism)? Were their reforms a half-baked compromise? From an Anglo-Saxon capitalism yardstick, probably bad, yes and yes. Nowhere was the contrast between the two more visible than in profits, as the Japanese media liked to point out.[19] As GE's profits grew sharply through the 1980s, Hitachi's steadily declined and by 2003, at least, the reforms had yet to establish a new upward trajectory.

Questioning whether Japanese companies can compete in the twenty-first century, Porter et al. (2000) argue that a new differentiating strategy-based approach is needed, and that:

> Profitability is the only reliable guide to developing strategy. Pursuing the goal of profitability will require fundamental shifts in the values that underlie Japanese business practice. Earning a good return on investment must be seen as the ultimate test of a company's success in creating economic, customer and social value. Capital must be seen as a valuable resource to be used efficiently. Prestige and rewards come not from size but uniqueness.[20]

A weak interpretation of this statement is that a greater strategic emphasis on profitability is necessary. Hitachi's managers have arguably recognized, or rediscovered, this. A strong interpretation is that the greater the profitability, the more successful and the more valuable, implying that profit *maximization* should be Hitachi's goal. References by Porter et al. to Harley Davidson as a champion of uniqueness are of little use to a giant like Hitachi, but the implication is that Hitachi should have much more aggressively pruned its activities, and thought twice about diversifying into new areas like life sciences (which are likely to be a net drain for many years. For that matter, it should probably not have diversified into computers in the 1960s, as returns did not justify the investment for more than ten years.). In fact, the best thing Hitachi could have done

---

[19] Cf. *Nikkei shinbun*, 12 January 2001; also Sasaki (1999).

[20] Porter et al., 2000: 170–1. A similar view is expressed by Owen with regards Siemens in Germany. He argues that: 'The merit of the Anglo-American financial system is that it forces firms to specialize in businesses where they have a reasonable chance of competing profitably.' He notes that 'Siemens increased its sales faster than GEC between the 1970s and the 1990s, but its profitability was much lower . . . It is not easy to see what benefits accrued to the shareholders in the company, or to the German economy, from Siemens' heavy investments, over a period of many years, in loss-making activities such as semiconductors' (Owen, 1999, 292–3). GEC has virtually disappeared, Siemens is still around.

would have been to recruit Jack Welch upon his retirement from GE in 2001.[21]

Even if profit maximization *were* the goal, however, questions would remain about the relevant time frame – maximization in the short-term versus long-term – and unit – from individual activities within a division through to the consolidated Group. It might also be questioned whether an individual company or even group is the appropriate unit of assessment; individual companies might grow, in the short term at least, through exploiting resources in their environment, and imposing costs on the environment which increase their own profits. At the very least, the adverse consequences of aggressive profit maximizing, individual-enriching, governance and incentive structures symbolized by Enron should give pause for thought.[22]

Finally, leadership is not just about defining uniqueness, and decisiveness, but about balance as well. One set of balances is between individuals and the company. Another is between the demands of various stakeholders, and another is between short-term and long-term demands. An important balance in a time of reform is between decisiveness and balance itself. It may well be that erring towards balance limited the impact of the reforms, but the objectives themselves were different from GE.

A new model?

Our final evaluation asks whether the reforms challenged Hitachi's community firm classic model in a fundamental way. Did they destroy it, modify it, or perhaps even extend it? Can we see a new model in the making?

The company has tried to reshape the employment relationship. Top managers believed that the implicit contract had resulted in psychological comfort, and in some cases apathy; they sought to create a new tension, or edge, in the relationship. Loyalty was indirectly de-emphasized. Employees were urged to take responsibility for their own career development, to stand on their own feet, and to work more reflexively, more attuned to the environment outside the company.[23]

Nonetheless, the contract itself was not thrown out. There seems to have been a 'morale line' which top managers were not keen to breech.

[21] The authors might deny this is their implication. They later attempt to balance their prescription with an acknowledgement of the enabling resources Japanese companies have to bring about a transition.

[22] These are the kinds of criticisms leveled at GE by O'Boyle, 1998.

[23] As Gerstner says: 'As long as IBMers remain focused outwards, the world will keep them on their toes' (2002: 215).

Morale is closely linked with notions of fairness, which were not disregarded. (If anything, employees felt the company needed to make more concerted efforts at reform, including de-emphasizing seniority and rewarding performance.) Long-term employment was attenuated, but the core workforce was still employed on long-term assumptions. The living security principle was not seriously breached, and *nenko* was shackled, not slain. It is difficult to argue that in these respects the new employment relationship is fundamentally different from that of the classic model.

The employment relationship began to change in another sense as well, with a shift in emphasis from uniformity to flexibility and recognition of diversity (and perhaps the beginnings of welcoming diversity as a source of new ideas and perspectives which will stimulate creativity). Recognizing diversity means greater acceptance of individual differences, or individualization of employment. This in turn begins to blur the boundaries of employment types, and consequently categories of membership. Female employees, notably, edge closer to full membership. In addition, increasing movement of personnel and synergy projects began to blur community boundaries.

On the other hand, the 2004 reforms deliberately reintroduced standardization (though not uniformity), in the form of a common HRM framework, and a common understanding of that framework. It is significant that this once more encompassed both white- and blue-collar workers, and managers as well. There seems to be a line here, too, which managers did not want traversed, a point in which 'we-consciousness' begins to transmute or fracture.

With regards corporate governance, Hitachi culminated a series of reforms with the early introduction of the US-style committee system, in 2003, not only for itself, but for eighteen listed subsidiaries. At Hitachi this resulted in the appointment of four external directors, and one from a Group company. The institutional form may have been US-inspired, but the composition reflected a continuing desire for greater openness, and to draw in external *stakeholder* views more speedily.

The company did seek to strengthen investor relations, and also to encourage managers – and indeed employees – to 'imagine (themselves) in the shoes of shareholders'. The latter was done through stock options and new employee shareholding measures (and arguably allowing employees to convert part of their lump sum retirement money into a 401K-type pension, which involved creating the Hitachi Financial Community). But this was not a wholesale conversion to shareholder capitalism. The stock option scheme and new employee shareholding measures were largely symbolic. The company bought back a large chunk of shares in 2003, presumably to boost ROE, but it spent much more on its purchase of IBM's hard disk drive business around the same time. And its decision to lower its 20% divestment target in 2004 could not have been designed to please shareholders.

Here, too, there seems to be a line which top managers did not want to cross. Higher profits were needed for the long-term health of the company and all its stakeholders, including shareholders, but the preferred means was through high road measures – new value creation – which would enliven and not undermine the community firm.

Hitachi's future is clearly linked to its ability to develop and commercialize technology. To prosper in the future, it requires a governance structure, innovative organization architecture and HRM policies to support the development and commercialization of technology. It needs complementary structures and processes to ensure accountability to stakeholders. In principle, top managers now have the tools to create a different model to achieve these ends, but by their choices, they still believe that they are best accomplished by a modified, and not fundamentally different, version of the classic model.

We would like to close with some comments on Hitachi's global operations, which have not figured prominently in our analysis.[24] This is not just the result of omission; the reforms were very much driven by domestic concerns. In the words of one manager: 'If we don't change ourselves in our home base, there won't be anything left to globalize.' Domestically focused reforms, however, threatened to impact negatively on foreign operations, in the short to medium term at least, in contradiction to the i.e. Hitachi Plan goal of raising overseas sales share.

Common problems of managing global operations in diversified companies were magnified in the case of Hitachi. Many overseas operations were set up by operating divisions, and both regional headquarters and corporate headquarters played a secondary role. In the late 1980s and 1990s, however, there were attempts to strengthen regional headquarters and move towards new business creation rather than discrete sales or manufacturing operations. This created conflicting demands. On the one hand, it needed managers conversant with internal organizational complexities, and preferably with leverage in Japan, and on the other, it needed managers competent to do business in foreign settings, with strategic local networks.

Even Japanese managers abroad, however, complained that organizational complexity and the pace of decision-making in Japan killed many

---

[24] These comments are based on interviews at Hitachi America Ltd in October, 1998 and Hitachi Europe Ltd in October 1998 and March 1999. They do not necessarily apply to Asian operations.

chances of developing new business abroad. They wanted greater independence to develop new initiatives, but were reliant on the Japanese divisions and headquarters for funds, which came under sudden strain with the semiconductor losses in the mid-1990s. This strain, the loss of 1998, and the subsequent reforms, moreover, unwittingly sent the message to nervous foreign employees that the company was 'battening down the hatches', especially as some local operations were closed down or restructured. Capable managers and employees left. For corporate headquarters intent on saving money, this was not necessarily a bad thing, but for the overseas operations, it was very debilitating.

In principle, the organization and governance reforms designed to speed up decision-making and make the organization transparent will benefit not just investors, but foreign employees as well. The company began to work on a Global Grade System for HRM, and the i.e. Hitachi Plan II demonstrated a new realism about which products or technologies could be globalized. These may facilitate global operations in the long term, but the tensions and dilemmas are far from resolved. And it will be some time before there is a significant reverse flow of talent and ideas into Japanese operations to create this kind of enrichment through diversity. In this sense, too, there has not been a fundamental break from the classic model. In Part 3 we shall examine the grounds for calling this a 'reformed model' of the community firm.

Part 3

The Reformed Model

14 New Model in the Making?

In Part 3 we seek, first of all, to link the conclusions of Parts 1 and 2, to discuss change and continuity in the community firm, and prospects for its future. We begin with a brief reflection on the rise of the classic model and its association with producer-oriented industrial capitalism, and the problems encountered by both, which led to concerted efforts at reform in the late 1990s. The result, as we saw in Parts 1 and 2 was not fundamental discontinuity; the community firm has survived, but it has changed in several crucial respects.

If we conceive of the changes as movement along a continuum between a community pole and a market pole, most firms find themselves somewhere in between, but nearer to the community pole than the market one. This is not necessarily an unstable position to be in, as firms have good reasons to try to balance market forces with community dynamics, and vice versa. We explore this middle ground to better understand the nature of what we will call the 'reformed model'.

In section three we examine marketization's companion, financialization (Dore, 2000), and whether shareholders will bring fundamental change where product markets and internal reform have not. Japan's financial sector has been in crisis, and is undergoing great changes, but these, we argue, will not necessarily mirror those in the USA and UK in the 1980s and 1990s. Japan's future does not necessarily lie in financial capitalism.

Finally, we ask if the reformed community firm model is sufficiently reformed to answer the critics, both in terms of economic efficiency or vitality, and in terms of social fairness. As the model is still in its early stages of evolution, we cannot offer a definitive view, but we will offer some preliminary observations.

The rise and fall of the 'classic model'

The material fruits of Japan's remarkable postwar growth are still evident in every town and city across the country, but psychologically, the postwar era seems an age ago, separated from the twenty-first century by the chasm of the troubled 1990s. Japan's corporate champions rose from the devastation of the Second World War, and the turmoil and social conflict which followed, by selectively maintaining past institutions and practices, and introducing new ones. This was especially evident in many, though not all, manufacturing industries, where shopfloor-based innovation brought about dramatic productivity gains while labour costs were still low by international standards.

The history of Japan's postwar productivity movement shows innovative twists to many ideas originating in the USA. Productivity improvement did not remain the province of production engineering or specialist quality control offices, but spread to the shopfloor, where it became institutionalized in zero defect and quality control circles. 'Soft' innovation was combined with 'hard' technological innovation, which created the foundations for international competitiveness in the machine industries.

This innovation dynamic was supported by complementary innovations in employment relations. The burgeoning postwar labour movement pressed for employment security, living wages and the abolition of white-collar–blue-collar status differentials. Managers were forced to give significant concessions in these areas, which were not overturned when they regained the initiative in the 1950s. The mitigation of status – or class – differentials most probably facilitated the spread of quality control concepts to the shopfloor and the development of new shopfloor institutions by ameliorating the 'them and us' divide that remained a feature of employment relations in countries like the UK (cf. Udagawa et al., 1995). And employment security no doubt made it easier for workers to co-operate over the introduction of new technologies in the 1950s, or at least not to oppose it.

Nonetheless, it took further innovations (and considerable arm twisting – cf. Gordon, 1998) in managing blue-collar workers, such as the new foreman system which opened the way for promotion of veteran workers to lower management ranks, before the high growth 'co-operate over pie production, bargain over the distribution' dynamic was finally established. These innovations were introduced in the late 1950s and early 1960s and were subsequently refined and systematized, creating the finishing touches to Japan's postwar community firms. Encompassing both white-collar and blue-collar regular (male) employees, community firms were a crucial foundation for Japan's postwar reconstruction and growth.

These were complemented, in turn, by innovations in other institutions and practices, such as 'patient' indirect financing and stable, reciprocal shareholding, as well as subcontracting and inter-firm relations.

Combined, they created a dynamic form of industrial capitalism that became the focus of world attention, and consternation, in the 1980s.

Indeed, as large businesses in the UK and USA embarked on restructuring in the 1980s, often with mass redundancies, and as these spread from blue-collar workers into white-collar offices and middle manager ranks, the Japanese industrial and corporate community model seemed superior to many in terms of both economic efficiency *and* social fairness (justice).

Within Japan, there were those who saw this form of capitalism, and community firms, as a decidedly mixed blessing, as we saw in chapter 1. Criticism coalesced around three issues: community companies may have encompassed both white-collar and blue-collar employees, but they discriminated against quasi-members and non-members – *exclusion*; they gave the semblance of allowing bottom-up participation, but within prescribed parameters in which individual needs could be overridden in favour of the 'public' (corporate) good – *enforcement*; and they externalized problems arising from exclusive corporate-centredness, retarding the development of civil society – *externalities*. While conceding economic efficiency, critics saw this as being gained at the expense of social fairness.

These concerns grew in the 1980s. Even leaders of the productivity movement became concerned that there was an important ingredient missing from the postwar success formula. The Japan Productivity Centre commissioned studies on the 'humanization of work', and public campaigns were launched to reduce working hours and make Japan a 'giant in living' as well as production. At the time there was little alternative inspiration to be gained from restructuring in the USA and UK, though, and considerable resistance to tampering with a successful formula. Concerns about social fairness alone could not provide the impetus to overcome this resistance. This is not surprising since many successful companies were now run by senior managers who had spent their whole working lives in those companies, and as junior managers had been involved in the very innovations which had made them successful.

Success is a fickle friend, however. It often produces the seeds of its own transformation, and sometimes destruction. It encourages adherence to strategies which outlive their day. Mature leaders of mature companies often responded to challenges of the late 1980s, especially those unleashed by the post-Plaza Accord yen appreciation, with institutionalized innovation which had worked in the past. This brought temporary relief, but pushed the yen ever higher, creating more demanding treadmill pressures.

Productivity advances and the shifting of production offshore to counter the strong yen and trade friction, meanwhile, reduced the weight of direct production in corporate activities. By the early 1990s, blue-collar workers constituted a relatively small share of employees in many large manufacturers, even though personnel practices and were still oriented towards their management and needs. The importance of white-collar creativity and productivity was recognized, but to the extent that it supported production activities. New thinking and organizational responses, necessary to cope with technological and competitive challenges in the ICT industries, were largely missing.

In terms of both social fairness and productive efficiency, therefore, problems had emerged which were not dealt with decisively. In the 1990s they were compounded by new problems, such as financial crisis, prolonged recession and deflation. By the late 1990s it was clear to many companies that sitting tight and hoping for things to improve was no longer a viable option, but that strategic and organizational reforms were needed, as well as reforms to employment practices. The Japan Federation of Employers' Association's employment 'portfolio' advocacy (Nikkeiren, 1995) reflected this change in thinking, as well as conceptual fuzziness about what should be done.

Individual employers started to embark on organization reform, consolidated management, and to introduce new governance structures and HRM practices. Changes to the Commercial Code and related laws facilitated these management reforms, while a series of new employment-related laws shifted the policy emphasis from employment stability through corporations to individual employability and facilitating restructuring. Media opinion, too, shifted to advocacy of 'bold' restructuring and castigation of those seen as procrastinators.

In this book we set out to identify just how much change there has been to the community firm, particularly through changes in employment relations, corporate governance and managers' priorities, as a result. In Part 1 we examined statistical and survey evidence of change. We saw that there had been some weakening of long-term employment and *nenko*, particularly with regards attitudes, but not sufficient to justify claims of collapse. Although problems were identified in organization and management, the rise of white-collar workers and 'creative work' were not seen as incompatible with community firm employment practices. More employees were now aspiring to become specialists, but the work ethic remained strong. 'Company man' had changed, but not disappeared.

In terms of corporate governance, too, increasing attention was being paid to shareholders and investor relations, amidst a decline of stable and reciprocal shareholding. We found a growing willingness to strengthen supervision and auditing mechanisms. The overall result may be a movement on the part of some top managers towards the 'enlightened shareholder value model', but hardly a conversion to shareholder or financial capitalism. Critically, the employee characteristics of top managers had been weakened, but not firmly changed. We also found loose coupling between corporate governance orientations and attitudes towards the reform of employment relations.

By some measures, managers' priorities had shifted, from favouring sales growth to profitability. Relatedly, managers had been implementing consolidated management and restructuring group orientations. But as our case studies showed, this was typically not constructed as a zero-sum trade-off with maintaining employment opportunities. Consolidated management limited opportunities for employment adjustment through quasi internal labour markets, but in terms of strategic HRM, these had matured rather than withered.

The picture that emerges from the detailed case study is basically similar. Our focus was on a series of reforms introduced by Hitachi in the wake of its 1998 loss, and these were both broad and deep. The HRM system was transformed, supposedly killing seniority considerations, the (US-inspired) committee system of corporate governance adopted, and consolidated management pursued. But after an initial period of ambivalence, the reforms generally took what we called a 'high road' direction, which stressed new value creation rather than single-minded cost cutting. This direction was influenced by industrial relations and morale considerations, and consequently did not fatally undermine the sense of community.

In terms of production in manufacturing companies, too, we see attempts to modify the overwhelming emphasis on development and production-related processes, and mobilize white-collar workers as professionals in the pursuit of 'total value creation'. But this may be viewed as the extension of productionist principles or their modification, rather than their abandonment. Here, too, there is continuity amidst change.

We conclude that the community firm will persist, but the classic model may be giving way to what may be called, for want of a better term, a *reformed model*. This presents us with a conceptual challenge. We argue that the community firm is being modified or reformed but not abandoned, but just when does the former give way to the latter? And how would we recognize a fundamentally new model if we saw it? Second, we have looked at changes to employment practices, corporate governance and managers' priorities or ideologies, but our concept of the community firm is still vague. Just what type of community are we left with?

Between community and market

We argued in chapter 1 that greater openness and mobility would weaken the sense of community. In addition, individualization, choice and emphasis on performance will shift the balance in the individual–community relationship. Involvement will become more conditional. We can get a sense of this from Hitachi's large-scale employee survey. Asked what was important for them in company life, twice as many employees chose 'fulfilling work' ('work worth doing') than the next choice, 'balance between work and private life', which in turn beat 'personal growth through raising ability', 'workplace human relations' and 'remuneration levels'. When asked what they thought about continuing to work for the company, not surprisingly more older than younger workers wrote they wanted to continue working there until retirement. What was surprising was the scale of the difference, suggesting greater conditionality of tenure as far as younger workers were concerned. Asked why they might change jobs, the most commonly cited reason was 'work is not fulfilling', followed by 'too busy', and for younger employees, 'want to improve skill levels' and 'dissatisfaction with wages'.

Greater conditionality in involvement has diverse manifestations. Capable employees in successful operations are likely to be less tolerant of management which seeks to preserve community at the expense of economic vigour, by continued support of weak operations, for instance, or diffuse R&D which creates a competitive disadvantage in the area they work in vis-à-vis their competitors.

The changes we have described in the book should not be seen simply as a weakening of commitment and community. There may well be a rebalancing of community occurring, between workplace community, firm-level community, and occupation-based or professional community, which Hazama lamented had been tilted decisively towards the firm level in the postwar period.

Another way of looking at the changes is along a continuum between two poles, one the community firm, and as its polar opposite, a firm characterized by a series of contracts undertaken on behalf of the shareholders, where employment relations are 'market oriented'. The closest empirical expressions are to be found in the Anglo Saxon USA, UK, New Zealand, etc. Dore (2000) uses a similar conceptual scheme to examine how far the twin forces of financialization and marketization have eroded the community basis of Japanese firms and transformed welfare capitalism. He argues that Japan is advancing along the road to market individualism, although the change is more in attitudes than actual practice (cf. Dore, 2000).

Although the extent of change may be debated, few would doubt that there has been some movement in the market direction. In Parts 1 and 2 we found penetration of market forces in group management and accounting practices, greater referencing of wages and conditions to competitor companies, of what work should be done internally versus externally, and so on. But most would also argue that Japanese companies remain some distance from the market pole. In fact, it is precisely in what appears to be the middle ground between markets and community that many of the reforms discussed in this book appear destined. In some cases this is because the reforms are tentative or superficial, but there may be good reasons for genuine reformers to seek out this middle ground. Granovetter, for instance, has argued convincingly that entrepreneurship flourishes where there is a balance between 'coupling' and 'decoupling'.[1]

A number of positions in this middle ground may be possible, weighted towards either the community or the market. US firms, for instance, are allegedly well along the road to marketization. Many writers have claimed the implicit or psychological contract for white-collar workers was broken in the late 1980s and 1990s, creating a contradiction of lost loyalty and employee instrumentalism on the one hand, with a requirement for greater commitment and creative contributions on the other.[2] Various approaches were taken to deal with this contradiction. AT&T, for instance, shed some 100,000 employees during restructuring in the 1980s, and was faced with the problem of low morale and insecurity among those left:

[T]he company met a significant competitive challenge by attempting to change the attitude and work practices of its own employees. It viewed its employees as important consumers of company products, specifically employment and compensation, and sought to influence employees by changing these products. (Albert and Bradley, 1997: 109)

Another 'market'-based solution widely used was equity-based compensation packages. Some companies, on the other hand, tried to reknit torn social fabric through a 'partnership' approach (cf. Kochan and Osterman, 1994).

Heckscher (1995) depicted the decline in paternalism associated with traditional 'communities of loyalty', but not their replacement by

---

[1] E.g. Granovetter, 2000.

[2] 'When employers backed away from their traditional obligations and offered nothing in return, employee commitment collapsed . . . How employers will operate with sharply lower employee commitment is an important issue, especially given that they have moved toward work systems that demand greater commitment through greater autonomy and reduced supervision' (Cappelli et al., 1997: 10–11; see also Blair and Kochan, 2000, including Baron's critique of the marketization thesis).

free agents and market forces. Some middle managers in his study – 'loyalists' – put their heads down and tried to shut themselves off from increasing organizational turbulence. Some became cynical and withdrawn. Others, in dynamic organizations, began to redefine their work, and their relationship with the company in a more constructive way. The new ethic espoused by the third type of middle manager was a 'professional' ethic, balancing the freedom of the individual with commitment to co-operation in 'communities of purpose'.[3]

This has clear similarities with our account, but is a 'community' in which people come together for specific purposes and continue to do so only as long as there are overlapping interests, or 'mutual gains', really a community? In sociology, this has long been referred to as 'association'.[4] As far as the Japanese companies we have been describing are concerned, there is still arguably a strong sense of membership, of 'we-consciousness', and this fosters a commitment which, for better or worse, goes beyond the pursuit of individual interests. It would seem that such companies are still on the community side of the fence, even if the balance between the different types of community is changing.

Diversity

A second area of both similarity and difference between US and Japanese companies concerns diversity. Kanter (1977) and others have documented increasing diversity in US companies. Heckscher argues that this was one factor in driving changes in the companies he studied. The reverse could apply, however – changing environments and ways of work increase the importance of diversity; homogeneity can actually become a liability. This appears to be the case at Hitachi, where one of the three key concepts to emerge from the second large-scale employee survey conducted in 2002 was the importance of 'diversity'. Relatedly, one of the other two key concepts to emerge from the survey was 'openness'. (The third was 'challenge'.) Greater openness is a natural partner of diversity. The dilemma, of course, is that greater diversity and openness may weaken internal cohesion. Diversity has yet to proceed this far at companies like Hitachi, and may well not do so. In this respect, too, they are still on the community side of the fence.

---

[3] 'The fundamental strength of the professional ethic, as I have described it, is that it balances the sense of meeting one's own needs with that of contributing to something larger, in a way that allows for dynamic change' (Heckscher, 1995: 156).

[4] Tönnies' *Gemeinschaft und Gesellschaft* (1887) is the most famous of many community-association ideal typical contrasts, sometimes with a continuum inserted in between.

In a third aspect of positioning in the middle ground, on the other hand, Japanese companies exhibit greater diversity. 'Communities of purpose' in the USA, like 'communities of loyalty' before them, tend to be limited to select white-collar workers or managers. Blue-collar workers seldom belong. It is significant that many large US companies began to outsource their manufacturing operations to contract manufacturers in the 1990s, or conversely, to contract in. This may represent a process of marketization. It might also, however, make it easier to create overlapping interests, communities even, among those left, with greater homogeneity, and without traditional 'them and us' conflict.[5]

In Japanese manufacturing companies, by contrast, although white-collarization is well advanced and is one pressure for reform, blue-collar employees are still part of the community firm. Indeed as they become a minority, special care is often taken to ensure that they are not disproportionately affected by reform and restructuring. Significantly, the contract manufacturing (EMS) model has been much slower to take root in Japan, although internal contracting has re-emerged. This may not simply be the result of enduring productionism, but of community as well.

If we extend this observation, in general Japanese companies have been reluctant to exclude or downgrade the status of member categories which raise fundamental questions of fairness. They are also reluctant to reward categories, teams or members to the extent that similar questions are raised.

Dilemmas of the middle ground

Being on the community side of the fence (or 'morale line' – the line managers have tried not to breech so as to mobilize employees willingly behind reform), and maintaining continuity in the face of change, (many) Japanese companies and their employees do not face the broken implicit or psychological contract contradiction referred to above. Instead, they face a different contradiction or dilemma. Employees are expected to break out of the introversion that can lurk in the community firm, to stand on their own feet and become more creative, while still knowing that they belong. Belonging can generate psychological comfort, and this in turn can create dependence.[6]

---

[5] If this is so, the changes have been driven by a combination of marketization and communitization of sorts.

[6] At a strategic level, the synergy dilemma is similar; it relies on creating new opportunities without fundamentally pruning weaker operations.

Some companies have been working hard to address this dilemma. They find a ready audience among younger employees, who prefer the new balance. Thus, for instance, Fuji Xerox has created a President's Academy to develop 'change leaders' (*henkaku rida*), who are selected on the basis of proposal submission following their initial three-year training period, and encouraged to identify, study and tackle problems or opportunities facing the company (mostly in their own time, on their own initiative, but with interaction and support from top managers). They are subsequently given job assignments to develop their leadership skills with a view to producing department managers in their 30s and directors in their 40s. Similarly, Denso has a mechanism for selecting and challenging 'high talent' employees in their early 30s, some of whom will eventually become 'core managers' or 'core specialists' with special assignments.[7]

Such mechanisms depart from the OJT-(*nenko* sensitive) job postings described in chapter 2. They rely on individual (white-collar) employees stepping forward and using their own initiative individually or in small groups. The rewards are still long-term, but they come quicker than in the past. The company benefits from the employees' initiative, and rejuvenation. It is significant that they target younger employees, who want challenging jobs, and appear to be more willing than in the past to quit if they don't get them. More broadly, internal job posting and 'free agent' systems encourage and reward individual initiative. In many ways they simulate market mechanisms, but within company or enterprise group communities.[8]

The diversity and openness dilemma is a knotty one. It is particularly important for Japanese companies aspiring to develop globally, and where competitive advantage is not strongly linked to shopfloor production processes. Early selection, individualization of employment, new working practices and increased mid-term hiring increase diversity to some extent, as can family friendly policies. Ethnic diversity is another matter. Fujitsu notably hired a Korean – at the time a managing director of Samsung – and in 2001 appointed him to head business strategies for the Asia-Pacific region. Matsushita has appointed a Korean female to develop its global HRM system. But these are as yet isolated cases. In principle the reforms we have described should make it easier to accommodate diversity, but this will not come about easily.

Third, membership and fairness dilemmas have to do with employees who become surplus to requirements, or fail to perform on the one hand,

---

[7] Presentations by Y. Otake and H. Kawachi respectively at the Japan Management Association's Human Resources Development 2004 Conference, 3–6 February 2004.

[8] This is different from trying to introduce partnership or mutual gains into market-based or adversarial relationships.

and very high performers on the other. These are partially resolvable. As we saw, notions of fairness are changing on the part of both employees and managers, by and large in the same direction. Other studies have suggested that rising income and status tilts notions of fairness from need to merit (e.g. Alves and Rossi, 1978), or effort to performance. As long as efforts are expended to help lesser-performers, and high performers' rewards are not astronomical, community norms can remain intact. The rub, no doubt, comes when very high performers think they deserve more, as in the celebrated case of Nakamura versus Nichia (cf. chapter 4), and this rub may become more severe with moves afoot to legislate on intellectual property rights for employees.

Finally, while many Japanese companies are still on the community side of the fence, some will be nearer the market pole than others. This is particularly so in the financial sector, in which non-Japanese companies have a significant presence, and present an alternative model to the community firm. This leads to the question of 'financialization'.

Financialization and managers

If 'marketization' has not destroyed the community firm, how about its companion, 'financialization', brought on by financial liberalization, global capital flows, increasing wealth and ageing? Will shareholders force Japanese managers to introduce far-reaching changes they would rather not undertake themselves?

The case should not be underestimated. Until the early 1990s, most companies only shed employees through early retirement, voluntary or involuntary redundancies in rather exceptional circumstances, and their share price generally dropped. By the turn of the century, labour shedding had begun to exert a positive influence on share prices. As consciousness of share prices itself had risen, this may have encouraged pro-active labour shedding. For those managers still not tuned into such changes, the hostile takeover bid by US buy-out fund Steel Partners for Yushiro Chemical and Sotoh in early 2004 cannot have gone unnoticed. The bids were only repulsed after the companies massively raised their dividends, prompting financial analysts to declare another victory for shareholder activism and shareholder value.[9] Lists were soon created of new takeover candidates – companies with low price-to-book value ratios, high retained earnings against total assets or surplus funds to market capitalization – and some of these were household names.

---

[9] E.g. Goldman Sach's chief strategist in Tokyo, quoted in *Financial Times*, 17 February 2004.

The question is, how will managers respond? In fact here, too, we can identify a position between that of the classic model of the community firm on the one hand, and shareholder primacy on the other. The position is both old and new; we could argue that the wheel is coming a full circle, to the position advocated by many executives in the early postwar period, when labour rather than capital was on the offensive. In 1947, the newly formed Keizai Doyukai (Japan Committee for Economic Development) argued that the firm should be seen as a community comprising capital, management and labour, each entitled to a 'fair' share of profits and say in management. In this conception of 'modified capitalism' (*shusei shihonshugi*), two parties would be able to provide checks and balances on excessive demands by the third party, but by and large, it was the job of managers to mediate interests and resolve conflicts in a way conducive to corporate development and economic reconstruction.[10]

Recent management and governance reforms have weakened the employee characteristics of managers somewhat, but have hardly thrust them into the role of agents of shareholders. This trend is likely to continue as the job of executives becomes more complex and demanding. Intensified, global competition, deregulation, rapid developments and changes in technologies, shortened product cycles and associated risks with R&D all call for faster, responsive decision-making, and sometimes restructuring, or spinning out operations into joint ventures with former rivals. Consolidated management and focus is another challenge.

Managers climbing corporate hierarchies in community firms are not always well equipped to deal with these challenges. They may lack the necessary perspective on change, or be too entrenched or inexperienced to bring it about. The most celebrated example of an outsider brought in to carry out changes people knew needed to be done but couldn't accomplish was Carlos Ghosn at Nissan; less famous but also significant were quasi-insiders (or quasi-outsiders) with broader experience in enterprise groups brought in – or back – to restructure core companies in retailing, pharmaceutical and other industries (Probert, 2002).

In merged companies, the community-respecting formula of balancing parties proportionately in the top management structure can be highly debilitating. Nowhere is this more dramatically illustrated than in Elpida, the merged DRAM operations of NEC and Hitachi, where world market share plunged from 15% to 4% in just two years prior to the arrival of Sakamoto Yukio (formerly of Texas Instruments and UMC) in 2002. Sakamoto reduced intervention by the 'parent' firms, raised

---

[10] Cf. Okazaki et al., 1996; Tsutsui, 1998: 122–9.

funds which had been denied the new company, clarified objectives and responsibilities, and replaced many of the senior managers. Elpida gradually began to regain lost market share.[11]

Restructuring, mergers, acquisitions, not to mention various kinds of alliance, may have been exceptional in the past, but have become more common, and call for new management skills, especially with a backdrop of consolidated management, and heightened shareholder and media scrutiny. Consolidated management has forced executives to think, and to some extent *behave*, like shareholders in their enterprise groups. These developments are likely to reduce the employee representative, senior community member characteristics of managers, and increase the difference between senior managers and employees.

Ideologically, too, it is not surprising to see some repositioning – though generally on the community side of the fence – particularly in view of the global tide of corporate governance reform which hit Japan in the 1990s. From the mid-to-late 1990s, the Japan Federation of Employers' Associations advocated making companies attractive to both capital and labour markets (e.g. Nikkeiren, 1998). As we noted in chapter 5, in March 2002 the Japan Association of Corporate Directors was launched, to study and improve corporate governance practice in Japan. It was headed by the chairman of the Japan Corporate Governance Forum, Miyauchi Yoshihiko, who believes 'simply put, corporate governance is executives managing their companies effectively for the profit of shareholders, and supervised from the shareholder perspective' (Nihon torishimariyaku kyokai, 2002: 10). Significantly, however, committee heads of the Association, writing in the same publication, demurred. As Idei, chairman and CEO of Sony – which has higher consolidated sales in the USA than Japan – put it: 'There is no global standard of corporate governance' (pp. 165–6).

Indeed, Enron, WorldCom and other corporate scandals took the shine off the US version of 'global standards', but that did not put an end to corporate governance reform. A string of corporate scandals in Japan, often involving corporate irresponsibility towards customers, highlighted the need to review 'inside virtue–outside vice' dynamics, risk management and corporate social responsibility. As a result, executives themselves became concerned about the efficacy of their corporate governance institutions, and set about implementing changes.

---

[11] T. Yunogami, 'Technology Management in the IT Sector: The Case of Semiconductors', presentation to ITEC International Forum, Kyoto, 12 March 2004. Sakamoto reflected that one of his biggest challenges was to replace an inward (Elpida/NEC/Hitachi) focus with an outward-oriented one; discussion, 16 March 2004.

This has produced innovations to the full circle. The number of stakeholders has now been extended. We can see this, again, in JCED publications, such as its 2003 Corporate White Paper (Keizai Doyukai 2003). Titled 'Market Evolution and Corporate Social Responsibility Management: Toward Building Integrity and Creating Stakeholder Value', it starts with the importance of profitability and competitiveness, and then argues that managers have responsibilities to all stakeholders, and as they manage public bodies, they must attempt to meet all of them. Corporations must go beyond the pursuit of economic value, and be responsible for creating social value and human value as well. The danger of prioritizing shareholder interests is that:

> corporations may veer drastically from social needs and values, which reflect Japan's unique culture, traditions and customs. In this sense, it is necessary to promote the evolution of the market so that the market is capable and geared towards rendering a more comprehensive evaluation of corporations and corporate behaviour. (p. 2)

This reformulation of 'modified capitalism' argues that performance should be measured as the 'total impact of corporate activities on stakeholders, as seen in the context of the corporation's own mission' (ibid.: 12).[12]

Of course this might be executives' preferred position, but these might be overwhelmed by shareholder activism. It is difficult to predict what will happen when or if individual investors begin diverting savings away from banks and into equity markets, but it is worth noting that from within shareholder activism, a current of socially responsible investment (SRI) has emerged. Eco-funds were launched in Japan in 1999, but 2003 was dubbed the 'birth year' of SRI, when Morningstar Japan launched the first SRI index (covering corporate social responsibility, corporate governance, employment, consumer services, the environment and social contributions), and funds and investors increased sharply. It is still too early to say what the impact of SRI will be in Japan, but it is likely to reinforce the emerging stakeholder ideology, which is compatible with the reformed model of the community firm. Financialization will most probably develop differently from the USA and UK in the 1980s and 1990s.

---

[12] This, of course, is easier said than done. Berle and Means, too, argued that corporations should ultimately be subject to the claims of the community, and that managers should balance to claims of various groups, but Berle argued that in the absence of a well-defined system of responsibilities to society, accountability should be to shareholders: Berle and Means, 1932: 312–13; Berle, 1932: 1365, cited in Learmount and Roberts, 2002: 2–3. Hitachi intended to introduce performance indices reflecting stakeholder interests, but initially, at least, introduced a variant of EVA.

Normative questions

The classic model of the community firm played an important role in Japan's emergence as an economic powerhouse, and raising living standards while maintaining social cohesion. Can the revised model play a similar role in a new growth dynamic, while addressing some of the long-standing criticisms of the classic model, as well as emerging issues of social fairness? Let us look at the economic vitality question first.

Japanese corporate managers have been castigated for their failure to downsize decisively, for investing in new business areas rather than cutting back to the bone, for mollycoddling mediocre managers and workers rather than casting them aside. Such castigation is sometimes tinged with a Machiavellian barb that good intentions and indecision pave the road to ruin. At the very least, concerted restructuring – or creative destruction – would free up resources and space for startups, of which Japan has shown a relative dearth in recent years.

But the persistence of large firms, and their employment share, does not prove they are laggards. On the contrary, it could be argued that many have been relatively more successful at adapting to new conditions than their UK and US counterparts which restructured in the 1980s and 1990s. And to some degree, at least, this success is linked to efforts to maintain a sense of community, and draw upon this, in the midst of reform. Corporate managers can hardly be blamed for failing to take a macro-view of startups, and for attempting to rekindle entrepreneurship internally, and through spinoffs.[13]

That said, we recognize that Japan's large firms are by no means homogeneous in terms of both need and effectiveness of reforms. Some are successfully navigating turbulent business environments and internal challenges, and the dilemmas we have outlined, while others are not. Some have succeeded in restoring outward responsiveness and reflexivity, while others have not.

In the latter type of firm, managers hard pressed to produce results today will be tempted to reduce headcounts and intensify work, seeking to mobilize workers to greater effort through appeals to common destiny and loyalty, but at the expense of creating conditions for more creative work which might boost performance in the long term.[14] We have no wish

---

[13] Actually a case can be made that it is in the self-interest of large companies to promote or at least condone employee spinouts, as often happened in the past, as it creates a more fertile and flexible business environment, which they can ultimately benefit from, but this is not the same as blaming managers for the problem.

[14] Surveys show a sharp rise in unreported overtime from the mid-1990s, concentrated in white-collar occupations and among male workers Dai-ichi seimei kenkyusho, 2003; Suzuki, 2003.

to be apologists for the interia-bound, work intensifiers, but it is unfair to tar all Japanese firms and managers with the same brush.

Second, there will be some sectors in which the reformed community firm will flourish, and others where it will not. We have already suggested that the deregulated financial sector will be less conducive to the survival of the community firm, reformed or not. Anecdotal evidence suggests there is less 'after 5' socializing with colleagues, labour turnover is comparatively high, and strongly influenced by individual remuneration packages. Even in the technology-manufacturing sector, there will be some diversity. Some companies like Toyota, which still derives strong competitive strength from productionist methods it honed, are likely to remain close to the classic model, while others pare down their regular employees to a very small core.

It is reasonable to argue, *a priori*, that community firms are more likely to survive and thrive in markets characterized by low-to-medium-scale volatility, but where very rapid decision-making is needed, and rapid and sometime risky redeployment of resources, they will be less successful. But even if this is broadly so, there are other sources of competitive strength such firms can call upon. There are powerful incentives for community firms to develop new technologies, experiment with new business models and enter new markets where standing still is not an option (or rather, is agreed not to be an option). There is no compelling reason why the community firm can only achieve incremental innovation and not fundamental breakthroughs.

It might also be argued that they will fare less well where business success is reliant on high performing individuals (the upper right corner of figure 11.3), but this will depend on how the balance is struck between individual employees and the community firm. There is no *a priori* reason why the reformed community firm is inimical to individual creativity.

And what of social fairness – the problems of exclusion, enforcement (or patriarchy), and externalities we identified earlier in the chapter, for instance? In principle, some of these criticisms will be ameliorated, as company boundaries become more porous, diversity becomes more widely accepted, and employees gain greater choice in the way they work and are employed. Problems remain, however, and some may intensify.

The rise of the company professional is often associated with more flexible forms of working, and hence improved compatibility between working and family life. On the other hand, company professionals are just as likely as company men to put in long hours of work. This is not simply problematic for their families. As the MHLW's 2003 White Paper notes, birth rates tend to be lowest where working hours are longest. Low birth rates accelerate demographic ageing. Problems associated with working hours, and hence externalities in this sense, are unlikely to be resolved by the emergence of the reformed model of the community firm.

Next, reforms in employment practices for core workers, and maintenance of community, have been accompanied by a parallel trend of casualization. As we saw in chapter 3, there has been a significant rise in the number of part-time and other non-regular workers, more than offsetting the decline in family labour. Non-regular workers now comprise over 27% of the labour force, and relaxation of the Worker Dispatching Law in 2004 will no doubt push the figure higher.

The privileges of full community firm members are to some extent secured at the expense of non-regular employees, many of whom are women. The distinction in working hours and content between the two groups is not always clear, and indeed has become increasingly blurred, but wages and conditions are very different. This is increasingly seen as unfair, but it is difficult for employers and unions to address it decisively, as doing so could adversely affect vested interests for both parties. For unions in particular, it raises the thorny issue of undermining the breadwinner's ('living') wage.

Third, youth are now over-represented in both non-regular employment and unemployment, with middle school and high school graduates finding it particularly difficult to get regular jobs. This corresponds with the curtailment of hiring in the 1990s, the increase in hiring of experienced workers, and of part-timers. In some cases, youth unemployment coexists with the availability of job openings, indicating a 'disconnect' between employers and young people, expressed in the '7-5-3' phenomenon (of 70% of middle school leavers quitting their first job within three years, 50% of high school leavers and 30% of university graduates).

With social fairness – social sustainability even – as with economic efficiency or vitality, some issues cannot be addressed fundamentally by individual employers. Business organizations are beginning to address some of these in the context of corporate social responsibility, but it is too early to anticipate concrete outcomes. Labour policy is coming to place less emphasis on full employment and job security, and more on 'fair' employment. Part-timer legislation looks increasingly likely, and may well be followed by reforms to spouse tax and social security regulations. It will be interesting to see to what extent such developments, and the corporate social responsibility movement, bring such issues on to the reform agenda of the community firm, providing a spur to further reform.

Criticism of the community firm and its deleterious links with the wider society is not limited to employment and labour market-related issues (or indeed capital market-related issues), but extends to relations with consumers. While not directed at Japanese firms in particular, in their critique of managerial capitalism and the enterprise logic, Zuboff and Maxmin (2002) argue that the maleness of producer organizations, and their tendency for introversion and narcissism, creates a fundamental disconnect with consumers, who are primarily women.[15] This disconnect leads to a variety of pathologies which can only be rectified, they argue, by a new type of capitalism – 'distributed capitalism' – not reform.

Community firms developed essentially as producer organizations, and by and large, this remains the case even under the reformed model. It is highly unlikely that we will see the next episode of capitalism as envisaged by Zuboff and Maxmin being born in Japan, even if support networks for consumers improve. We can, however, expect a different balance between community firms and the wider society, especially as mediated through product, labour and capital markets. The people inside the firms themselves are, after all, not just producers, but to an increasing extent consumers and holders of capital as well.

---

[15] They paraphrase sociologist Harrison White: 'Markets are tangible cliques of producers observing each other. Pressure from the buyer side creates a mirror in which producers see themselves, not consumers' (Zuboff and Maxmin, 2002: 243).

Appendix   Changes in Job Tenure

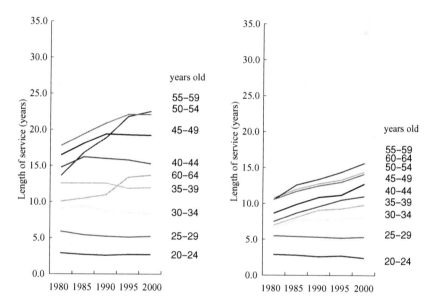

A–1–1 All industries, all sizes, males

A–1–2 All industries, all sizes, females

Note: Large company – 1,000 employees
Source: Rodosho/Kosei rodosho, *Chingin kozo kihon tokei chosa*, respective years

255

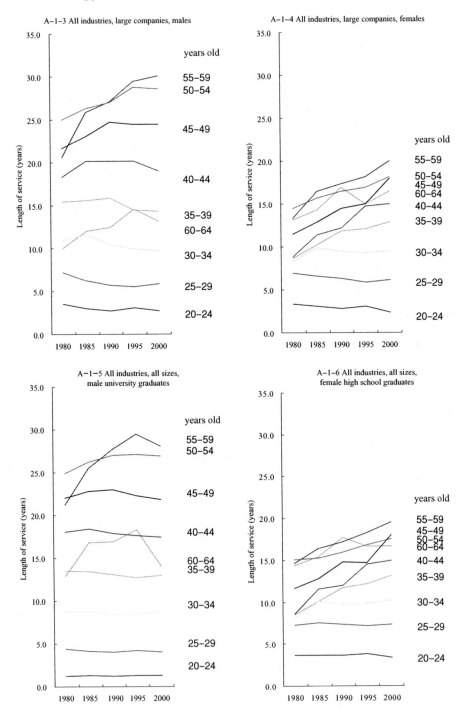

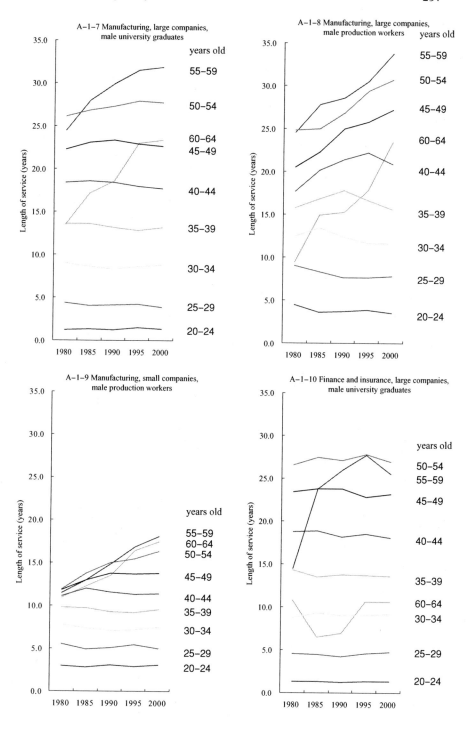

A–1–7 Manufacturing, large companies, male university graduates

A–1–8 Manufacturing, large companies, male production workers

A–1–9 Manufacturing, small companies, male production workers

A–1–10 Finance and insurance, large companies, male university graduates

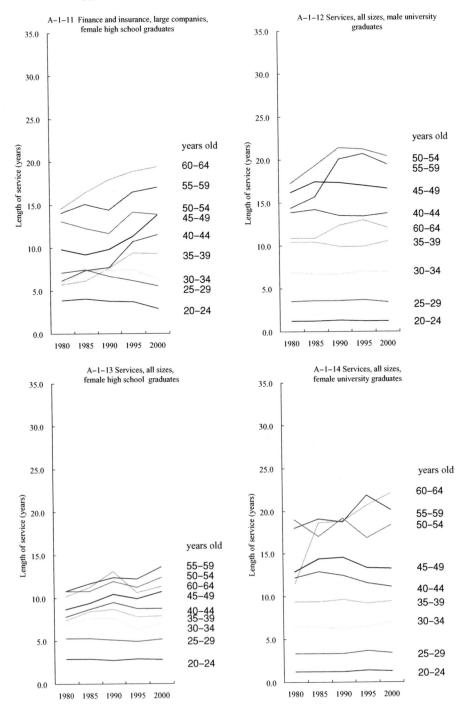

A–1–11 Finance and insurance, large companies, female high school graduates

A–1–12 Services, all sizes, male university graduates

A–1–13 Services, all sizes, female high school graduates

A–1–14 Services, all sizes, female university graduates

References

Abeggsen, J. (1958), *The Japanese Factory*, Glencoe Il: Free Press.

Albert, M. (1991), *Capitalisme contre capitalisme*, Paris: Edition du Seuil.

Albert, S. and K. Bradley (1997), *Managing Knowledge: Experts, Agencies and Organizations*, Cambridge: Cambridge University Press.

Allen, S., R. Clark and S. Schieber (1999), 'Has Job Security Disappeared in Large Corporations?', NBER Working Paper No. 6966. Cambridge, MA: National Bureau of Economic Research.

Alves, W. and P. Rossi (1978), 'Who Should Get What? Fairness Judgements of the Distribution of Earnings', *American Journal of Sociology*, Vol. 84, No. 3, pp. 541–64.

American Law Institute (1992), *Principles of Corporate Governance: Analysis and Recommendations*, Washington, DC: ALI Publishers.

Aoki, M. (1994), 'Toward an Economic Model of the Japanese Firm', in K. Imai and R. Komiya eds., *Business Enterprise in Japan: Views of Leading Japanese Economists*, Cambridge, MA: MIT Press.

Appleyard, M., C. Brown and L. Sattler (2002), 'An International Investigation of Creative Performance in the Semiconductor Industry', unpublished manuscript.

Araki, T. (2001), *Koyo shisutemu to rodo joken henko hori* (Employment System and Legal Principles of Altering Working Conditions), Tokyo: Yuhikaku.

— (2002), *Labor and Employment Law in Japan*, Tokyo: Japan Institute of Labour.

Atkinson, J. (1985), *Flexibility, Uncertainty and Manpower*, IMS Report, No. 89, Brighton: Institute of Manpower Studies.

Auer, P. (2000), *Employment Revival in Europe: Labour Market Success in Austria, Denmark, Ireland and the Netherlands*, Geneva: ILO.

Auer, P. and S. Cazes (2000), 'The Resilience of the Long-term Employment Relationship: Evidence from the Industrialized Countries', *International Labour Review*, Vol. 139, No. 4, pp. 379–408.

— (2003), *Employment Stability in an Age of Flexibility: Evidence from Industrialised Countries*, Geneva: ILO.

Baba, Y. (1997), 'Manufacturing Technologies', in Japan Commission on Industrial Performance, *Made in Japan*, Cambridge, MA: MIT Press.

Bennett, A. (1990), *The Death of the Organization Man*, New York: Touchstone.

Berger, S. and R. Dore eds. (1996), *National Diversity and Global Capitalism*, Ithaca: Cornell University Press.

Berle, A. (1932), 'For Whom Corporate Managers are Trustees: A Note', *Harvard Law Review*, 45, pp. 1365–72.

Berle, A. and G. Means (1932), *The Modern Corporation and Private Property*, New York: Macmillan.

Bertelsmann Stiftung und Hans Böckler Stiftung hrsg. (1998), *Mitbestimmung und neue Unternehmenskulturen – Bilanz und Perspektiven: Bericht der Kommission Mitbestimmung*, Köln: Bertelsmann Stiftung.

Best, M. (1990), *The New Competition: Institutions of Industrial Restructuring*, Cambridge: Polity Press.

Blair, M. and T. Kochan eds. (2000), *The New Relationship: Human Capital in the American Corporation*, Washington, DC: Brookings Institution Press.

Brown, W., S. Deakin, M. Hudson, C. Pratten and P. Ryan (1998), 'The Individualization of Employment Contracts in Britain', DTI Research Paper, June.

Business Roundtable (1997), *Statement on Corporate Governance*, Washington, DC: The Business Roundtable.

Business Sector Advisory Group on Corporate Governance (1998), *Corporate Governance: Improving Competitiveness and Access to Capital in Global Markets* (Millstein Report), Paris: OECD.

Cadbury Report – *see* Committee on the Financial Aspects of Corporate Governance.

Cain, P. and A. Hopkins (1993), *British Imperialism*, 2 vols., London: Longman.

CalPERS (California Public Employee Retirement System) (1998), *Corporate Governance: Core Principles and Guidelines*, Sacramento: CalPERS.

Cappelli, P. (1999a), *The New Deal at Work*, Boston: Harvard Business School Press.

— (1999b), 'Career Jobs are Dead', *California Management Review*, Vol. 41, No. 1, pp. 146–67.

Cappelli, P., L. Bassi, H. Katz, D. Knoke, P. Osterman and M. Useem (1997), *Change at Work*, New York: Oxford University Press.

Charkham, J. (1995), *Keeping Good Company: A Study of Corporate Governance in Five Countries*, Oxford: Oxford University Press.

Chikudate, N. (1999), 'The State of Collective Myopia in Japanese Business Communities: A Phenomenological Study for Exploring Blocking Mechanisms for Change', *Journal of Management Studies*, Vol. 36, No. 1, pp. 69–86.

Christensen, C. (1997), *The Innovator's Dilemma: When New Technologies Cause Great Firms to Fail*, Boston: Harvard Business School Press.

Clark, R. (1979), *The Japanese Company*, New Haven: Yale University Press.

Cole, R. (2003), 'Japanese Manufacturing Dilemmas: The ICT Industries', paper for Institutional Change in East Asia Conference, Cornell University, 3–5 April.

Collins, M. (1991), *Banks and Industrial Finance in Britain: 1800–1939*, Cambridge: Cambridge University Press.

Committee on Corporate Governance (1998), *Final Report* (Hampel Report), London: Gee Publishing.

Committee on the Financial Aspects of Corporate Governance (1992), *Financial Aspects of Corporate Governance* (Cadbury Report), London: Gee Publishing.

Conyon, M. and K. Murphy (2000), 'The Prince and the Pauper?: CEO Pay in the United States and United Kingdom', *Economic Journal*, 110, November, F670–671.

Coser, L. (1956), *The Functions of Social Conflict*, London: Routledge & Kegan Paul.

— (1974), *Greedy Institutions*, New York: Free Press.

Dai-ichi seimei kenkyusho (2003), 'Fukyoka de zoka suru sabisu zangyo' (Increasing Unpaid Overtime in the Recession), *Makuro keizai bunseki ripoto*, N-24, June.

Deery, S. and R. Mitchell eds. (1999), *Employment Relations: Individualisation and Union Exclusion*, Sydney: Federation Press.

Department of Trade and Industry (DTI, UK) (1998a), *Modern Company Law for a Competitive Economy*, London: DTI.

— (1998b), *Modern Company Law for a Competitive Economy: International Survey of Company Law in the Commonwealth, North America, Asia and Europe*, London: DTI.

— (1999), *Modern Company Law for a Competitive Economy: The Strategic Framework*, London: DTI.

— (2001), *Business and Society: Developing Corporate Social Responsibility in the UK*, London: DTI.

Dore, R. (1958; 1999), *City Life in Japan: A Study of a Tokyo Ward*, Berkeley: University of California Press.

— (1973; 1990), *British Factory – Japanese Factory: The Origins of National Diversity in Industrial Relations*, London: Allen and Unwin, and Berkeley: University of California Press.

— (1987), *Taking Japan Seriously: A Confucian Perspective on Leading Economic Issues*, London: Athlone Press.

— (1989), 'Where Are We Now? Musings of an Evolutionist', *Work, Employment and Society*, Vol. 3, No. 4, pp. 425–46.

—(2000), *Stock Market Capitalism, Welfare Capitalism: Japan and Germany versus the Anglo-Saxons*, Oxford: Oxford University Press.

Durkheim, E. (1893), *De la division du travail social*, Paris: PUF.

European Commission (2001), *Promoting a European Framework for Corporate Social Responsibility: Green Paper*, Luxembourg: Office for Official Publications of the European Community.

Foster, R. (1986), *Innovation: The Attacker's Advantage*, New York: Summit Books.

Fransman, M. (1995), *Japan's Computer and Communications Industry*, Oxford: Oxford University Press.

Freeman, R. (1998), 'War of the Models: Which Labour Market Institutions for the 21st Century?', *Labour Economics*, Vol. 5, pp. 1–24.

— (2000), 'The US Economic Model at Y2K: Lodestar for Advanced Capitalism?', National Bureau of Economic Research Working Paper 7757, Cambridge, MA: NBER.

Fruin, M. (1992), *The Enterprise System: Competitive Strategies and Cooperative Structures*, Oxford: Clarendon Press.

— (1997), *Knowledge Works: Managing Intellectual Capital at Toshiba*, New York: Oxford University Press.

Fujimoto, M. (2000), 'Kabunushi jushi keiei to keiei soshiki kaikaku' (Shareholder-favouring Management and Innovation in Management Organization), *Jinji romu kanri kenkyu*, pp. 95–118.

Fujimoto, T. (2001), 'The Case for Cautious Optimism', *Look Japan*, May, pp. 12–16.

Fujita, S. (1982), *Seishinshi teki kosatsu* (Essay on Spiritual History), Tokyo: Heibun-sha.

Gerschenkron, A. (1962), *Economic Backwardness in Historical Perspective*, New York: Praeger.

Gerstner, L. (2002), *Who Says Elephants Can't Dance? Inside IBM's Historic Turnaround*, New York: Harper Business.

Ghoshal, S. (2001), 'GE as the Best Practice of the Individualized Corporation', *Diamond Harvard Business Review* (Japanese), January, pp. 126–35.

Ghoshal, S. and C. Bartlett (1997), *The Individualized Corporation*, New York: Random House.

Goh, K. (2000), 'Beikoku senmon jinzai ikusei shisutemu kara erareru inpurikeshon: Kinyu gyokai wo chushin ni shite' (Implications from the System of Professional Human Resource Development in the American Finance Industry), in Nissei kiso kenkyusho ed., pp. 100–23.

Goldthorpe, J., D. Lockwood, F. Bechhofer and J. Platt (1968a), *The Affluent Worker: Industrial Attitudes and Behaviour*, Cambridge: Cambridge University Press.

— (1968b), *The Affluent Worker: Political Attitudes and Behaviour*, Cambridge: Cambridge University Press.

— (1969), *The Affluent Worker in the Class Structure*, Cambridge: Cambridge University Press.

Gordon, A. (1985), *The Evolution of Labour Relations in Japan: Heavy Industry, 1853–1955*, Cambridge, MA: Harvard University Press.

— (1998), *The Wages of Affluence: Labor and Management in Postwar Japan*, Cambridge, MA: Harvard University Press.

Gouldner, A. (1957–58), 'Cosmopolitans and Locals: Toward an Analysis of Latent Social Roles', 1–2, *Administrative Science Quarterly*, December 1957; March 1958.

Granovetter, M. (2000), 'Economic Sociology of Firms and Entrepreneurs', in R. Swedberg ed., *Entrepreneurship: The Social Science View*, Oxford: Oxford University Press.

Greenbury Report – *see* Study Group on Directors' Remuneration

Hall, P. and D. Soskice eds. (2001), *Varieties of Capitalism: The Institutional Foundations of Comparative Advantage*, Oxford: Oxford University Press.

Hamaguchi, E. (1977), *'Nihon rashisa' no saihakken* (Rediscovering 'Japaneseness'), Tokyo: Nihon keizai shinbunsha.

Hamaguchi, E. and S. Kumon eds (1982), *Nihonteki shudanshugi* (Japanese-style Groupism), Tokyo: Yuhikaku.

Hampel Report – *see* Committee on Corporate Governance

Hazama, H. (1960), 'Keiei kazoku-shugi no ronri to sono keisei katei' (Logic and Emergence of Managerial Familism), *Shakaigaku hyoron* (Japanese Sociological Review), Vol. 11, No. 1, pp. 2–18.

— (1963), *Nihonteki keiei no keifu* (Origins and Development of Japanese-style Management), Tokyo: Nihon Noritsu Kyokai.

— (1964), *Nihon romu kanrishi kenkyu* (Study on the Development of Labour Management in Japan), Tokyo: Daiyamondo-sha.

— (1974), *Igirisu no shakai to roshi kankei* (Society and Industrial Relations in Britain), Tokyo: Japan Institute of Labour.

— (1979), *Keiei fukushi-shugi no susume* (Recommendations for Welfare Managerialism), Tokyo: Toyo keizai shinpo-sha.

Heckscher, C. (1995), *White Collar Blues: Management Loyalties in an Age of Corporate Restructuring*, New York: Basic Books.

Hitachi Ltd ed. (1990), *Introduction to Hitachi and Modern Japan*, Tokyo: Hitachi.

— (1949; 1960; 1971; 1985), *Hitachi seisakushoshi* (Hitachi: Company History, Vols. 1–4), Tokyo: Hitachi.

Hitachi rodo undoshi hensan iinkai ed. (1980), *Hitachi Rodo Undoshi* (History of Hitachi Labour Movement), 2nd edition, vol. 2, Hitachi: Hitachi Workers' Union.

Hitachi Workers' Union (1996), *Hitachi rodo undoshi* (A History of the Hitachi Labour Movement), 3rd edition, vols. 1 and 2, Hitachi: HWU.

— (various years), *Teiki taikai giansho* (Report to Annual Mass Meeting), Hitachi: HWU.

Hitachi Works ed. (1985), *Hitachi kojo 75 nenshi* (75 Year History of the Hitachi Works), Ibaragi: Hitachi.

Imano, K. et al. (2000), 'Joho sangyo no jinteki shigen kanri to rodo shijo' (Human Resource Management and Labour Markets in the Information Industries), JIL Research Paper Series, No. 134, March, 2000, Tokyo: Japan Institute of Labour.

Inagami, T. (1981), *Roshi kankei no shakaigaku* (Sociology of Industrial Relations), Tokyo: University of Tokyo Press.

— (1985), 'Rodo Sekai no Henyo' (Transformations of the World of Work), *Ekonomisuto*, 8 January, pp. 56–63.

— (1989), *Tenkanki no rodo sekai* (The World of Work in an Age of Transition), Tokyo: Yushin-do.

— ed. (1995), *Seijuku shakai no naka no kigyobetsu kumiai* (Enterprise Unions in Mature Society), Tokyo: Japan Institute of Labour.

— (1998), 'Labour Market Policies in Asian Countries: Diversity and Similarity among Singapore, Malaysia, the Republic of Korea and Japan', Employment and Training Paper 34, Geneva: ILO.

— (1999), 'Soron: Nihon no sangyo shakai to rodo' (Introduction: Japanese Industrial Society and Work), in Inagami and Kawakita eds., pp. 1–31.

— (2001), 'From Industrial Relations to Investor Relations?: Persistence and Change in Japanese Corporate Governance, Employment Practices and Industrial Relations', *Social Science Japan Journal*, Vol. 4, No. 2, pp. 225–41.

— (2002), 'Shukko, tenseki to iu koyo kanko' (Employment Practices of Secondment and Transfer), *Nihon Rodo Kenkyu Zasshi*, No. 501, April, pp. 57–9.

— (2003), *Kigyo gurupu keiei to shukko tenseki kanko* (Corporate Group Management and Employee Transfer Practices), Tokyo: University of Tokyo Press.

Inagami, T. and H. Ide (1995), 'Kigyobetsu kumiai no shoruikei' (Types of Enterprise Unionism) in Inagami ed., 1995, pp. 235–73.

Inagami, T. and T. Kawakita, eds. (1987), *Ridinguou: Nihon no shakaigaku 91–1 sangyo, rodo* (Readings in Japanese Sociology 9: Industry, Work), Tokyo: University of Tokyo Press.

— (1988), *Union Aidentiti* (Union Identity), Tokyo: Japan Institute of Labour.

— (1999), *Rodo* (Work), Vol. 6 of Sociology Series, Tokyo: University of Tokyo Press.

Inagami, T. and Rengo Soken (RIALS) eds. (2000), *Gendai Nihon no koporeto gabanansu* (Contemporary Corporate Governance in Japan), Tokyo: Toyo keizai shinpo-sha.

Inagami, T., D. Whittaker, N. Ohmi, T. Shinoda, Y. Shimodaira and Y. Tsujinaka (1994), *Neo-koporatizumu no kokusai hikaku* (An International Comparison of Neo-Corporatism), Tokyo: Japan Institute of Labour.

Inagami, T. and Yahata, S. eds. (1999) *Chusho kigyo no kyosoryoku kiban to jinteki shigen* (Competitive Basis and Human Resources in Small and Medium-Sized Enterprises), Tokyo: Bunshin-do.

Ingham, G. (1984), *Capitalism Divided?: The City and Industry in British Social Development*, London: Macmillan.

Ishida, M. (2003), *Shigoto no shakai kagaku* (The Social Science of Work), Kyoto: Minerva shobo.

Iwahara, S. (2000), 'Reform of Company Law', *Junkan shoji homu* (Commercial Law Review), No. 1569, August, pp. 4–16.

Iwahori, Y. (1978), *Hitachi no keiei* (Hitachi's Management), Tokyo: Nihon jitsugyo shuppansha.

Iwata, R. (1977), *Nihonteki keiei no hensei genri* (Organising Principles of Japanese-style Management), Tokyo: Bunshin-do.

— (1978), *Gendai Nihon no keiei fudo* (Management Climate in Contemporary Japan), Tokyo: Toyo Keizai Shinposha.

Jacoby, S. (1997), *Modern Manors: Welfare Capitalism Since the New Deal*, Princeton: Princeton University Press.

— (1999), 'Are Career Jobs Headed for Extinction?', *California Management Review*, Vol. 41, No. 1, pp. 123–45.

— (2004), 'The Embedded Corporation: Corporate Governance and Employment Relations in Japan and the United States.' Princeton: Princeton University Press.

Japan Institute of Labour (JIL) ed. (2002), *Yusufuru rodo tokei 2002* (Useful Labour Statistics 2002), Tokyo: Japan Institute of Labour.

Japan Productivity Centre (JPC, Special Research Committee of Humanisation of Work) (1988), *Rodo no ningenka to seisansei undo* (Humanisation of Work and Movement of Productivity Improvement), Tokyo: JPC.

Jensen, M. and J. Fuller (2002), 'Just Say No to Wall Street', *Journal of Applied Finance*, Winter, pp. 41–6.

Jinji romu kenkyu-kai (JRK: Research Committee on Personnel and Labour Management) (1999), *Shin-seiki ni mukete no Nihonteki koyo kanko no henka to tenbo* (Change and Future of Japanese-style Employment Practices in the New Century), Tokyo: Institute of Labour.

— (2000a), *Shinseiki howaito kara no koyo jittai to roshi kankei: Genjo to tenbo* (Present and Future of White-collar Employees: Employment and Industrial Relations in the New Century), Tokyo: Japan Institute of Labour.

— (2000b), 'Shinseiki no keiei senryaku, koporeto gabanansu, jinji senryaku' (New Century Management Strategies, Corporate Governance and Personnel Strategies), Research Paper Series No. 133, March 2000, Tokyo: Japan Institute of Labour.

Kagono, T. and T. Kobayashi (1994), 'The Provision of Resources and Barriers to Exit', in K. Imai and R. Komiya eds., *Business Enterprise in Japan*, Cambridge, MA: MIT Press.

Kamata, A. (1999), 'Chusho seizogyo monozukuri kino no saihensei' (Reconstruction of Manufacturing Function in Small Industries) in Inagami and Yahata eds., pp. 1–26.

Kanter, R. M. (1977), *Men and Women of the Corporation*, New York: Basic Books.

— (1989), *When Giants Learn to Dance*, New York, Simon & Schuster.

Kato, K. (1996), *Hitachi no chosen* (Hitachi's Challenge), Tokyo: Bijinesu sha.

Katz, H. and O. Darbishire (2000), *Converging Divergences: Worldwide Changes in Employment Systems*, Ithaca: ILR Press.

Kawakita, T. (1990), *Sangyo hendo to romu kanri* (Industrial Change and Labour Management), Tokyo: Japan Institute of Labour.

Kawakita, T., M. Iwamura, H. Takagi, H. Nagano and H. Fujimura (1997), *Gurupu keiei to jinzai senryaku* (Enterprise Group Management and Human Resource Management Strategy), Tokyo: Sogo rodo kenkyujo.

Kawanishi, H. (1992), *Enterprise Unionism in Japan*, London: Kegan Paul International.

Keizai Doyukai (1998), *Dai 13 kai kigyo hakusho: Shihon koritsu jushi keiei* (The 13th Corporate White Paper: Capital Efficiency-Oriented Management), Tokyo: Keizai Doyukai.

— (2002), *Kigyo kyosoryoku no kiban kyoka o mezashita koporeto gabanansu kaikaku* (Reform of Corporate Governance for Improving Firms' Competitiveness), Tokyo: Keizai Doyukai.

— (2003), *Dai 15 kai kigyo hakusho: Shijo shinka to shakaiteki sekinin keiei* (The 15th Corporate White Paper: Market Evolution and CSR Management), Tokyo: Keizai Doyukai.

Kochan, T. and P. Osterman (1994), *The Mutual Gains Enterprise: Forging a Winning Partnership among Labor, Management and Government*, Boston: Harvard Business School Press.

Koike, K. (1977), *Shokuba no rodo kumiai to sanka* (Labour Unions at the Workplace and Participation), Tokyo: Toyo keizai shinposha.

— (1981), *Nihon no jukuren: sugureta jinzai keisei shisutemu* (Skill in Japan: An Outstanding HRD System), Tokyo: Yuhikaku.

— (1983), 'Josetsu: howaitokara ka kumiai moderu' (Introduction: Union Model of White-collarisation), in Japan Institute of Labour ed., 1980, pp. 225–46.

— (1988), *Understanding Industrial Relations in Modern Japan*, New York: Macmillan.

— (1991), *Shigoto no keizaigaku* (Economics of Work), Tokyo: Toyo keizai shinposha.

Kono, H. (2000), *Hitachi: Joho, kin'yu okoku e no yabo* (Hitachi: Ambitions to Become a Major Information and Financial Power), Tokyo: Yell Books.

Konzelmann, S. and R. Forrant (2000), 'Creative Work Systems in Destructive Markets', CBR Working Paper Series No. 187, University of Cambridge.

Kosei nenkin kikin rengokai (Pension Fund Association) (2001), *Kabunushi giketsuken koshi ni kansuru jitsumu gaidorain* (Practical Guidelines for Shareholders' Voting), Tokyo: KNKR.

Kosei rodosho (MWLH) (2000), *Koyo Kanri Chosa* (Survey of Employment Management), Tokyo: Kosei rodosho.

Kumazawa, M. (1996), *Portraits of the Japanese Workplace: Labour Movements, Workers and Managers*, New York: Westview Press.

—— (2000), *Josei rodo to kigyo shakai* (Female Work and Corporate Society), Tokyo: Iwanami-shoten.

Kyochokai (Industrial Harmony Association) ed. (1938), *Jikyoku taisaku iinkai kankei shiryo tsuzuri* (Collected Materials of Committee on Current Issues), Tokyo: Kyochokai.

Lave, J. and E. Wenger (1991), *Situated Learning: Legitimate Peripheral Participation*, New York: Cambridge University Press.

Learmount, S. (2002), *Corporate Governance: What Can be Learned from Japan?*, Oxford: Oxford University Press.

Learmount, S. and J. Roberts (2002), 'Meanings of Ownership of the Firm', Centre for Business Research Working Paper Series No. 238, University of Cambridge.

Lee, M. (2001), 'Heisei fukyoka no roso no keiei sanka no jittai to seika' (Reality and Achievements of Union Participation in Management during the Heisei Recession), in Research Committee on the Future of Labour Unions, *Rodo kumiai no mirai o saguru* (In Search of the Future of Labour Unions), Tokyo: RIALS, pp. 57–151.

Lipset, S. (1996), *American Exceptionalism: A Double-Edged Sword*, New York: W. W. Norton.

Lowe, J. (2001), *Welch: An American Icon*, New York: J. Wiley and Sons.

Machin, S. (1996), 'Are the Fat Cats Getting Fatter?', *Centre Piece*, Issue 1, February, pp. 7–9.

Magota, R. (1978), *Nenko chingin no shuen* (The End of Nenko Wages), Tokyo: Nihon keizai shinbun-sha.

Maruyama, M. (1984), 'Genkei, koso to shitsuyo eion' (Prototype, Classical Base and Basso-ostinato) in K. Takeda ed., *Nihon bunka no kakureta katachi* (Hidden Form of Japanese Culture), Tokyo: Iwanami shoten, pp. 87–152.

Matsushima, S. (1951), *Rodo shakaigaku josetsu* (Introduction to Sociology of Labour), Tokyo: Fukumura shoten.

—— (1962), *Romu kanri no Nihonteki tokushitsu to hensen* (Characteristics and Change in Japanese Labour Management), Tokyo: Daiyamondo-sha.

—— (1971), 'Nihonteki romu kanri ni henshitu o ataeru shojoken' (Conditions to Change Japanese-style Labour Management), in S. Matsushima and K. Noda eds., *Keiei to rodosha* (Management and Workers), Tokyo: Chuo koron-sha.

McCormick, K. (2000), *Engineers in Japan and Britain: Education, Training and Employment*, London: Routledge.

Merton, R. (1948 [1968]), 'The Self-Fulfilling Prophecy', *Antioch Review*, Summer, pp. 193–210 (reprinted in Merton, 1968, pp. 475–90).

—— (1968), *Social Theory and Social Structure* (enlarged edition), New York: Free Press.

Michino, M. (1995), 'Jugyoin mochikabu seido no kenkyu: Doitsu tono hikaku ni yoru seido mokuteki no saikento o chushin nishite', 1–3 (Inquiry into Employee Shareholding: Reconsidering Institutional Purpose Through Comparison with Germany), *Ritsumeikan hogaku* (Ritsumeikan Jurisprudence), Nos. 240–2.

Millstein Report – *see* Business Sector Advisory Group on Corporate Governance

Ministry of Labour – *see* Rodosho

Ministry of Welfare, Labour and Health – *see* Kosei rodosho

Mito, H. (1976), *Oyake to watakushi* (The Public and the Private), Tokyo: Mirai-sha.

— (1991a), *Ie no ronri 1: Nihonteki keieiron josetsu* (Logic of the 'Ie' 1: Introduction to the Theory of Japanese-style Management), Tokyo: Bunshin-do.

— (1991b), *Ie no ronri 2: Nihonteki keiei no seiritsu* (Logic of the 'Ie' 2: Formation of Japanese-style Management), Tokyo: Bunshin-do.

— (1994), *'Ie' toshite no Nihon shakai* (Japanese Society as 'Ie'), Tokyo: Yuhikaku.

Mizuno, Y. (2004), *Hitachi: Gijutsu okoku saiken e no ketsudan* (Hitachi: Rebuilding a Technological Powerhouse), Tokyo: Nihon keizai shinbunsha.

Morishima, M. (1982), *Why has Japan Succeeded? Western Technology and the Japanese Ethos*, Cambridge: Cambridge University Press.

Murakami, Y., S. Kumon and S. Sato (1979), *Bunmei toshite no Ie-shakai* (Ie-Society as a Civilization), Tokyo: Chuo koron-sha.

Myners, P. (2001), *Institutional Investment in the United Kingdom: A Review*, London: DTI.

Nagano, H. (1989), *Kigyo gurupu nai jinzai ido no kenkyu* (Study on the Mobility of Human Resources in Corporate Groups), Tokyo: Taga shuppan.

Nakamura, K. (1996), *Nihon no shokuba to seisan shisutemu* (Workplace and Production System in Japan), Tokyo: University of Tokyo Press.

Nakano, T. (1968), *Shoka dozokudan no kenkyu* (Study on Extended Quasi-Family Coalitions in Commerce Industry), Tokyo: Mirai-sha.

Nihon kansayaku kyokai (Japan Corporate Auditors Association) (2002), *Shoho kaisei ni kansuru net anketo shukei kekka* (Net Questionnaire Survey on Commercial Law Reform), Tokyo: JCAA.

Nihon keieishi kenkyusho (Japan Institute of Management History) ed. (1997), *Tore 70-nenshi* (70 Years of Toray Inc.), Tokyo: Toray.

Nihon koporeto gabanansu foramu (Japan Corporate Governance Forum) (1998), *Koporeto gabanansu gensoku: Atarashii Nihon-gata kigyo tochi o kangaeru, saishu hokoku* (Principles of Corporate Governance: Thinking of New Japanese-style Corporate Governance, Final Report), Tokyo: JCGF.

— (2001), *Kaitei koporeto gabanansu gensoku* (Revised Principles of Corporate Governance), Tokyo: JCGF.

Nihon noritsu kyokai ed. (1982), *Hitachi no seisan kakumei* (Hitachi's Production Revolution), Tokyo: Nihon noritsu kyokai.

Nihonteki koyo seido kenkyukai (Research Group on the Japanese Employment System) (1994), 'Kigyo, jugyoin grupu chosa kenkyu hokokusho' (Report of the Research Survey on Firms and Employees), Tokyo: Sanwa sogo kenkyujo.

Nihon torishamariyaku kyokai ed. (2002), *Torishimariyaku no joken* (Leaders of Corporate Governance), Tokyo: Nikkei BP.

Nikkei bijinesu (1998), 'Shizumuna Hitachi' (Don't Sink, Hitachi), 1 June, feature article, pp. 20–34.

Nikkeiren ed. (1995), *Shinjidai no Nihonteki keiei* (Japanese-style of Management in a New Era), Tokyo: Nikkeiren.

— (1997), *Koyo antei to kokumin seikatsu no shitsuteki kaizen o mezasu kozo kaikaku: 'daisan no michi' no mosaku* (Structural Reform Aiming at Qualitative Improvements in Peoples' Living and Employment Stability: Searching for a 'Third Way'), Tokyo: Nikkeiren.

— (1998), *Nihon kigyo no koporeto gabanansu kaikaku no hoko: Shihon shijo karamo rodo shijo karano sentaku sareru kigyo o mezashite* (Directions of Corporate Governance Reform of Japanese Firms: Towards a Firm Favoured by Both Capital Markets and Labour Markets), Tokyo: Nikkeiren.

Nikkeiren and Kanto keieisha kyokai eds. (1996), *Shinjidai no Nihonteki keiei ni tsuiteno foroappu chosa hokoku* (Follow-up Survey of 'Japanese-style Management in a New Era'), Tokyo: Nikkeiren.

Nissei kiso kenkyusho (Nissei Basic Research Institute) (2000), 'Gurobaruka jidai no senmon jinzai no ikusei ni mukete: Kinyu kikan no senmon jinzai ikusei o chushin nishite' (Toward Professional Human Resource Development in an Era of Globalization: Focusing on Professionals in Financial Institutions), *Shaho*, Special Issue, January, Tokyo: NBRI.

Nishiyama, T. (1980), *Shihai koso-ron: Nihon shihon-shugi no hokai* (Considerations on the Structure of Control: Collapse of Japanese Capitalism), Tokyo: Bunshin-do.

— (1983), *Datsu shihon-shugi bunseki* (Analysis of Post-capitalism), Tokyo: Bunshin-do.

Nitta, M. (1987), *Nihon no rodosha sanka* (Worker Participation in Japan), Tokyo: University of Tokyo Press.

— (1999), 'Tenkeiteki koyo to hitenkeiteki koyo: Nihon no keiken' (Typical Work and Atypical Work: Japan's Experience), paper submitted to Japan-Europe Symposium on Multiple Patterns of Employment and Changes in the Labour Market, Japan Productivity Centre, Tokyo.

— (1998), 'Roshi kankeiron to shakai seisaku ni kansuru oboegaki' (Notes on Theories of Industrial Relations and Social Policy) in Shakai seisaku sosho henshu iinkai (Editorial Committee of Social Policy Series) ed., *Shakai seisaku-gakkai 100-nen* (One Hundred Years of the Association of Social Policy), pp. 109–30.

Nomura soken (NRI) ed. (1981), *Hitachi seisakusho no kenkyu: gijutsu rikkoku jidai no top runner* (Research on Hitachi Ltd: Top runner in an age of technological standing), Tokyo: V Books.

Norton, R. (2001), *Creating the New Economy: The Entrepreneur and the US Resurgence*, Cheltenham: Edward Elgar.

O'Boyle, T. (1998), *At Any Cost: Jack Welch, General Electric and the Pursuit of Profit*, New York: Random House.

Odaka, K. (1981), *Sangyo shakaigaku kogi* (Lectures on Industrial Sociology), Tokyo: Iwanami-shoten.

— (1984), *Nihonteki keiei: sono shinwa to genjitsu* (Japanese-style Management: Myth and Reality), Tokyo: Chuo koron-sha.

— (1995), *Nihonteki keiei* (Japanese-style Management), Collected Works of Odaka Kunio, Vol. 5, Tokyo: Muso-sha.

OECD (1984), *Employment Outlook 1984*, Paris: OECD.

— (1993), *Employment Outlook 1993*, Paris: OECD.

— (1997), *Employment Outlook 1997*, Paris: OECD.

— (1999), 'OECD Principles of Corporate Governance', Paris: OECD (pamphlet).

Okamoto, H. (1965: 1987), 'Roshi kankei' (Labour and Capital Relations), in R. Kitagawa ed., *Rodo shakaigaku nyumon* (Introduction to Sociology of Labour), Tokyo: Yuhikaku, pp. 117–55 (included in Inagami and Kawakita eds., 1987, pp. 126–36).

— (1966), *Kogyoka to genba kantokusha* (Industrialization and Foreman), Tokyo: Japan Institute of Labour.

Okamoto, Y. (1979), *Hitachi to Matsushita* (Hitachi and Matsushita, Vols. 1 and 2), Tokyo: Chuo koronsha.

Okazaki, T. (1994), 'The Japanese Firm Under the Wartime Planned Economy', in M. Aoki and R. Dore eds., *The Japanese Firm: Sources of Competitive Strength*, Oxford: Oxford University Press.

Okazaki, T., S. Sugayama, T. Nishizawa and S. Yonekura (1996), *Sengo Nihon keizai to Keizai Doyukai* (Postwar Japanese Economy and the JCED), Tokyo: Iwanami shoten.

Okochi, K., S. Ujihara and W. Fujita eds. (1959), *Rodo kumiai no kozo to kino* (Structure and Function of Labour Unions), Tokyo: University of Tokyo Press.

Okumura, H. (1975), *Hojin shihonshugi no kozo* (The Structure of Corporate Capitalism), Tokyo: Nihon Hyoron-sha. (English edition: *Corporate Capitalism in Japan*, trans. D. Anthony, D. and N. Brown, London: Macmillan, 2000).

— (1984), *Hojin shihonshugi* (Corporate Capitalism), Tokyo: Ochanomizu-shobo.

— (1992), *Kaitai suru 'Keiretsu' to hojin shihonshugi* (Dismantling Keiretsu and Corporate Capitalism), Tokyo: Shakai shisosha.

Ono, A. (1989), *Nihonteki koyo kanko to rodo shijo* (Japanese-style Employment Practices and Labour Markets), Tokyo: Toyo Keizai Shipo-sha.

Osawa, M. (1993), *Kigyo-chushin shakai o koete* (Beyond the Corporate-Centred Society), Tokyo: Jiji tsushin-sha.

Ouchi, W. (1981), *Theory Z*, New York: Addison Wesley.

Owen, G. (1999), *From Empire to Europe: The Decline and Revival of British Industry Since the Second World War*, London: HarperCollins.

Pahl, J. and R. Pahl (1971), *Managers and Their Wives: A Study of Career and Family Relationships*, London: Allen Lane.

Parsons, T. (1951), *The Social System*, New York: Free Press.

Pascale, R. and A. Athos (1981), *The Art of Japanese Management*, New York: Simon and Schuster.

Patrick, H. and M. Aoki eds. (1995), *The Japanese Main Bank System: Its Relevance for Developing and Transforming Economies*, New York: Oxford University Press.

Porter, M. (1990), *The Competitive Advantage of Nations*, Basingstoke: Macmillan.

Porter, M., H. Takeuchi and M. Sakakibara (2000), *Can Japan Compete?* Basingstoke: Macmillan.

Probert, J. (2002), 'Organizational Change and the Strategic Renewal Process: Innovation, Stability and Inertia in Japanese Companies', Ph.D. dissertation, University of Cambridge.

Riesman, D. (1950), *The Lonely Crowd: A Study of the Changing American Character*, New Haven: Yale University Press.

Rodo horei kyokai (Association of Labour Ordinance) ed. (1964), *Shukko seido no jissai* (Realities of Employee Secondment), Tokyo: ALO.

Rodosho (MOL) ed. (1987), *Nihonteki koyo kanko no henka to tenbo: Chosahen* (Change and Future of Japanese-style Employment Practices: Survey Results), Tokyo: Okurasho insatsu kyoku.

— (1991), 'Toshi tsukin no genjo to kinrosha seikatsu e no eikyo ni kansuru chosa hokokusho' (Research Report on Urban Commuting and its Effects on Workers' Lives), Tokyo: Rodosho.

— (1995), *Nihonteki koyo seido no genjo to tenbo* (The Present State and Future of the Japanese-style Employment System), Tokyo: Okurasho insatsu kyoku.

— (1996), *Chiteki sozogata rodo to jinji kanri* (Knowledge-creative Work and Personnel Management), Tokyo: Okurasho insatsu kyoku.

— (1999, 2000), *Josei koyo kanri chosa* (Survey on Employment Management of Women), Tokyo: Rodosho.

Roshi kankei chosa iinkai (Research Committee on Industrial Relations) ed. (1981), *Tenkanki ni okeru roshi kankei no jittai* (Reality of Industrial Relations in an Age of Transition), Tokyo: University of Tokyo Press.

Rubinstein, W. (1977), 'Wealth, Elites and the Class Structure of Modern Britain', *Past and Present*, No. 76, August, pp. 99–126.

Sako, M. and H. Sato (2000), 'Union Networks in the Extended Enterprise in Japan: Evidence from the Automobile and Electrical Machinery Industries', paper submitted to the 12th IRRA International Conference, 27 May–1 June, Tokyo.

Sampson, A. (1995), *Company Man: The Rise and Fall of Corporate Life*, New York: Times Business.

Sasaki, H. (1999) *GE tsuyosa no shikumi* (Mechanisms of GE's Strength), Tokyo: Chukei shuppan.

Sato, A. (2001), *Howaito kara no sekai: Shigoto to kyaria no supekutoramu* (The World of White-collar Employees: Spectrum of Work and Careers), Tokyo: Japan Institute of Labour.

Sato, H. (2000), 'Keiei mokuhyo no henka to kigyo tochi, koyo, roshi kankei heno eikyo' (Change in Management Objectives and its Effects on Corporate Governance, Employment and Industrial Relations), in Jinji romu kenkyukai ed., 2000a, pp. 51–65.

Sato, H. and T. Umezawa (1983), 'Rodo kumiai no hatsugen to kumiai ruikei' (Union Voice and Types of Labour Unions), in Japan Institute of Labour ed., pp. 396–452.

Schein, E. (1992), *Organizational Culture and Leadership*, 2nd edition, New York: Jossey Bass.

Secretary of State for Trade and Industry (UK) (2002), *Modern Company Law*, presented to Parliament, July 2002.

Seike, A. (1998), *Shogai geneki shakai no joken* (Conditions for Lifelong Active Society), Tokyo: Chuo koron-sha.

Sekijima, Y. (2001), 'Koporeto yunibashitei toshite no Hitachi keiei kenshujo no keiei kanbu ikusei senryaku' (Corporate University Hitachi Institute of Management Development's Executive Development Strategy), *Kigyo to jinzai*, 5 May, pp. 10–17.

Shapira, P. ed. (1995), *The R&D Workers: Managing Innovation in Britain, Germany, Japan and the United States*, New York: Quorum Books.

Simmel, G. (1955), *Conflict*, trans. Kurt H. Wolff, New York: Free Press. (ch. 4 of *Soziologie* (1908), Leipzig: Duncker & Humboldt).

Slater, R. (1999), *Jack Welch and the GE Way*, New York: McGraw-Hill.

Streeck, W. (1989), 'Skills and the Limits of Neo-liberalism: The Enterprise of the Future as a Place of Learning', *Work, Employment and Society*, Vol. 3, No. 1, pp. 89–104.

— (1996), 'Lean Production in the German Automobile Industry: A Test Case for Convergence Theory', in Berger and Dore eds., pp. 138–70.

Study Group on Directors Remuneration (Greenbury Report) (1995), *Directors' Remuneration: Report of a Study Group Chaired by Sir Richard Greenbury*, London: Burgess Science Press.

Sugayama, S. (1991), 'The Bureaucratization of Japanese Firms and Academic Credentialism: A Case Study of Hitachi Ltd', in Japanese Business History Institute ed., *Japanese Yearbook on Business History*, Vol. 8, Tokyo.

Sugeno, K. (2002a), *Shin koyo shakai no ho* (Employment Society and Law, revised edition), Tokyo: Yuhikaku.

— (2002b), *Japanese Employment and Labour Law*, trans. L. Kanowitz, Durham, NC: Carolina Academic Press.

Sugimoto, N., S. Kono, A. Hiramoto and N. Ogura (1990), *Johoka e no kigyo senryaku: Hitachi no jirei kenkyu* (Corporate Strategies for Informationization: A Case Study of Hitachi), Tokyo: Dobunkan.

Suwa, Y. (1994), 'Koyo seisakuho no kozo to kino' (Structure and Function of Employment Policy), *Nihon Rodo Kenkyu Zasshi* (Monthly Journal of the Japan Institute of Labour), Vol. 37, No. 6, pp. 4–15.

Suzuki, F. (2003), 'Sabisu zangyo no jittai to rodo kumiai no taio' (The Situation of Unpaid Overtime and the Response of Labour Unions), *Nihon rodo kenkyu zasshi*, No. 519, October.

Tekkororen and Rodo Chosa Kyogikai eds. (1980), *Tekko sangyo no roshi kankei to rodo kumiai* (Industrial Relations and Labour Unions in the Iron and Steel Industry), Tokyo: Nihon Rodo Kyokai.

TIAA-CREF (Teachers Insurance and Annuity Association-College Retirement Equities Fund) (1997), *TIAA-CREF Policy Statement on Corporate Governance*, Washington, DC: TIAA-CREF.

Tokunaga, S. and N. Sugimoto eds. (1990), *FA kara CIM e: Hitachi no jirei kenkyu* (From Factory Automation to Computer Integrated Manufacturing: A Case Study of Hitachi), Tokyo: Dobunkan.

Tokyo shoken torihikijo (Tokyo Stock Exchange) (2002), *Heisei 13 nendo jugyoin mochikabukai jokyo chosa kekka no gaiyo ni tuite* (Summary of Survey Results on Employee Shareholding in 2001), Tokyo: TSE.

Tore kabushiki gaisha shashi hensan iinkai (Editorial Committee of History of Toray Inc.) ed. (1977), *Tore 50-nenshi* (50 Years of Toray), Tokyo: Toray.

Tsuchiya, M. and Y. Konomi (1997), *Shaping the Future of Japanese Management: New Leadership to Overcome the Impending Crisis*, Tokyo: LTCB International Library Foundation (orig. *Korekara no Nihonteki keiei*, 1995).

Tsuda, M. (1976), *Nihonteki keiei no yogo* (Defence of Japanese-style Management), Tokyo: Toyo keizai shinpo-sha.

— (1977), *Nihonteki keiei no ronri* (Logic of Japanese-style Management), Tokyo: Chuo keizai-sha.

— (1981), *Gendai keiei to kyodo seikatsutai: Nihonteki keiei no riron no tameni* (Contemporary Management and Community: For a Theory of Japanese-style Management), Tokyo: Dobunkan.

— (1994), *Nihon no keiei bunka: 21-seiki no soshiki to hito* (Management Culture in Japan: People and Organization of the 21st Century), Kyoto: Minerva shobo.

Tsujimura, K. (1998), 'Kanko ni yosete' (Foreword) in Tsusansho (MITI) ed., *Sozo-kakushin gata koporeto sisutemu* (Creative and Innovative-type of Corporate System), Tokyo: Toyo-keizai shinpo-sha, pp. v–vi.

Tsutsui, W. (1998), *Manufacturing Ideology: Scientific Management in Twentieth-Century Japan*, Princeton: Princeton University Press.

Udagawa, S., H. Sato, K. Nakamura and I. Nonaka (1995), *Nihon kigyo no hinshitsu kanri* (The Quality Management of Japanese Companies), Tokyo: Yuhikaku.

Ujihara, S. (1953), 'Daikojo rodosha no seikaku' (Characteristics of Workers of Big Factories); included in S. Ujihara, *Nihon rodo mondai kenkyu* (Studies of Labour Problems in Japan), Tokyo: University of Tokyo Press, 1956, pp. 351–401.

— (1989 [1980]), 'Nenko chingin, shogai koyo, kigyobetsu kumiai wa sanmi-ittai ka?' (Are *nenko* Wages, Lifetime Employment and Enterprise Unions an Indivisible Trinity?), in Ujihara, *Nihon no roshi kankei to rodo seisaku* (Industrial Relations and Labour Policy in Japan), Tokyo: University of Tokyo Press, pp. 232–8.

Veblen, T. (1904), *The Theory of Business Enterprise*, New York: Charles Scribner's Sons.

Welch, J. with J. Byrne (2001), *Jack: Straight from the Gut*, New York: Warner Books.

Wenger, E. (1998), *Communities of Practice: Learning, Meaning, and Identity*, New York: Cambridge University Press.

Westney, E. (1992), 'Country Patterns in R&D Organization: The United States and Japan', in B. Kogut ed., *Country Competitiveness: Technology and the Organizing of Work*, New York: Oxford University Press.

Whitby, R. (1999), *Divergent Capitalisms: The Social Structuring and Change of Business Systems*, Oxford: Oxford University Press.

Whittaker, D. H. (1990a), *Managing Innovation: A Study of British and Japanese Factories*, Cambridge: Cambridge University Press.

— (1990b), 'The End of Japanese-Style Employment?', *Work, Employment and Society*, Vol. 4, No. 3, pp. 321–47.

— (1997), *Small Firms in the Japanese Economy*, Cambridge: Cambridge University Press.

Whyte, W. Jr. (1956), *The Organization Man*, New York: Simon and Schuster.

Wolferen, K. van (1989), *The Enigma of Japanese Power: People and Politics in a Stateless Nation*, London: Macmillan.

Yahata, S. (1999a), 'Jukuren keisei to kokusaika' (Skill Formation and Internationalisation), in Inagami and Kawakita eds., pp. 105–42.

— (1999b), 'Mono zukuri kiban no shorai sekkei to jinteki shigen' (Future Design of the Manufacturing Base and Human Resources), in Inagami and Yahata eds., pp. 27–50.

Yamakawa, R. (2001), 'Gurupu keiei to rodoho' (Corporate Group Management and Labour Law), in Dentsu soken ed., *Kigyo gurupu renketsu keiei to jinji romu kanri ni kansuru chosa kenkyu hokokusho* (Research Report on Corporate Group Management and Personnel and Labour Management), Tokyo: Dentsu soken, pp. 190–205.

Zaimusho (2003), *Shinten suru koporeto gabanansu kaikaku to Nihon kigyo saisei* (Developing Corporate Governance Reform and Company Regeneration), Tokyo: Zaimusho.

Zuboff, S. and J. Maxmin (2002), *The Support Economy: Why Corporations are Failing Individuals and the Next Episode of Capitalism*, London: Penguin/Allen Lane.

Index